GW00675789

FRIEDRICH NIETZSCHE

Friedrich Nietzsche

SELECTIONS FROM

Human, All Too Human
Miscellaneous Maxims and Opinions
Thus Spake Zarathustra
Beyond Good and Evil
Twilight of the Idols and
The Antichrist

The Collector's Library of
ESSENTIAL THINKERS

This edition published in 2005 by
The Collector's Library of Essential Thinkers
an imprint of CRW Publishing Limited
69 Gloucester Crescent, London NW1 7EG

ISBN 1 904919 63 4

Text © CRW Publishing Limited 2005

1 3 5 7 9 10 8 6 4 2

Typeset in Great Britain by Antony Gray
Printed and bound in China by Imago

Contents

Introduction

Nietzsche was not a systematic thinker, and therefore my aim in this introduction is not to give a summary of his thought, but to try and counter some of the prejudice which attaches to his name, and which may sometimes have put people off reading this most entertaining and stimulating of writers. I shall also, more positively, try to suggest a reason why one *should* read him.

There are, in particular, three prejudices I would like to deal with. The first is that Nietzsche was a friend of Wagner, that Hitler liked Wagner, and that therefore Nietzsche, by association, is implicated in the crimes of Nazism. The second concerns Nietzsche's views on religion. Nietzsche claimed that God was dead, the argument goes, and since he was wrong about that, we can disregard a lot of other things he says as well. The third objection is that he is difficult to read.

I shall give a brief account of Nietzsche's life, and then deal with these three prejudices in turn. For the first and second, I believe a small fragment of truth has been overlaid by a hundred years of misconception. If we look carefully at what Nietzsche wrote and believed, the misconceptions drop away of their own accord. For the third, all I shall need to do is allow Nietzsche to speak for himself, and the absurdity of the prejudice will be apparent.

NIETZSCHE'S LIFE

Nietzsche was born in 1844, in Prussia. When he was five, his father died, and Nietzsche was brought up in a household of women – mother, grandmother, two aunts, and a sister. Despite this, or because of it, he seems throughout his life to have been wary of women.

He studied classics at Bonn and Leipzig, and at the age of twenty-four, after a brief period in the army, was appointed professor of classical philology at the University of Basel. He also met Richard Wagner, and became friendly with him. But things did not run smoothly for very long. Nietzsche's health was never good, and he struggled to lead a normal life in the university. In 1873, as his eyesight started to fail, he started lecturing without notes, and in 1876 was forced to give up teaching completely. 1876 was also the year in which Nietzsche realised that his friendship with Wagner was not going to produce the artistic and philosophical collaboration he had hoped for.

The break with Wagner, and the end of his teaching responsibilities, prompted a great surge in creativity and productivity. In a little over a decade Nietzsche produced a string of works of extraordinary power and originality: *Human All Too Human* (1878), *Assorted Opinions and Maxims* (1878), *The Wanderer and His Shadow* (1878), *The Gay Science* (1882; Book 5 in 1886), *Thus Spake Zarathustra* (1883–85), *Beyond Good and Evil* (1886), *The Genealogy of Morals* (1888), *Twilight of the Idols* (1888), *The Antichrist* (1889), *Ecce Homo*, his autobiography (1889), *The Will to Power* (1901). The urgency with which he worked suggests that he may somehow have realised he was working against time. In 1889 he suffered a mental breakdown which stopped him writing, and from which he never recovered. He died in Weimar in 1900.

The cause of his breakdown is uncertain, but there is a poignant paragraph ('The Saddest Destiny of a Prophet') in Part 2 of *Human All Too Human*:

> He has worked twenty years to convince his contemporaries, and succeeds at last, but in the meantime his adversaries have also succeeded – he is no longer convinced of himself.　　(MMO 193)

NIETZSCHE AND TOTALITARIANISM

Nietzsche and Wagner

Nietzsche was first drawn to Wagner by his admiration for the music of *Tristan und Isolde*; Wagner in his turn was struck by Nietzsche's ideas on the need for a new morality. And so, despite a thirty-year disparity in age, the two quickly became close friends – close enough for Nietzsche to spend two Christmases with the Wagners.

But Nietzsche expected more from the friendship than Wagner was prepared or able to give. He believed that Wagner shared his views on the Dionysian element in art and life, and seems to have expected Wagner to be a kind of 'musical apostle' for this new morality; hence he felt betrayed (quite unreasonably) when Wagner the artist continued, in his music-dramas, to use the values of the 'old' morality: humility, renunciation, and the redeeming power of love – values which have a clear dramatic and artistic function.

The Superman

What was this new morality? According to Nietzsche, Christian morality is slave morality, a morality created by weak and resentful individuals who encouraged gentleness, kindness, humility, forgiveness because such behaviour gave them some protection against the bold and the strong. Slave morality is essentially a willingness (born of fear) to give up on life in its entirety. By contrast, Nietzsche's superman ('übermensch') is secure and independent. He feels deeply, but his passions are rationally controlled. Concentrating on this world, not on the rewards of the next, the superman accepts and welcomes life, including the suffering and pain that accompany human existence. His superman creates his own values, a 'master morality' that reflects the strength and independence of one who is liberated from all values except those that he himself deems valid. The essential thing is the will to power. In its positive sense, this will to power is not simply power over others, but power over oneself, as manifested in the superman's independence, creativity, and originality.

It is easy to see how talk of 'master morality' and 'slave morality' can be conflated with Hitler's ideas about the master race and slave races. So it is important to emphasise that this is not the kind of thing Nietzsche is talking about. According to Nietzsche, the superman has not yet appeared, but he mentions individuals who might serve as models: Socrates, Jesus, Leonardo, Michelangelo, Shakespeare, Goethe, Julius Caesar, Napoleon. Two teachers, two painters, two writers, two soldier-statesmen. This is hardly the stuff of racist supremacy or totalitarian dictatorship.

NIETZSCHE AND RELIGION

God is dead?

'Nietzsche said "God is dead." Now Nietzsche is dead, and GOD LIVES.' That was the message outside churches in London, some years ago. *Did* Nietzsche say 'God is dead'? If he did, what did he mean by it?

The most famous assertion that God is dead comes not from Nietzsche speaking in his own person, but from the 'madman who lit a lantern in the bright morning hours'. But there are places where, speaking for himself, he comes close to saying the same thing.

> A Christian . . . might well ask himself on some occasion whether it is really necessary that there should be a God, side by side with a representative Lamb, if faith in the existence of these beings suffices to produce the same influences . . . It is here as in another well-known case – there were indeed no witches, but the terrible effects of the belief in witches were the same as if they really had existed. For all occasions where the Christian awaits the immediate intervention of a God, though in vain (for there is no God), his religion is inventive enough to find subterfuges and reasons for tranquillity.
>
> (MMO 225)

Was Nietzsche an atheist? One thing we have to keep in mind is that, more than anything else, Nietzsche likes to shock and startle his reader. He recognised, as the modern Christian church for the most part refuses to do, that a pictorial representation of God which was convincing to many people in the middle east 2000 years ago is likely to be unconvincing to a large number of people today, just as the Olympian gods of the ancient Greeks are no longer convincing to many people today.

He was well aware, however, that the gods whose pictorial form is now obsolete do represent something real in the world. Dionysus and Apollo are not living creatures resembling their statues, but there are still many things which can best be explained by reference to what they represent. Much the same applies, in Nietzsche's view, to the Judaeo-Christian god.

Dionysus and Apollo

In his study of the ancients, Nietzsche was responsible for a perception which has been of profound importance both in the realm of classical scholarship and in our understanding of the world at large. In his own words:

> I was the first who, in order to understand the ancient, still rich and even superabundant Hellenic instinct, took that marvellous phenomenon, which bears the name of Dionysus, seriously . . .
>
> (TI 4)

As Nietzsche saw it, there were two opposing strands in the psychology of the ancient Greeks: the life-affirming, yes-saying irrationalism represented by the god Dionysus; and the life-denying, no-saying rationalism of Apollo.

This was at odds with the received wisdom of the nineteenth century, which saw only the Apolline element. For nineteenth century scholars, the classical Greek world was characterised by its cool, calm rationality. Its defining symbols were Socrates, with his contempt for death; Plato, distrusting the body and its pleasures; the funeral speech of Pericles; the Hermes of Praxiteles; the dazzling bleached marble of the Parthenon. This view ignored the darker, wilder side of Greek life, a side brilliantly illuminated by E. R. Dodds, in 1951, in his *The Greeks and the Irrational*. In essentials, however, Nietzsche was eighty years ahead of him, in *The Birth of Tragedy*. Europe's tragedy, for Nietzsche, was that it was the Apolline element which eventually triumphed, making its way via Plato into the gloomy self-denials of Christianity.

A *new* morality?

I mentioned Nietzsche's 'new' morality, yet in some ways it was not a new morality at all; it was a very, very old morality – that found in the Homeric poems. Listen to Nietzsche's description of the archaic view of goodness:

> Whoever has the power of returning good for good, evil for evil, and really practises requital, and who is, therefore, grateful and revengeful, is called good; whoever is powerless, and unable to requite, is reckoned as bad . . . the enemy is not looked upon as evil, he can requite. In Homer the Trojan and the Greek are both good.
>
> (HH 45)

When we read the *Iliad*, in other words, we find only heroes and no villains, whereas in Wagner there are heroes *and* villains. And in Christianity, of course, we are all villains.

The same idea, that we define who we are by our relation to our enemies, more than to our friends, comes up again in *Zarathustra*:

By our best enemies we do not want to be spared, nor by those either whom we love from the very heart. So let me tell you the truth!

My brethren in war! I love you from the very heart. I am, and was ever, your counterpart. And I am also your best enemy. So let me tell you the truth! . . .

. . . I spare you not, I love you from my very heart, my brethren in war!

(Z 1.10)

This Homeric, or heroic, view of morality leads inevitably to the conclusion that what is good is strength, and what is bad is weakness.

What is good? All that enhances the feeling of power, the Will to Power, and power itself in man. What is bad? All that proceeds from weakness. What is happiness? The feeling that power *is increasing* – that resistance has been overcome.

Not contentment, but more power; not peace at any price, but war; not virtue, but efficiency (virtue in the Renaissance style, *virtù*, free from all moralic acid). The weak and the botched shall perish: first principle of our humanity. And they ought even to be helped to perish.

What is more harmful than any vice? Practical sympathy with all the botched and the weak – Christianity.

(AC 2)

READING NIETZSCHE

Is Nietzsche difficult to read?

Not at all. It is hard to give a systematic account of his thought, but that is because he is not a systematic thinker. It does not mean the things he says are difficult to understand. And his lack of system can be something of an advantage. It matters much less if you allow your attention to wander while you are reading. You may miss a few things, but you won't miss a vital step in an argument. What is more, Nietzsche offers so many striking insights that if you miss one on this page, there is certain to be another, equally striking, on the next. This makes him, if anything, the easiest of all philosophers to read.

Why then does he have the reputation of being difficult? Much of the blame lies with *Zarathustra*, his best-known (and most unreadable) book. It is hard to like the central character in *Zarathustra*, who, for my taste at least, is far too aware of his own superiority, and spends far too much time striding over the mountains, communing with eagles. If that is what the superman is going to be like, he is a poor advertisement for it. But *Zarathustra* is far from typical of Nietzsche's writing. In his other books, he makes his observations and reflections, and simply leaves you to draw your own conclusions from them.

Or is he difficult because he is hard to classify? What kind of philosopher is he? An idealist? An empiricist? An existentialist? If you want to put his philosophy in a nutshell, what label would that nutshell have on it? Perhaps the best answer is that we should not see Nietzsche as a philosopher at all, but rather as a prophet.

Nietzsche as prophet

Nietzsche is a prophet in two senses. First, in the Old Testament sense: one who speaks out and tells us uncomfortable truths.

> When a rich man deprives a poor man of a possession (for instance, a prince taking the sweetheart of a plebeian), an error arises in the mind of the poor man; he thinks that the rich man must be utterly infamous to take away from him the little that he has. But the rich man does not estimate so highly the value of a *single* possession, because he is accustomed to have many; hence he cannot imagine himself in the poor man's place, and does not commit nearly so great a wrong as the latter supposes. (HH 81)

I said earlier that Nietzsche liked to shock, and that is what he is doing here. He does not approve of the rich man, nor does he say the rich man is justified. But he does refuse to slip into the conventional platitudes of popular morality. You don't like what he says here, but you have an uncomfortable feeling there might be some truth in it. Or worse, take what he says about Europe and War:

> it will become more and more obvious that such a highly cultivated and therefore necessarily enfeebled humanity as that of modern Europe not only needs wars, but the greatest and most terrible wars – consequently occasional relapses into barbarism – lest, by the means of culture, it should lose its culture and its very existence. (HH 477)

Yes, he wants to surprise you and shock you – to reach out and grab your attention. But there is always at least a half-truth in the aphorism or paradox by which he achieves his aim.

However, Nietzsche is also a prophet in the modern sense – someone with an acute ability to foresee events in the future.

> . . . and in some far-off future there will be a new language, used at first as a language of commerce, then as a language of intellectual intercourse generally, then for all, as surely as some time or other there will be aviation.
>
> (HH 267)

He was clearly right about air travel. And we may well be in the process of seeing him proved right about a new language. What is US English, after all, if not a new language for everybody, used at first as a language of commerce, then as a language of intellectual intercourse?

Or listen to him predicting the horrors of twentieth-century socialism:

> Socialism is the fantastic younger brother of almost decrepit despotism, which it wants to succeed; its efforts are, therefore, in the deepest sense reactionary. For it desires such an amount of State power as only despotism has possessed . . . it requires the most submissive prostration of all citizens before the absolute State, such as has never yet been realised; and as it can no longer even count upon the old religious piety towards the State . . . [Socialism] can only hope for existence occasionally, here and there for short periods, by means of the extremest terrorism.
>
> (HH 473)

Those who would like to see Nietzsche as a proto-

Nazi should remind themselves that Nazism too, like Soviet communism, was a form of socialism.

Insights

I said I would offer a reason why one *should* read Nietzsche. We should read him, I would suggest, for his insights. These come in many shapes and forms. Sometimes they are simple truths expressed with great clarity:

> One may promise actions but no sentiments.
>
> (HH 58)

> Convictions are more dangerous enemies of truth than lies.　　　　　(HH 483)

Sometimes they are simply humorous:

> We are so fond of being out among Nature, because it has no opinions about us.　　(HH 508)

And sometimes they provoke thought because they are striking, and we simply cannot decide whether they are true or not:

> If she is to become beautiful a woman must not want to be considered pretty.　　(AOM 292)

> Profundity of thought belongs to youth, clarity of thought to old age.　　(AOM 289)

> The undissolved dissonances in the relation of the character and sentiments of the parents survive in the nature of the child and make up the history of its inner sufferings.　　(HH 379)

> One person sticks to an opinion because he takes pride in having acquired it himself – another sticks

to it because he has learnt it with difficulty and is proud of having understood it; both of them, therefore, out of vanity. (HH 527)

Do not expect to find nothing in Nietzsche with which you will disagree. And do not necessarily expect to like Nietzsche as a person. But as a writer, he is superb. He sets out to startle, to shock, to annoy. And he *will* shock and annoy you. What he won't do is bore you. And for every time you disagree with him, there will be half a dozen where you marvel at a perception you would never have arrived at for yourself.

Nietzsche may be, of all philosophers, the most difficult to spell, but he is among the easiest, and most enjoyable, to read.

TOM GRIFFITH

Abbreviations

A	*The Antichrist*
MMO	*Miscellaneous Maxims and Opinions*
BGE	*Beyond Good and Evil*
HH	*Human All Too Human*
Z	*Thus Spake Zarathustra*
TI	*Twilight of the Idols*

Further Reading

Dostoevsky, Fyodor, *Devils*

Dostoevsky, Fyodor, *The Brothers Karamazov*

Hesse, Hermann, *Narziss and Goldmund* (the Apollo and Dionysus motif)

Hesse, Hermann, *Magister Ludi* (*The Glass Bead Game*)

Homer, *Iliad*

Kaufmann, Walter A., *Nietzsche, Philosopher, Psychologist, Antichrist*

Kierkegaard, Søren, *Fear and Trembling*

Kierkegaard, Søren, *Either/Or*

Nietzsche, Friedrich, *Ecce Homo*

Schopenhauer, Arthur, *The World as Will and Idea*

Sartre, Jean-Paul, *Being and Nothingness*

Wagner, Richard, *The Nibelung's Ring*

HUMAN, ALL-TOO-HUMAN

First and last things

I

Chemistry of ideas and sensations – Philosophical problems adopt in almost all matters the same form of question as they did two thousand years ago; how can anything spring from its opposite? For instance, reason out of unreason, the sentient out of the dead, logic out of unlogic, disinterested contemplation out of covetous willing, life for others out of egoism, truth out of error? Metaphysical philosophy has helped itself over those difficulties hitherto by denying the origin of one thing in another, and assuming a miraculous origin for more highly valued things, immediately out of the kernel and essence of the 'thing in itself'. Historical philosophy, on the contrary, which is no longer to be thought of as separate from physical science, the youngest of all philosophical methods, has ascertained in single cases (and presumably this will happen in everything) that there are no opposites except in the usual exaggeration of the popular or metaphysical point of view, and that an error of reason lies at the bottom of the opposition: according to this explanation, strictly understood, there is neither an unegoistical action nor an entirely disinterested point of view, they are both only sublimations in which the fundamental element appears almost evaporated, and is only to be discovered by the closest observation. All that we require, and which can only be given us by the present advance of the single sciences, is a *chemistry* of the moral, religious, aesthetic ideas and sentiments, as also of those emotions which we experience in ourselves both in the great and in the small phases of social and intellectual intercourse, and even in solitude; but what if this chemistry should result in the fact that also in this case the most beautiful colours have been obtained from base, even despised materials? Would many be inclined to pursue such examinations? Humanity likes to put all questions as to origin and beginning out of its mind; must one not be almost dehumanised to feel a contrary tendency in one's self?

2

Inherited faults of philosophers – All philosophers have the common fault that they start from man in his present state and hope to attain their end by an analysis of him. Unconsciously they look upon 'man' as an *aeterna veritas*, as a thing unchangeable in all commotion, as a sure standard of things. But everything that the philosopher says about man is really nothing more than testimony about the man of a *very limited* space of time. A lack of the historical sense is the hereditary fault of all philosophers; many, indeed, unconsciously mistake the very latest variety of man, such as has arisen under the influence of certain religions, certain political events, for the permanent form from which one must set out. They will not learn that man has developed, that his faculty of knowledge has developed also; whilst for some of them the entire world is spun out of this faculty of knowledge. Now everything *essential* in human development happened

24

in pre-historic times, long before those four thousand years which we know something of; man may not have changed much during this time. But the philosopher sees 'instincts' in the present man and takes it for granted that this is one of the unalterable facts of mankind, and, consequently, can furnish a key to the understanding of the world; the entire teleology is so constructed that man of the last four thousand years is spoken of as an *eternal* being, towards which all things in the world have from the beginning a natural direction. But everything has evolved; there are *no eternal facts*, as there are likewise no absolute truths. Therefore, *historical philosophising* is henceforth necessary, and with it the virtue of diffidence.

3

Appreciation of unpretentious truths – It is a mark of a higher culture to value the little unpretentious truths, which have been found by means of strict method, more highly than the joy-diffusing and dazzling errors which spring from metaphysical and artistic times and peoples. First of all one has scorn on the lips for the former, as if here nothing could have equal privileges with anything else, so unassuming, simple, bashful, apparently discouraging are they, so beautiful, stately, intoxicating, perhaps even animating, are the others. But the hardly attained, the certain, the lasting, and therefore of great consequence for all wider knowledge, is still the higher; to keep one's self to what is manly and shows bravery, simplicity, and forbearance. Gradually not only single individuals but the whole of mankind will be raised to this manliness, when it has at last accustomed itself to the higher appreciation of durable, lasting knowledge, and has lost all belief in inspiration and the miraculous communication of truths. Respecters of *forms*, certainly, with their standard of the beautiful and noble, will first of all have good reasons for mockery, as soon as the appreciation of unpretentious truths, and the scientific spirit, begin to obtain the mastery; but only because their eye has either not yet recognised the charm of the *simplest* form, or because men educated in that spirit are not yet completely and inwardly saturated by it, so that they still thoughtlessly imitate old forms (and badly enough, as one does who no longer cares much about the matter). Formerly the spirit was not occupied with strict thought, its earnestness then lay in the spinning out of symbols and forms. This is changed; that earnestness in the symbolical has become the mark of a lower culture. As our arts themselves grow ever more intellectual, our senses more spiritual, and as, for instance, people now judge concerning what sounds well to the senses quite differently from how they did a hundred years ago, so the forms of our life grow ever more *spiritual*, to the eye of older ages perhaps *uglier*, but only because it is incapable of perceiving how the kingdom of the inward, spiritual beauty constantly grows deeper and wider, and to what extent the inner intellectual look may be of more importance to us all than the most beautiful bodily frame and the noblest architectural structure.

23

The age of comparison – The less men are fettered by tradition, the greater becomes the inward activity of their motives; the greater, again, in proportion thereto, the outward restlessness, the confused flux of mankind, the polyphony of strivings. For whom is there still an absolute compulsion to bind himself and his descendants to one place? For whom is there still anything strictly compulsory? As all styles of arts are imitated simultaneously, so also are all grades and kinds of morality, of customs, of cultures. Such an age obtains its importance because in it the various views of the world, customs, and cultures can be compared and experienced simultaneously – which was formerly not possible with the always localised sway of every culture, corresponding to the rooting of all artistic styles in place and time. An increased aesthetic feeling will now at last decide amongst so many forms presenting themselves for comparison; it will allow the greater number, that is to say all those rejected by it, to die out. In the same way a selection amongst the forms and customs of the higher moralities is taking place, of which the aim can be nothing else than the downfall of the lower moralities. It is the age of comparison! That is its pride, but more justly also its grief. Let us not be afraid of this grief! Rather will we comprehend as adequately as possible the task our age sets us: posterity will bless us for doing so – a posterity which knows itself to be as much above the terminated original national cultures as above the culture of comparison, but which looks back with gratitude on both kinds of culture as upon antiquities worthy of veneration.

24

The possibility of progress – When a scholar of the ancient culture forswears the company of men who believe in progress, he does quite right. For the greatness and goodness of ancient culture lie behind it, and historical education compels one to admit that they can never be fresh again; an unbearable stupidity or an equally insufferable fanaticism would be necessary to deny this. But men can *consciously* resolve to develop themselves towards a new culture; whilst formerly they only developed unconsciously and by chance, they can now create better conditions for the rise of human beings, for their nourishment, education and instruction; they can administer the earth economically as a whole, and can generally weigh and restrain the powers of man. This new, conscious culture kills the old, which, regarded as a whole, has led an unconscious animal and plant life; it also kills distrust in progress – progress is *possible*. I must say that it is over-hasty and almost nonsensical to believe that progress must *necessarily* follow; but how could one deny that it is possible? On the other hand, progress in the sense and on the path of the old culture is not even thinkable. Even if romantic fantasy has also constantly used the word 'progress' to denote its aims (for instance, circumscribed primitive national cultures), it borrows the picture of it in any case from the past; its thoughts and ideas on this subject are entirely without originality.

25

Private and oecumenical morality – Since the belief has ceased that a God directs in general the fate of the world and, in spite of all apparent crookedness in the path of humanity, leads it on gloriously, men themselves must set themselves oecumenical aims embracing the whole earth. The older morality, especially that of Kant, required from the individual actions which were desired from all men – that was a delightfully naïve thing, as if each one knew off-hand what course of action was beneficial to the whole of humanity, and consequently which actions in general were desirable; it is a theory like that of free trade, taking for granted that the general harmony *must* result of itself according to innate laws of amelioration. Perhaps a future contemplation of the needs of humanity will show that it is by no means desirable that all men should act alike; in the interest of oecumenical aims it might rather be that for whole sections of mankind, special, and perhaps under certain circumstances even evil, tasks would have to be set. In any case, if mankind is not to destroy itself by such a conscious universal rule, there must previously be found, as a scientific standard for oecumenical aims, a *knowledge of the conditions of culture* superior to what has hitherto been attained. Herein lies the enormous task of the great minds of the next century.

26

Reaction as progress – Now and again there appear rugged, powerful, impetuous, but nevertheless backward-lagging minds which conjure up once more a past phase of mankind; they serve to prove that the new tendencies against which they are working are not yet sufficiently strong, that they still lack something, otherwise they would show better opposition to those

29

exorcisers. Thus, for example, Luther's Reformation bears witness to the fact that in his century all the movements of the freedom of the spirit were still uncertain, tender, and youthful; science could not yet lift up its head. Indeed the whole Renaissance seems like an early spring which is almost snowed under again. But in this century also, Schopenhauer's Metaphysics showed that even now the scientific spirit is not yet strong enough; thus the whole mediaeval Christian view of the world and human feeling could celebrate its resurrection in Schopenhauer's doctrine, in spite of the long achieved destruction of all Christian dogmas. There is much science in his doctrine, but it does not dominate it: it is rather the old well-known 'metaphysical requirement' that does so. It is certainly one of the greatest and quite invaluable advantages which we gain from Schopenhauer, that he occasionally forces our sensations back into older, mightier modes of contemplating the world and man, to which no other path would so easily lead us. The gain to history and justice is very great – I do not think that any one would so easily succeed now in doing justice to Christianity and its Asiatic relations without Schopenhauer's assistance, which is specially impossible from the basis of still existing Christianity. Only after this great *success of justice*, only after we have corrected so essential a point as the historical mode of contemplation which the age of enlightenment brought with it, may we again bear onward the banner of enlightenment, the banner with the three names, Petrarch, Erasmus, Voltaire. We have turned reaction into progress.

27

A substitute for religion – It is believed that something good is said of philosophy when it is put forward as a substitute for religion for the people. As a matter of fact, in the spiritual economy there is need, at times, of an *intermediary* order of thought: the transition from religion to scientific contemplation is a violent, dangerous leap, which is not to be recommended. To this extent the recommendation is justifiable. But one should eventually learn that the needs which have been satisfied by religion and are now to be satisfied by philosophy are not unchangeable; these themselves can be *weakened* and *eradicated*. Think, for instance, of the Christian's distress of soul, his sighing over inward corruption, his anxiety for salvation – all notions which originate only in errors of reason and deserve not satisfaction but destruction. A philosophy can serve either to *satisfy* those needs or to *set them aside*; for they are acquired, temporally limited needs, which are based upon suppositions contradictory to those of science. Here, in order to make a transition, *art* is far rather to be employed to relieve the mind over-burdened with emotions; for those notions receive much less support from it than from a meta-physical philosophy. It is easier, then, to pass over from art to a really liberating philosophical science.

28

Ill-famed words – Away with those wearisomely hackneyed terms Optimism and Pessimism! For the occasion for using them becomes less and less from day to day; only the chatterboxes still find them so absolutely necessary. For why in all the world should any one wish to be an optimist unless he had a God to defend who *must* have created the best of worlds if he himself be goodness and perfection – what thinker, however, still needs the hypothesis of a God? But every occasion for a pessimistic confession of faith is also lacking when one has no interest in being annoyed at the advocates of God (the theologians, or the theologising philosophers), and in energetically defending the opposite view, that evil reigns, that pain is greater than pleasure, that the world is a bungled piece of work, the manifestation of an ill-will to life. But who still bothers about the theologians now – except the theologians? Apart from all theology and its contentions, it is quite clear that the world is not good and not bad (to say nothing of its being the best or the worst), and that the terms 'good' and 'bad' have only significance with respect to man, and indeed, perhaps, they are not justified even here in the way they are usually employed; in any case we must get rid of both the calumniating and the glorifying conception of the world.

29

Intoxicated by the scent of the blossoms – It is supposed that the ship of humanity has always a deeper draught, the heavier it is laden; it is believed that the deeper a man thinks, the more delicately he feels, the higher he values himself, the greater his distance from the other animals – the more he appears as a genius amongst the animals – all the nearer will he approach the real essence of the world and its knowledge; this he actually does too, through science, but he *means* to do so still more through his religions and arts. These certainly are blossoms of the world, but by no means any *nearer to the root of the world* than the stalk; it is not possible to understand the nature of things better through them, although almost every one believes he can. *Error* has made man so deep, sensitive, and inventive that he has put forth such blossoms as religions and arts. Pure knowledge could not have been capable of it. Whoever were to unveil for us the essence of the world would give us all the most disagreeable disillusionment. Not the world as thing-in-itself, but the world as representation (as error) is so full of meaning, so deep, so wonderful, bearing happiness and unhappiness in its bosom. This result leads to a philosophy of the logical denial of the world, which, however, can be combined with a practical world-affirming just as well as with its opposite.

30

Bad habits in reasoning – The usual false conclusions of mankind are these: a thing exists, therefore it has a right to exist. Here there is inference from the ability to live to its suitability; from its suitability to its rightfulness. Then: an opinion brings happiness; therefore it is the true opinion. Its effect is good; therefore it is itself good and true. To the effect is here assigned the predicate beneficent, good, in the sense of the useful, and the cause is then furnished with the same predicate good, but here in the sense of the logically valid. The inversion of the sentences would read thus: an affair cannot be carried through, or maintained, therefore it is wrong; an opinion causes pain or excites, therefore it is false. The free spirit who learns only too often the faultiness of this mode of reasoning, and has to suffer from its consequences, frequently gives way to the temptation to draw the very opposite conclusions, which, in general, are naturally just as false: an affair cannot be carried through, therefore it is good; an opinion is distressing and disturbing, therefore it is true.

31

The illogical necessary – One of those things that may drive a thinker into despair is the recognition of the fact that the illogical is necessary for man, and that out of the illogical comes much that is good. It is so firmly rooted in the passions, in language, in art, in religion, and generally in everything that gives value to life, that it cannot be withdrawn without thereby hopelessly injuring these beautiful things. It is only the all-too-naïve people who can believe that the nature of man can be changed into a purely logical one; but if there were degrees of proximity to this goal, how many things would not have to be lost on this course! Even the most rational man has need of nature again from time to time, *i.e.* his *illogical fundamental attitude* towards all things.

32

Injustice necessary – All judgments on the value of life are illogically developed, and therefore unjust. The inexactitude of the judgment lies, firstly, in the manner in which the material is presented, namely very imperfectly; secondly, in the manner in which the conclusion is formed out of it; and thirdly, in the fact that every separate element of the material is again the result of vitiated recognition, and this, too, of necessity. For instance, no experience of an individual, however near he may stand to us, can be perfect, so that we could have a logical right to make a complete estimate of him; all estimates are rash, and must be so. Finally, the standard by which we measure our nature, is not of unalterable dimensions – we have moods and vacillations, and yet we should have to recognise ourselves as a fixed standard in order to estimate correctly the relation of any thing whatever to ourselves. From this it will, perhaps, follow that we should make no judgments at all; if one could only live without making estimations, without having likes and dislikes! For all dislike is connected with an estimation, as well as all inclination. An impulse towards or away from anything without a feeling that something advantageous is desired, something injurious avoided, an impulse without any kind of conscious valuation of the worth of the aim does not exist in man. We are from the beginning illogical, and therefore unjust beings, *and can recognise this*; it is one of the greatest and most inexplicable discords of existence.

The History of the Moral Sentiments

39

The fable of intelligible freedom – The history of the sentiments by means of which we make a person responsible consists of the following principal phases. First, all single actions are called good or bad without any regard to their motives, but only on account of the useful or injurious consequences which result for the community. But soon the origin of these distinctions is forgotten, and it is deemed that the qualities 'good' or 'bad' are contained in the action itself without regard to its consequences, by the same error according to which language describes the stone as hard, the tree as green – with which, in short, the result is regarded as the cause. Then the goodness or badness is implanted in the motive, and the action in itself is looked upon as morally ambiguous. Mankind even goes further, and applies the predicate good or bad no longer to single motives, but to the whole nature of an individual, out of whom the motive grows as the plant grows out of the earth. Thus, in turn, man is made responsible for his operations, then for his actions, then for his motives, and finally for his nature. Eventually it is discovered that even this nature cannot be responsible, inasmuch as it is an absolutely necessary consequence concreted out of the elements and influences of past and present things – that man, therefore, cannot be made responsible for anything, neither for his nature, nor his motives, nor his actions, nor his effects. It has therewith come to be recognised that the history of moral valuations is at the same time the history of an error, the error of responsibility, which is based upon the error of the freedom of will. Schopenhauer thus decided against it: because certain actions bring ill humour ('consciousness of guilt') in their train, there must be a responsibility; for there would be *no reason* for this ill humour if not only all human actions were not done of necessity – which is actually the case and also the belief of this philosopher – but man himself from the same necessity is precisely the *being* that he is – which Schopenhauer denies. From the fact of that ill humour Schopenhauer thinks he can prove a liberty which man must somehow have had, not with regard to actions, but with regard to nature; liberty, therefore, to *be* thus or otherwise, not to *act* thus or otherwise. From the *esse*, the sphere of freedom and responsibility, there results, in his opinion, the *operari*, the sphere of strict causality, necessity, and irresponsibility. This ill humour is apparently directed to the *operari* – in so far it is erroneous – but in reality it is directed to the *esse*, which is the deed of a free will, the fundamental cause of the existence of an individual; man becomes that which he *wishes* to be, his will is anterior to his existence. Here the mistaken conclusion is drawn that from the fact of the ill humour, the justification, the reasonable *admissableness* of this ill humour is presupposed; and starting from this mistaken conclusion, Schopenhauer arrives at his fantastic sequence of the so-called intelligible freedom. But the ill humour after the deed is not necessarily reasonable, indeed it is assuredly not reasonable, for it is based upon the erroneous presumption that the action need *not* have inevitably followed. Therefore, it is only because man *believes* himself to be free, not because he is free, that he experiences remorse and pricks of conscience. Moreover, this ill humour is a habit that can be broken off; in many people it is entirely absent in connection with actions where others experience it. It is a very changeable thing, and one which is connected with the development of customs and culture, and probably only existing during a comparatively short period of the world's history. Nobody is responsible for his actions, nobody for his nature; to judge is identical with being unjust. This also applies when an individual judges himself. The theory is as clear as sunlight, and yet every one prefers to go back into the shadow and the untruth, for fear of the consequences.

40

The super-animal – The beast in us wishes to be deceived; morality is a lie of necessity in order that we may not be torn in pieces by it. Without the errors which lie in the assumption of morality, man would have remained an animal. Thus, however, he has considered himself as something higher and has laid strict laws upon himself. Therefore he hates the grades which have remained nearer to animalness, whereby the former scorn of the slave, as a not-yet-man, is to be explained as a fact.

41

The unchangeable character – That the character is unchangeable is not true in a strict sense; this favourite theory means rather, that during the short lifetime of an individual the new influencing motives cannot penetrate deeply enough to destroy the ingrained marks of many thousands of years. But if one were to imagine a man of eighty thousand years, one would have in him an absolutely changeable character, so that a number of different individuals would gradually develop out of him. The shortness of human life misleads us into forming many erroneous ideas about the qualities of man.

42

The order of possessions and morality – The once-accepted hierarchy of possessions, according as this or the other is coveted by a lower, higher, or highest egoism, now decides what is moral or immoral. To prefer a lesser good (for instance, the gratification of the senses) to a more highly valued good (for instance, health) is accounted immoral, and also to prefer luxury to liberty. The hierarchy of possessions, how-ever, is not fixed and equal at all times; if any one prefers vengeance to justice he is moral according to the standard of an earlier civilisation, but immoral according to the present one. To be 'immoral', therefore, denotes that an individual has not felt, or not felt sufficiently strongly, the higher, finer, spiritual motives which have come in with a new culture; it marks one who has remained behind, but only according to the difference of degrees. The order of possessions itself is *not* raised and lowered according to a moral point of view; but each time that it is fixed it supplies the decision as to whether an action is moral or immoral.

43

Cruel people as those who have remained behind – People who are cruel nowadays must be accounted for by us as the grades of earlier civilisations which have survived; here are exposed those deeper formations in the mountain of humanity which usually remain concealed. They are backward people whose brains, through all manner of accidents in the course of inheritance, have not been developed in so delicate and manifold a way. They show us what we all *were* and horrify us, but they themselves are as little responsible as is a block of granite for being granite. There must, too, be grooves and twists in our brains which answer to that condition of mind, as in the form of certain human organs there are supposed to be traces of a fish-state. But these grooves and twists are no longer the bed through which the stream of our sensation flows.

44

Gratitude and revenge – The reason why the powerful man is grateful is this: his benefactor, through the benefit he confers, has mistaken and intruded into the sphere of the powerful man – now the latter, in return, penetrates into the sphere of the benefactor by the act of gratitude. It is a milder form of revenge. Without the satisfaction of gratitude, the powerful man would have shown himself powerless, and would have been reckoned as such ever after. Therefore every society of the good, which originally meant the powerful, places gratitude amongst the first duties. Swift propounded the maxim that men were grateful in the same proportion as they were revengeful.

45

The twofold early history of good and evil – The conception of good and evil has a twofold early history, namely, *once* in the soul of the ruling tribes and castes. Whoever has the power of returning good for good, evil for evil, and really practises requital, and who is, therefore, grateful and revengeful, is called good; whoever is powerless, and unable to requite, is reckoned as bad. As a good man one is reckoned among the 'good', a community which has common feelings because the single individuals are bound to one another by the sense of requital. As a bad man one belongs to the 'bad', to a party of subordinate, powerless people who have no common feeling. The good are a caste, the bad are a mass like dust. Good and bad have for a long time meant the same thing as noble and base, master and slave. On the other hand, the enemy is not looked upon as evil, he can requite. In Homer the Trojan and the Greek are both good. It is not the one who injures us, but the one who is despicable, who is called bad. Good is inherited in the community of the good; it is impossible that a bad man could spring from such good soil. If, nevertheless, one of the good ones does something which is unworthy of the good, refuge is sought in excuses; the guilt is thrown upon a god, for instance; it is said that he has struck the good man with blindness and madness –

Then in the soul of the oppressed and powerless. Here every *other* man is looked upon as hostile, inconsiderate, rapacious, cruel, cunning, be he noble or base; evil is the distinguishing word for man, even for every conceivable living creature, *e.g.* for a god;

human, divine, is the same thing as devilish, evil. The signs of goodness, helpfulness, pity, are looked upon with fear as spite, the prelude to a terrible result, stupefaction and outwitting – in short, as refined malice. With such a disposition in the individual a community could hardly exist, or at most it could exist only in its crudest form, so that in all places where this conception of good and evil obtains, the downfall of the single individuals, of their tribes and races, is at hand. Our present civilisation has grown up on the soil of the *ruling* tribes and castes.

46

Sympathy stronger than suffering – There are cases when sympathy is stronger than actual suffering. For instance, we are more pained when one of our friends is guilty of something shameful than when we do it ourselves. For one thing, we have more faith in the purity of his character than he has himself; then our love for him, probably on account of this very faith, is stronger than his love for himself. And even if his egoism suffers more thereby than our egoism, inasmuch as it has to bear more of the bad consequences of his fault, the un-egoistic in us – this word is not to be taken too seriously, but only as a modification of the expression – is more deeply wounded by his guilt than is the un-egoistic in him.

47

Hypochondria – There are people who become hypochondriacal through their sympathy and concern for another person; the kind of sympathy which results therefrom is nothing but a disease. Thus there is also a Christian hypochondria, which afflicts those solitary, religiously-minded people who keep constantly before their eyes the sufferings and death of Christ.

48

Economy of goodness – Goodness and love, as the most healing herbs and powers in human intercourse, are such costly discoveries that one would wish as much economy as possible to be exercised in the employment of these balsamic means; but this is impossible. The economy of goodness is the dream of the most daring Utopians.

49

Goodwill – Amongst the small, but countlessly frequent and therefore very effective, things to which science should pay more attention than to the great, rare things, is to be reckoned goodwill; I mean that exhibition of a friendly disposition in intercourse, that smiling eye, that clasp of the hand, that cheerfulness with which almost all human actions are usually accompanied. Every teacher, every official, adds this to whatever is his duty; it is the perpetual occupation of humanity, and at the same time the waves of its light, in which everything grows; in the narrowest circle, namely, within the family, life blooms and flourishes only through that goodwill. Kindliness, friendliness, the courtesy of the heart, are ever-flowing streams of un-egoistic impulses, and have given far more powerful assistance to culture than even those much more famous demonstrations which are called pity, mercy, and self-sacrifice. But they are thought little of, and, as a matter of fact, there is not much that is un-egoistic in them. The *sum* of these small doses is nevertheless mighty, their united force is amongst the strongest forces. Thus one finds much more happiness in the world than sad eyes see, if one only reckons rightly, and does not forget all those moments of comfort in which every day is rich, even in the most harried of human lives.

50

The wish to arouse pity – In the most remarkable passage of his auto-portrait (first printed in 1658), La Rochefoucauld assuredly hits the nail on the head when he warns all sensible people against pity, when he advises them to leave that to those orders of the people who have need of passion (because it is not ruled by reason), and to reach the point of helping the suffering and acting energetically in an accident; while pity, according to his (and Plato's) judgment, weakens the soul. Certainly we should *exhibit* pity, but take good care not to feel it, for the unfortunate are so *stupid* that to them the exhibition of pity is the greatest good in the world. One can, perhaps, give a more forcible warning against this feeling of pity if one looks upon that need of the unfortunate not exactly as stupidity and lack of intellect, a kind of mental derangement which misfortune brings with it (and as such, indeed, La Rochefoucauld appears to regard it), but as something quite different and more serious. Observe children, who cry and scream *in order* to be pitied, and therefore wait for the moment when they will be noticed; live in intercourse with the sick and mentally oppressed, and ask yourself whether that ready complaining and whimpering, that making a show of misfortune, does not, at bottom, aim at *making the spectators miserable*; the pity which the spectators then exhibit is in so far a consolation for the weak and suffering in that the latter recognise therein that they *possess still one power*, in spite of their weakness, *the power of giving pain*. The unfortunate derives a sort of pleasure from this feeling of superiority, of which the exhibition of pity makes him conscious; his imagination is exalted, he is still powerful enough to give the world pain. Thus the thirst for pity is the thirst for self-gratification, and that, moreover, at the expense of his fellow-men; it shows man in the whole inconsiderateness of his own dear self, but not exactly in his 'stupidity', as La Rochefoucauld thinks. In society-talk three-fourths of all questions asked and of all answers given are intended to cause the interlocutor a little pain; for this reason so many people pine for company; it enables them to feel their power. There is a powerful charm of life in such countless but very small doses in which malice makes itself felt, just as goodwill, spread in the same way throughout the world, is the ever-ready means of healing. But are there many honest people who will admit that it is pleasing to give pain? That one not infrequently amuses one's self – and amuses one's self very well – in causing mortifications to others, at least in thought, and firing off at them the grapeshot of petty malice? Most people are too dishonest, and a few are too good, to know anything of this *pudendum*; these will always deny that Prosper Mérimée is right when he says, '*Sachez aussi qu'il n'y a rien de plus commun que de faire le mal pour le plaisir de le faire.*'

51

How appearance becomes actuality – The actor finally reaches such a point that even in the deepest sorrow he cannot cease from thinking about the impression made by his own person and the general scenic effect; for instance, even at the funeral of his child, he will weep over his own sorrow and its expression like one of his own audience. The hypocrite, who always plays one and the same part, ceases at last to be a hypocrite; for instance, priests, who as young men are generally conscious or unconscious hypocrites, become at last natural, and are then really without any affectation, just priests; or if the father does not succeed so far, perhaps the son does, who makes use of his father's progress and inherits his habits. If any one long and obstinately desires to *appear* something, he finds it difficult at last to *be* anything else. The profession of almost every individual, even of the artist, begins with hypocrisy, with an imitating from without, with a copying of the effective. He who always wears the mask of a friendly expression must eventually obtain a power over well-meaning dispositions without which the expression of friendliness is not to be compelled – and finally, these, again, obtain a power over him, he *is* well-meaning.

52

The point of honour in deception – In all great deceivers one thing is noteworthy, to which they owe their power. In the actual act of deception, with all their preparations, the dreadful voice, expression, and mien, in the midst of their effective scenery they are overcome by their *belief in themselves*; it is this, then, which speaks so wonderfully and persuasively to the spectators. The founders of religions are distinguished from those great deceivers in that they never awake from their condition of self-deception; or at times, but very rarely, they have an enlightened moment when doubt overpowers them; they generally console themselves, however, by ascribing these enlightened moments to the influence of the Evil One. There must be self-deception in order that this and that may *produce* great *effects*. For men believe in the truth of everything that is visibly, strongly believed in.

53

The nominal degrees of truth – One of the commonest mistakes is this: because some one is truthful and honest towards us, he must speak the truth. Thus the child believes in its parents' judgment, the Christian in the assertions of the Founder of the Church. In the same way men refuse to admit that all those things which men defended in former ages with the sacrifice of life and happiness were nothing but errors; it is even said, perhaps, that they were degrees of the truth. But what is really meant is that when a man has honestly believed in something, and has fought and died for his faith, it would really be too *unjust* if he had only been inspired by an error. Such a thing seems a contradiction of eternal justice; therefore the heart of sensitive man ever enunciates against his head the axiom: between moral action and intellectual insight there must absolutely be a necessary connection. It is unfortunately otherwise; for there is no eternal justice.

54

Falsehood – Why do people mostly speak the truth in daily life? Assuredly not because a god has forbidden falsehood. But, firstly, because it is more convenient, as falsehood requires invention, deceit, and memory. (As Swift says, he who tells a lie is not sensible how great a task he undertakes; for in order to uphold one lie he must invent twenty others.) Therefore, because it is advantageous in upright circumstances to say straight out, 'I want this, I have done that,' and so on; because, in other words, the path of compulsion and authority is surer than that of cunning. But if a child has been brought up in complicated domestic circumstances, he employs falsehood, naturally and unconsciously says whatever best suits his interests; a sense of truth and a hatred of falsehood are quite foreign and unknown to him, and so he lies in all innocence.

55

Throwing suspicion on morality for faith's sake – No power can be maintained when it is only represented by hypocrites; no matter how many 'worldly' elements the Catholic Church possesses, its strength lies in those still numerous priestly natures who render life hard and full of meaning for themselves, and whose glance and worn bodies speak of nocturnal vigils, hunger, burning prayers, and perhaps even of scourging; these move men and inspire them with fear. What if it were *necessary* to live thus? This is the terrible question which their aspect brings to the lips. Whilst they spread this doubt they always uprear another pillar of their power; even the freethinker does not dare to withstand such unselfishness with hard words of truth, and to say, 'Thyself deceived, deceive not others!' Only the difference of views divides them from him, certainly no difference of goodness or badness; but men generally treat unjustly that which they do not like. Thus we speak of the cunning and the infamous art of the Jesuits, but overlook the self-control which every individual Jesuit practises, and the fact that the lightened manner of life preached by Jesuit books is by no means for their benefit, but for that of the laity. We may even ask whether, with precisely similar tactics and organisation, we enlightened ones would make equally good tools, equally admirable through self-conquest, indefatigableness, and renunciation.

56

Victory of knowledge over radical evil – It is of great advantage to him who desires to be wise to have witnessed for a time the spectacle of a thoroughly evil and degenerate man; it is false, like the contrary spectacle, but for whole long periods it held the mastery, and its roots have even extended and ramified themselves to us and our world. In order to understand *ourselves* we must understand *it*; but then, in order to mount higher we must rise above it. We recognise, then, that there exist no sins in the metaphysical sense; but, in the same sense, also no virtues; we recognise that the entire domain of ethical ideas is perpetually tottering, that there are higher and deeper conceptions of good and evil, of moral and immoral. He who does not desire much more from things than a knowledge of them easily makes peace with his soul, and will make a mistake (or commit a sin, as the world calls it) at the most from ignorance, but hardly from covetousness. He will no longer wish to excommunicate and exterminate desires; but his only, his wholly dominating ambition, to *know* as well as possible at all times, will make him cool and will soften all the savageness in his disposition. Moreover, he has been freed from a number of tormenting conceptions, he has no more feeling at the mention of the words 'punishments of hell', 'sinfulness', 'incapacity for good', he recognises in them only the vanishing shadow-pictures of false views of the world and of life.

57

Morality as the self-disintegration of man – A good author, who really has his heart in his work, wishes that some one could come and annihilate him by representing the same thing in a clearer way and answering without more ado the problems therein proposed. The loving girl wishes she could prove the self-sacrificing faithfulness of her love by the unfaithfulness of her beloved. The soldier hopes to die on the field of battle for his victorious fatherland; for his loftiest desires triumph in the victory of his country. The mother gives to the child that of which she deprives herself – sleep, the best food, sometimes her health and fortune. But are all these un-egoistic conditions? Are these deeds of morality *miracles*, because, to use Schopenhauer's expression, they are 'impossible and yet performed'? Is it not clear that in all four cases the individual loves *something of himself*, a thought, a desire, a production, better than *anything else of himself*; that he therefore divides his nature and to one part sacrifices all the rest? Is it something *entirely* different when an obstinate man says, 'I would rather be shot than move a step out of my way for this man'? The *desire for something* (wish, inclination, longing) is present in all the instances mentioned; to give way to it, with all its consequences, is certainly not 'unegoistic'. – In ethics man does not consider himself as *individuum* but as *dividuum*.

58

What one may promise – One may promise actions, but no sentiments, for these are involuntary. Whoever promises to love or hate a person, or be faithful to him for ever, promises something which is not within his power; he can certainly promise such actions as are usually the results of love, hate, or fidelity, but which may also spring from other motives; for many ways and motives lead to one and the same action. The promise to love some one for ever is, therefore, really: so long as I love you I will act towards you in a loving way; if I cease to love you, you will still receive the same treatment from me, although inspired by other motives, so that our fellow-men will still be deluded into the belief that our love is unchanged and ever the same. One promises, therefore, the continuation of the semblance of love, when, without self-deception, one speaks vows of eternal love.

59

Intellect and morality – One must have a good memory to be able to keep a given promise. One must have a strong power of imagination to be able to feel pity. So closely is morality bound to the goodness of the intellect.

60

To wish for revenge and to take revenge – To have a revengeful thought and to carry it into effect is to have a violent attack of fever, which passes off, however – but to have a revengeful thought without the strength and courage to carry it out is a chronic disease, a poisoning of body and soul which we have to bear about with us. Morality, which only takes intentions into account, considers the two cases as equal; usually the former case is regarded as the worse (because of the evil consequences which may perhaps result from the deed of revenge). Both estimates are short-sighted.

70

Execution – How is it that every execution offends us more than does a murder? It is the coldness of the judges, the painful preparations, the conviction that a human being is here being used as a warning to scare others. For the guilt is not punished, even if it existed – it lies with educators, parents, surroundings, in ourselves, not in the murderer – I mean the determining circumstances.

71

Hope – Pandora brought the box of ills and opened it. It was the gift of the gods to men, outwardly a beautiful and seductive gift, and called the Casket of Happiness. Out of it flew all the evils, living winged creatures; thence they now circulate and do men injury day and night. One single evil had not yet escaped from the box, and by the will of Zeus Pandora closed the lid and it remained within. Now for ever man has the casket of happiness in his house and thinks he holds a great treasure; it is at his disposal, he stretches out his hand for it whenever he desires; for he does not know the box which Pandora brought was the casket of evil, and he believes the ill which remains within to be the greatest blessing – it is hope. Zeus did not wish man, however much he might be tormented by the other evils, to fling away his life, but to go on letting himself be tormented again and again. Therefore he gives man hope – in reality it is the worst of all evils, because it prolongs the torments of man.

74

The everyday standard – One will seldom go wrong if one attributes extreme actions to vanity, average ones to habit, and petty ones to fear.

80

Old age and death – Apart from the commands of religion, the question may well be asked, Why is it more worthy for an old man who feels his powers decline, to await his slow exhaustion and extinction than with full consciousness to set a limit to his life? Suicide in this case is a perfectly natural, obvious action, which should justly arouse respect as a triumph of reason, and did arouse it in those times when the heads of Greek philosophy and the sturdiest patriots used to seek death through suicide. The seeking, on the contrary, to prolong existence from day to day, with anxious consultation of doctors and painful mode of living, without the power of drawing nearer to the actual aim of life, is far less worthy. Religion is rich in excuses to reply to the demand for suicide, and thus it ingratiates itself with those who wish to cling to life.

81

Errors of the sufferer and the doer – When a rich man deprives a poor man of a possession (for instance, a prince taking the sweetheart of a plebeian), an error arises in the mind of the poor man; he thinks that the rich man must be utterly infamous to take away from him the little that he has. But the rich man does not estimate so highly the value of a *single* possession, because he is accustomed to have many; hence he cannot imagine himself in the poor man's place, and does not commit nearly so great a wrong as the latter supposes. They each have a mistaken idea of the other. The injustice of the powerful, which, more than anything else, rouses indignation in history, is by no means so great as it appears. Alone the mere inherited consciousness of being a higher creation, with higher claims, produces a cold temperament, and leaves the conscience quiet; we all of us feel no injustice when the difference is very great between ourselves and another creature, and kill a fly, for instance, without any pricks of conscience. Therefore it was no sign of badness in Xerxes (whom even all Greeks describe as superlatively noble) when he took a son away from his father and had him cut in pieces, because he had expressed a nervous, ominous distrust of the whole campaign; in this case the individual is put out of the way like an unpleasant insect; he is too lowly to be allowed any longer to cause annoyance to a ruler of the world. Yes, every cruel man is not so cruel as the ill-treated one imagines; the idea of pain is not the same as its endurance. It is the same thing in the case of unjust judges, of the journalist who leads public opinion astray by small dishonesties. In all these cases cause and effect are surrounded by entirely different groups of feelings and thoughts; yet one unconsciously takes it for granted that doer and sufferer think and feel alike, and according to this supposition we measure the guilt of the one by the pain of the other.

83

The sleep of virtue – When virtue has slept, it will arise again all the fresher.

84

The refinement of shame – People are not ashamed to think something foul, but they are ashamed when they think these foul thoughts are attributed to them.

85

Malice is rare – Most people are far too much occupied with themselves to be malicious.

86

The tongue in the balance – We praise or blame according as the one or the other affords more opportunity for exhibiting our power of judgment.

92

The origin of Justice – Justice (equity) has its origin amongst powers which are fairly equal, as Thucydides (in the terrible dialogue between the Athenian and Melian ambassadors) rightly comprehended: that is to say, where there is no clearly recognisable supremacy, and where a conflict would be useless and would injure both sides, there arises the thought of coming to an understanding and settling the opposing claims; the character of *exchange* is the primary character of justice. Each party satisfies the other, as each obtains what he values more than the other. Each one receives that which he desires, as his own henceforth, and whatever is desired is received in return. Justice, therefore, is recompense and exchange based on the hypothesis of a fairly equal degree of power – thus, originally, revenge belongs to the province of justice, it is an exchange. Also gratitude. – Justice naturally is based on the point of view of a judicious self-preservation, on the egoism, therefore, of that reflection, 'Why should I injure myself uselessly and perhaps not attain my aim after all?' So much about the *origin* of justice. Because man, according to his intellectual custom, has *forgotten* the original purpose of so-called just and reasonable actions, and particularly because for hundreds of years children have been taught to admire and imitate such actions, the idea has gradually arisen that such an action is un-egoistic; upon this idea, however, is based the high estimation in which it is held: which, moreover, like all valuations, is constantly growing, for something that is valued highly is striven after, imitated, multiplied, and increases, because the value of the output of toil and enthusiasm of each individual is added to the value of the thing itself. How little moral would the world look without this forgetfulness! A poet might say that God had placed forgetfulness as doorkeeper in the temple of human dignity.

93

The right of the weaker – When any one submits under certain conditions to a greater power, as a besieged town for instance, the counter-condition is that one can destroy one's self, burn the town, and so cause the mighty one a great loss. Therefore there is a kind of *equalisation* here, on the basis of which rights may be determined. The enemy has his advantage in maintaining it. In so far there are also rights between slaves and masters, that is, precisely so far as the possession of the slave is useful and important to his master. The *right* originally extends *so far as* one *appears* to be valuable to the other, essentially unlosable, unconquerable, and so forth. In so far the weaker one also has rights, but lesser ones. Hence the famous *unusquisque tantum juris habet, quantum potentia valet* (or more exactly, *quantum potentia valere creditur*).

102

'Man always acts rightly' – We do not complain of nature as immoral because it sends a thunderstorm and makes us wet – why do we call those who injure us immoral? Because in the latter case we take for granted a free will functioning voluntarily; in the former we see necessity. But this distinction is an error. Thus we do not call even intentional injury immoral in all circumstances; for instance, we kill a fly unhesitatingly and intentionally, only because its buzzing annoys us; we punish a criminal intentionally and hurt him in order to protect ourselves and society. In the first case it is the individual who, in order to preserve himself, or even to protect himself from worry, does intentional injury; in the second case it is the State. All morals allow intentional injury *in the case of necessity*, that is, when it is a matter of *self-preservation*! But these two points of view suffice to explain all evil actions committed by men against men, we are desirous of obtaining pleasure or avoiding pain. In any case it is always a question of self-preservation. Socrates and Plato are right: whatever man does he always does well, that is, he does that which seems to him good (useful) according to the degree of his intellect, the particular standard of his reasonableness.

Self-defence – If self-defence is allowed to pass as moral, then almost all manifestations of the so-called immoral egoism must also stand; men injure, rob, or kill in order to preserve or defend themselves, to prevent personal injury; they lie where cunning and dissimulation are the right means of self-preservation. *Intentional injury*, when our existence or safety (preservation of our comfort) is concerned, is conceded to be moral; the State itself injures, according to this point of view, when it punishes. In unintentional injury, of course, there can be nothing immoral, that is ruled by chance. Is there, then, a kind of intentional injury where our existence or the preservation of our comfort is *not* concerned? Is there an injuring out of pure *malice*, for instance in cruelty? If one does not know how much an action hurts, it is no deed of malice; thus the child is not malicious towards the animal, not evil; he examines and destroys it like a toy. But *do* we ever know entirely how an action hurts another? As far as our nervous system extends we protect ourselves from pain; if it extended farther, to our fellow-men, namely, we should do no one an injury (except in such cases as we injure ourselves, where we cut ourselves for the sake of cure, tire and exert ourselves for the sake of health). We *conclude* by analogy that something hurts somebody, and through memory and the strength of imagination we may suffer from it ourselves. But still what a difference there is between toothache and the pain (pity) that the sight of toothache calls forth! Therefore, in injury out of so-called malice the *degree* of pain produced is always unknown to us; but inasmuch as there is *pleasure* in the action (the feeling of one's own power, one's own strong excitement), the action is committed, in order to preserve the comfort of the individual, and is regarded, therefore, from a similar point of view as defence and falsehood in necessity. No life without pleasure; the struggle for pleasure is the struggle for life. Whether the individual so fights this fight that men call him good, or so that they call him evil, is determined by the measure and the constitution of his *intellect*.

106

At the waterfall – In looking at a waterfall we imagine that there is freedom of will and fancy in the countless turnings, twistings, and breakings of the waves; but everything is compulsory, every movement can be mathematically calculated. So it is also with human actions; one would have to be able to calculate every single action beforehand if one were all-knowing; equally so all progress of knowledge, every error, all malice. The one who acts certainly labours under the illusion of voluntariness; if the world's wheel were to stand still for a moment and an all-knowing, calculating reason were there to make use of this pause, it could foretell the future of every creature to the remotest times, and mark out every track upon which that wheel would continue to roll. The delusion of the acting agent about himself, the supposition of a free will, belongs to this mechanism which still remains to be calculated.

The Soul of Artists and Authors

176

Shakespeare as a moralist – Shakespeare meditated much on the passions, and on account of his temperament had probably a close acquaintance with many of them (dramatists are in general rather wicked men). He could, however not talk on the subject, like Montaigne, but put his observations thereon into the mouths of impassioned figures, which is contrary to nature, certainly, but makes his dramas so rich in thought that they cause all others to seem poor in comparison and readily arouse a general aversion to them. Schiller's reflections (which are almost always based on erroneous or trivial fancies) are just theatrical reflections, and as such are very effective; whereas Shakespeare's reflections do honour to his model, Montaigne, and contain quite serious thoughts in polished form, but on that account are too remote and refined for the eyes of the theatrical public, and are consequently ineffective.

178

The incomplete as the effective – Just as figures in relief make such a strong impression on the imagination because they seem in the act of emerging from the wall and only stopped by some sudden hindrance; so the relief-like, incomplete representation of a thought, or a whole philosophy, is sometimes more effective than its exhaustive amplification – more is left for the investigation of the onlooker, he is incited to the further study of that which stands out before him in such strong light and shade; he is prompted to think out the subject, and even to overcome the hindrance which hitherto prevented it from emerging clearly.

185

Authors' paradoxes – The so-called paradoxes of an author to which a reader objects are often not in the author's book at all, but in the reader's head.

187

Antithesis – Antithesis is the narrow gate through which error is fondest of sneaking to the truth.

189

Thoughts in poetry – The poet conveys his thoughts ceremoniously in the vehicle of rhythm, usually because they are not able to go on foot.

193

Draconian law against authors – One should regard authors as criminals who only obtain acquittal or mercy in the rarest cases – that would be a remedy for books becoming too rife.

The Signs of Higher and Lower Culture

224

Ennoblement through degeneration – History teaches that a race of people is best preserved where the greater number hold one common spirit in consequence of the similarity of their accustomed and indisputable principles: in consequence, therefore, of their common faith. Thus strength is afforded by good and thorough customs, thus is learnt the subjection of the individual, and strenuousness of character becomes a birth gift and afterwards is fostered as a habit. The danger to these communities founded on individuals of strong and similar character is that gradually increasing stupidity through transmission, which follows all stability like its shadow. It is on the more unrestricted, more uncertain and morally weaker individuals that depends the *intellectual progress* of such communities, it is they who attempt all that is new and manifold. Numbers of these perish on account of their weakness, without having achieved any specially visible effect; but generally, particularly when they have descendants, they flare up and from time to time inflict a wound on the stable element of the community. Precisely in this sore and weakened place the community is *inoculated* with something new; but its general strength must be great enough to absorb and assimilate this new thing into its blood. Deviating natures are of the utmost importance wherever there is to be progress. Every wholesale progress must be preceded by a partial weakening. The strongest natures *retain* the type, the weaker ones help it to *develop*. Something similar happens in the case of individuals; a deterioration, a mutilation, even a vice and, above all, a physical or moral loss is seldom without its advantage. For instance, a sickly man in the midst of a warlike and restless race will perhaps have more chance of being alone and thereby growing quieter and wiser, the one-eyed man will possess a stronger eye, the blind man will have a deeper inward sight and will certainly have a keener sense of hearing. In so far it appears to me that the famous Struggle for Existence is not the only point of view from which an explanation can be given of the progress or strengthening of an individual or a race. Rather must two different things converge: firstly, the multiplying of stable strength through mental binding in faith and common feeling; secondly, the possibility of attaining to higher aims, through the fact that there are deviating natures and, in consequence, partial weakening and wounding of the stable strength; it is precisely the weaker nature, as the more delicate and free, that makes all progress at all possible. A people that is crumbling and weak in any one part, but as a whole still strong and healthy, is able to absorb the infection of what is new and incorporate it to its advantage. The task of education in a single individual is this: to plant him so firmly and surely that, as a whole, he can no longer be diverted from his path. Then, however, the educator must wound him, or else make use of the wounds which fate inflicts, and when pain and need have thus arisen, something new and noble can be inoculated into the wounded places. With regard to the State, Machiavelli says that, 'the form of Government is of very small importance, although half-educated people think otherwise. The great aim of Statecraft should be duration, which outweighs all else, inasmuch as it is more valuable than liberty'. It is only with securely founded and guaranteed duration that continual development and ennobling inoculation are at all possible. As a rule, however, authority, the dangerous companion of all duration, will rise in opposition to this.

227

Conclusions drawn from the consequences and traced back to Reason and Un-reason – All states and orders of society, professions, matrimony, education, law: all these find strength and duration only in the faith which the fettered spirits repose in them – that is, in the absence of reasons, or at least in the averting of inquiries as to reasons. The restricted spirits do not willingly acknowledge this, and feel that it is a *pudendum*. Christianity, however, which was very simple in its intellectual ideas, remarked nothing of this *pudendum*, required faith and nothing but faith, and passionately repulsed the demand for reasons; it pointed to the success of faith: 'You will soon feel the advantages of faith', it suggested, 'and through faith shall ye be saved.' As an actual fact, the State pursues the same course, and every father brings up his son in the same way: 'Only believe this,' he says, 'and you will soon feel the good it does.' This implies, however, that the truth of an opinion is proved by its personal usefulness; the wholesomeness of a doctrine must be a guarantee for its intellectual surety and solidity. It is exactly as if an accused person in a court of law were to say, 'My counsel speaks the whole truth, for only see what is the result of his speech: I shall be acquitted.' Because the fettered spirits retain their principles on account of their usefulness, they suppose that the free spirit also seeks his own advantage in his views and only holds that to be true which is profitable to him. But as he appears to find profitable just the contrary of that which his compatriots or equals find profitable, these latter assume that his principles are dangerous to them; they say or feel, 'He must not be right, for he is injurious to us'.

228

The strong, good character – The restriction of views, which habit has made instinct, leads to what is called strength of character When any one acts from few but always from the same motives, his actions acquire great energy; if these actions accord with the principles of the fettered spirits they are recognised, and they produce, moreover, in those who perform them, the sensation of a good conscience. Few motives, energetic action, and a good conscience compose what is called strength of character. The man of strong character lacks a knowledge of the many possibilities and directions of action; his intellect is fettered and restricted, because in a given case it shows him, perhaps, only two possibilities; between these two he must now of necessity choose, in accordance with his whole nature, and he does this easily and quickly because he has not to choose between fifty possibilities. The educating surroundings aim at fettering every individual, by always placing before him the smallest number of possibilities. The individual is always treated by his educators as if he were, indeed, something new but should become a *duplicate*. If he makes his first appearance as something unknown, unprecedented, he must be turned into something known and precedented. In a child, the familiar manifestation of restriction is called a good character; in placing itself on the side of the fettered spirits the child first discloses its awakening common feeling; with this foundation of common sentiment, he will eventually become useful to his State or rank.

229

The standards and values of the fettered spirits – There are four species of things concerning which the restricted spirits say they are in the right. Firstly: all things that last are right; secondly: all things that are not burdens to us are right; thirdly: all things that are advantageous for us are right; fourthly: all things for which we have made sacrifices are right. The last sentence, for instance, explains why a war that was begun in opposition to popular feeling is carried on with enthusiasm directly a sacrifice has been made for it. The free spirits, who bring their case before the forum of the fettered spirits, must prove that free spirits always existed, that free-spiritism is therefore enduring, that it will not become a burden, and, finally, that on the whole they are an advantage to the fettered spirits. It is because they cannot convince the restricted spirits on this last point that they profit nothing by having proved the first and second propositions.

230

Esprit fort – Compared with him who has tradition on his side and requires no reasons for his actions, the free spirit is always weak, especially in action; for he is acquainted with too many motives and points of view, and has, therefore, an uncertain and unpractised hand. What means exist of making him *strong in spite of this*, so that he will, at least, manage to survive, and will not perish ineffectually? What is the source of the strong spirit (*esprit fort*)? This is especially the question as to the production of genius. Whence comes the energy, the unbending strength, the endurance with which the one, in opposition to accepted ideas, endeavours to obtain an entirely individual knowledge of the world?

237

Renaissance and reformation – The Italian Renaissance contained within itself all the positive forces to which we owe modern culture. Such were the liberation of thought, the disregard of authorities, the triumph of education over the darkness of tradition, enthusiasm for science and the scientific past of mankind, the unfettering of the Individual, an ardour for truthfulness and a dislike of delusion and mere effect (which ardour blazed forth in an entire company of artistic characters, who with the greatest moral purity required from themselves perfection in their works, and nothing but perfection); yes, the Renaissance had positive forces, which have, *as yet*, never become so mighty again in our modern culture. It was the Golden Age of the last thousand years, in spite of all its blemishes and vices. On the other hand, the

German Reformation stands out as an energetic protest of antiquated spirits, who were by no means tired of mediaeval views of life, and who received the signs of its dissolution, the extraordinary flatness and alienation of the religious life, with deep dejection instead of with the rejoicing that would have been seemly. With their northern strength and stiff-neckedness they threw mankind back again, brought about the counter-reformation, that is, a Catholic Christianity of self-defence, with all the violences of a state of siege, and delayed for two or three centuries the complete awakening and mastery of the sciences; just as they probably made for ever impossible the complete inter-growth of the antique and the modern spirit. The great task of the Renaissance could not be brought to a termination, this was prevented by the protest of the contemporary backward German spirit (which, for its salvation, had had sufficient sense in the Middle Ages to cross the Alps again and again). It was the chance of an extraordinary constellation of politics that Luther was preserved, and that his protest gained strength, for the Emperor protected him in order to employ him as a weapon against the Pope, and in the same way he was secretly favoured by the Pope in order to use the Protestant princes as a counterweight against the Emperor. Without this curious counter-play of intentions, Luther would have been burnt like Huss – and the morning sun of enlightenment would probably have risen somewhat earlier, and with a splendour more beauteous than we can now imagine.

247

The circulation of humanity – It is possible that all humanity is only a phase of development of a certain species of animal of limited duration. Man may have grown out of the ape and will return to the ape again, without anybody taking an interest in the ending of this curious comedy. Just as with the decline of Roman civilisation and its most important cause, the spread of Christianity, there was a general uglification of man within the Roman Empire, so, through the eventual decline of general culture, there might result a far greater uglification and finally an animalising of man till he reached the ape. But just because we are able to face this prospect, we shall perhaps be able to avert such an end.

252

The pleasure in discernment – Why is discernment, that essence of the searcher and the philosopher, connected with pleasure? Firstly, and above all, because thereby we become conscious of our strength, for the same reason that gymnastic exercises, even without spectators, are enjoyable. Secondly, because in the course of knowledge we surpass older ideas and their representatives, and become, or believe ourselves to be, conquerors. Thirdly, because even a very little new knowledge exalts us above *every one*, and makes us feel we are the only ones who know the subject aright. These are the three most important reasons of the pleasure, but there are many others, according to the nature of the discerner. A not inconsiderable index of such is given, where no one would look for it, in a passage of my parenetic work on Schopenhauer, with the arrangement of which every experienced servant of knowledge may be satisfied, even though he might wish to dispense with the ironical touch that seems to pervade those pages. For if it be true that for the making of a scholar 'a number of very human impulses and desires must be thrown together,' that the scholar is indeed a very noble but not a pure metal, and 'consists of a confused blending of very different impulses and attractions,' the same thing may be said equally of the making and nature of the artist, the philosopher and the moral genius – and whatever glorified great names there may be in that list. *Everything* human deserves ironical consideration with respect to its *origin* – therefore irony is so *superfluous* in the world.

253

Fidelity as a proof of validity – It is a perfect sign of a sound theory if during *forty years* its originator does not mistrust it; but I maintain that there has never yet been a philosopher who has not eventually deprecated the philosophy of his youth. Perhaps, however, he has not spoken publicly of this change of opinion, for reasons of ambition, or, what is more probable in noble natures, out of delicate consideration for his adherents.

255

The superstition of the simultaneous – Simultaneous things hold together, it is said. A relative dies far away, and at the same time we dream about him – Consequently! But countless relatives die and we do not dream about them. It is like shipwrecked people who make vows; afterwards, in the temples, we do not see the votive tablets of those who perished. A man dies, an owl hoots, a clock stops, all at one hour of the night – must there not be some connection? Such an intimacy with nature as this supposition implies is flattering to mankind. This species of superstition is found again in a refined form in historians and delineators of culture, who usually have a kind of hydrophobic horror of all that senseless mixture, in which individual and national life is so rich.

259

A male culture – The Greek culture of the classic age is a male culture. As far as women are concerned, Pericles expresses everything in the funeral speech: 'They are best when they are as little spoken of as possible amongst men.' The erotic relation of men to youths was the necessary and sole preparation, to a degree unattainable to our comprehension, of all manly education (pretty much as for a long time all higher education of women was only attainable through love and marriage). All idealism of the strength of the Greek nature threw itself into that relation, and it is probable that never since have young men been treated so attentively, so lovingly, so entirely with a view to their welfare (*virtus*) as in the fifth and sixth centuries B.C. – according to the beautiful saying of Hölderlin: '*denn liebend giebt der Sterbliche vom Besten.*' The higher the light in which this relation was regarded, the lower sank intercourse with woman; nothing else was taken into consideration than the production of children and lust; there was no intellectual intercourse, not even real love-making. If it be further remembered that women were even excluded from contests and spectacles of every description, there only remain the religious cults as

71

their sole higher occupation. For although in the tragedies Electra and Antigone were represented, this was only *tolerated* in art, but not liked in real life – just as now we cannot endure anything pathetic in *life* but like it in art. The women had no other mission than to produce beautiful, strong bodies, in which the father's character lived on as unbrokenly as possible, and therewith to counteract the increasing nerve-tension of such a highly developed culture. This kept the Greek culture young for a relatively long time; for in the Greek mothers the Greek genius always returned to nature.

260

The prejudice in favour of greatness – It is clear that men overvalue everything great and prominent. This arises from the conscious or unconscious idea that they deem it very useful when one person throws all his strength into one thing and makes himself into a monstrous organ. Assuredly, an *equal* development of all his powers is more useful and happier for man; for every talent is a vampire which sucks blood and strength from other powers, and an exaggerated production can drive the most gifted almost to madness. Within the circle of the arts, too, extreme natures excite far too much attention; but a much lower culture is necessary to be captivated by them. Men submit from habit to everything that seeks power.

263

Talents – In such a highly developed humanity as the present, each individual naturally has access to many talents. Each has an *inborn talent*, but only in a few is that degree of toughness, endurance, and energy born and trained that he really becomes a talent, *becomes* what he *is* – that is, that he discharges it in works and actions.

266

The undervalued effect of public-school teaching – The value of a public school is seldom sought in those things which are really learnt there and are carried away never to be lost, but in those things which are learnt and which the pupil only acquires against his will, in order to get rid of them again as soon as possible. Every educated person acknowledges that the reading of the classics, as now practised, is a monstrous proceeding carried on before young people are ripe enough for it by teachers who with every word, often by their appearance alone, throw a mildew on a good author. But therein lies the value, generally unrecognised, of these teachers who speak *the abstract language of the higher culture*, which, though dry and difficult to understand, is yet a sort of higher gymnastics of the brain; and there is value in the constant recurrence in their language of ideas, artistic expressions, methods and allusions which the young people hardly ever hear in the conversations of their relatives and in the street. Even if the pupils only *hear*, their intellect is involuntarily trained to a scientific mode of regarding things. It is not possible to emerge from this discipline entirely untouched by its abstract character, and to remain a simple child of nature.

267

Learning many languages – The learning of many languages fills the memory with words instead of with facts and thoughts, and this is a vessel which, with every person, can only contain a certain limited amount of contents. Therefore the learning of many languages is injurious, inasmuch as it arouses a belief in possessing dexterity and, as a matter of fact, it lends a kind of delusive importance to social intercourse. It is also indirectly injurious in that it opposes the acquirement of solid knowledge and the intention to win the respect of men in an honest way. Finally, it is the axe which is laid to the root of a delicate sense of language in our mother-tongue, which thereby is incurably injured and destroyed. The two nations which produced the greatest stylists, the Greeks and the French, learned no foreign languages. But as human intercourse must always grow more cosmopolitan, and as, for instance, a good merchant in London must now be able to read and write eight languages, the learning of many tongues has certainly become a necessary evil; but which, when finally carried to an extreme, will compel mankind to find a remedy, and in some far-off future there will be a new language, used at first as a language of commerce, then as a language of intellectual intercourse generally, then for all, as surely as some time or other there will be aviation. Why else should philology have studied the laws of languages for a whole century, and have estimated the necessary, the valuable, and the successful portion of each separate language?

277

Happiness and culture – We are moved at the sight of our childhood's surroundings – the arbour, the church with its graves, the pond and the wood – all this we see again with pain. We are seized with pity for ourselves; for what have we not passed through since then! And everything here is so silent, so eternal, only we are so changed, so moved; we even find a few human beings, on whom Time has sharpened his teeth no more than on an oak tree – peasants, fishermen, woodmen – they are unchanged. Emotion and self-pity at the sight of lower culture is the sign of higher culture; from which the conclusion may be drawn that happiness has certainly not been increased by it. Whoever wishes to reap happiness and comfort in life should always avoid higher culture.

282

Lamentation – It is, perhaps, the advantages of our epoch that bring with them a backward movement and an occasional undervaluing of the *vita contemplativa*. But it must be acknowledged that our time is poor in the matter of great moralists, that Pascal, Epictetus, Seneca, and Plutarch are now but little read, that work and industry – formerly in the following of the great goddess Health – sometimes appear to rage like a disease. Because time to think and tranquillity in thought are lacking, we no longer ponder over different views, but content ourselves with hating them. With the enormous acceleration of life, mind and eye grow accustomed to a partial and false sight and judgment, and all people are like travellers whose only acquaintance with countries and nations is derived from the railway. An independent and cautious attitude of knowledge is looked upon almost as a kind of madness; the free spirit is brought into disrepute, chiefly through scholars, who miss their thoroughness and ant-like industry in his art of regarding things and would gladly banish him into one single corner of science, while it has the different and higher mission of commanding the battalion rearguard of scientific and learned men from an isolated position, and showing them the ways and aims of culture. A song of lamentation such as that which has just been sung will probably have its own period, and will cease of its own accord on a forcible return of the genius of meditation.

283

The chief deficiency of active people – Active people are usually deficient in the higher activity, I mean individual activity. They are active as officials, merchants, scholars, that is as a species, but not as quite distinct separate and *single* individuals; in this respect they are idle. It is the misfortune of the active that their activity is almost always a little senseless. For instance, we must not ask the moneymaking banker the reason of his restless activity, it is foolish. The active roll as the stone rolls, according to the stupidity of mechanics. All mankind is divided, as it was at all times and is still, into slaves and freemen; for whoever has not two-thirds of his day for himself is a slave, be he otherwise whatever he likes, statesman, merchant, official, or scholar.

289

The value of disease – The man who is bedridden often perceives that he is usually ill of his position, business, or society, and through them has lost all self-possession. He gains this piece of knowledge from the idleness to which his illness condemns him.

291

Prudence of the free spirits – Free-thinkers, those who live by knowledge alone, will soon attain the supreme aim of their life and their ultimate position towards society and State, and will gladly content themselves, for instance, with a small post or an income that is just sufficient to enable them to live; for they will arrange to live in such a manner that a great change of outward prosperity, even an overthrow of the political order, would not cause an overthrow of their life. To all these things they devote as little energy as possible in order that with their whole accumulated strength, and with a long breath, they may dive into the element of knowledge. Thus they can hope to dive deep and be able to see the bottom. Such a spirit seizes only the point of an event, he does not care for things in the whole breadth and prolixity of their folds, for he does not wish to entangle himself in them. He, too, knows the weekdays of restraint, of dependence and servitude. But from time to time there must dawn for him a Sunday of liberty, otherwise he could not endure life. It is probable that even his love for humanity will be prudent and somewhat short-winded, for he desires to meddle with the world of inclinations and of blindness only as far as is necessary for the purpose of knowledge. He must trust that the genius of justice will say something for its disciple and protégé if accusing voices were to call him poor in love. In his mode of life and thought there is a *refined heroism*, which scorns to offer itself to the great mob-reverence, as its coarser brother does, and passes quietly through and out of the world. Whatever labyrinths it traverses, beneath whatever rocks its stream has occasionally worked its way – when it reaches the light it goes clearly, easily, and almost noiselessly on its way, and lets the sunshine strike down to its very bottom.

Man in Society

293

Well-meant dissimulation – In intercourse with men a well-meant dissimulation is often necessary, as if we did not see through the motives of their actions.

294

Copies – We not unfrequently meet with copies of prominent persons; and as in the case of pictures, so also here, the copies please more than the originals.

295

The public speaker – One may speak with the greatest appropriateness, and yet so that everybody cries out to the contrary – that is to say, when one does not speak to everybody.

296

Want of confidence – Want of confidence among friends is a fault that cannot be censured without becoming incurable.

297

The art of giving – To have to refuse a gift, merely because it has not been offered in the right way, provokes animosity against the giver.

298

The most dangerous partisan – In every party there is

one who, by his far too dogmatic expression of the party-principles, excites defection among the others.

299

Advisers of the sick – Whoever gives advice to a sick person acquires a feeling of superiority over him, whether the advice be accepted or rejected. Hence proud and sensitive sick persons hate advisers more than their sickness.

300

Double nature of equality – The rage for equality may so manifest itself that we seek either to draw all others down to ourselves (by belittling, disregarding, and tripping up), or ourselves and all others upwards (by recognition, assistance, and congratulation).

301

Against embarrassment – The best way to relieve and calm very embarrassed people is to give them decided praise.

302

Preference for certain virtues – We set no special value on the possession of a virtue until we perceive that it is entirely lacking in our adversary.

303

Why we contradict – We often contradict an opinion when it is really only the tone in which it is expressed that is unsympathetic to us.

304

Confidence and intimacy – Whoever proposes to command the intimacy of a person is usually uncertain of possessing his confidence. Whoever is sure of a person's confidence attaches little value to intimacy with him.

305

The equilibrium of friendship – The right equilibrium of friendship in our relation to other men is sometimes restored when we put a few grains of wrong on our own side of the scales.

306

The most dangerous physicians – The most dangerous physicians are those who, like born actors, imitate the born physician with the perfect art of imposture.

307

When paradoxes are permissible – In order to interest clever persons in a theory, it is sometimes only necessary to put it before them in the form of a prodigious paradox.

308

How courageous people are won over – Courageous people are persuaded to a course of action by representing it as more dangerous than it really is.

309

Courtesies – We regard the courtesies shown us by unpopular persons as offences.

310

Keeping people waiting – A sure way of exasperating people and of putting bad thoughts into their heads is to keep them waiting long. That makes them immoral.

311

Against the confidential – Persons who give us their full confidence think they have thereby a right to ours. That is a mistake; people acquire no rights through gifts.

312

A mode of settlement – It often suffices to give a person whom we have injured an opportunity to make a joke about us to give him personal satisfaction, and even to make him favourably disposed to us.

313

The vanity of the tongue – Whether man conceals his bad qualities and vices, or frankly acknowledges them, his vanity in either case seeks its advantage thereby – only let it be observed how nicely he distinguishes those from whom he conceals such qualities from those with whom he is frank and honest.

314

Considerate – To have no wish to offend or injure any one may as well be the sign of a just as of a timid nature.

315

Requisite for disputation – He who cannot put his thoughts on ice should not enter into the heat of dispute.

316

Intercourse and pretension – We forget our pretensions when we are always conscious of being amongst meritorious people; being alone implants presumption in us. The young are pretentious, for they associate with their equals, who are all ciphers but would fain have a great significance.

317

Motives of an attack – One does not attack a person merely to hurt and conquer him, but perhaps merely to become conscious of one's own strength.

318

Flattery – Persons who try by means of flattery to put us off our guard in intercourse with them, employ a dangerous expedient, like a sleeping-draught, which, when it does not send the patient to sleep, keeps him all the wider awake.

319

A good letter-writer – A person who does not write books, thinks much, and lives in unsatisfying society, will usually be a good letter-writer.

320

The ugliest of all – It may be doubted whether a person who has travelled much has found anywhere in the world uglier places than those to be met with in the human face.

321

The sympathetic ones – Sympathetic natures, ever ready to help in misfortune, are seldom those that participate in joy; in the happiness of others they have nothing to occupy them, they are superfluous, they do not feel themselves in possession of their superiority, and hence readily show their displeasure.

322

The relatives of a suicide – The relatives of a suicide take it in ill part that he did not remain alive out of consideration for their reputation.

323

Ingratitude foreseen – He who makes a large gift gets no gratitude; for the recipient is already overburdened by the acceptance of the gift.

324

In dull society – Nobody thanks a witty man for politeness when he puts himself on a par with a society in which it would not be polite to show one's wit.

325

The presence of witnesses – We are doubly willing to jump into the water after some one who has fallen in, if there are people present who have not the courage to do so.

326

Being silent – For both parties in a controversy, the most disagreeable way of retaliating is to be vexed and silent; for the aggressor usually regards the silence as a sign of contempt.

327

Friends' secrets – Few people will not expose the private affairs of their friends when at a loss for a subject of conversation.

328

Humanity – The humanity of intellectual celebrities consists in courteously submitting to unfairness in intercourse with those who are not celebrated.

329

The embarrassed – People who do not feel sure of themselves in society seize every opportunity of publicly showing their superiority to close friends, for instance by teasing them.

330

Thanks – A refined nature is vexed by knowing that some one owes it thanks, a coarse nature by knowing that it owes thanks to some one.

331

A sign of estrangement – The surest sign of the estrangement of the opinions of two persons is when they both say something ironical to each other and neither of them feels the irony.

332

Presumption in connection with merit – Presumption in connection with merit offends us even more than presumption in persons devoid of merit, for merit in itself offends us.

333

Danger in the voice – In conversation we are sometimes confused by the tone of our own voice, and misled to make assertions that do not at all correspond to our opinions.

334

In conversation – Whether in conversation with others we mostly agree or mostly disagree with them is a matter of habit; there is sense in both cases.

335

Fear of our neighbour – We are afraid of the animosity of our neighbour, because we are apprehensive that he may thereby discover our secrets.

336

Distinguishing by blaming – Highly respected persons distribute even their blame in such fashion that they try to distinguish us therewith. It is intended to remind us of their serious interest in us. We misunderstand them entirely when we take their blame literally and protest against it; we thereby offend them and estrange ourselves from them.

337

Indignation at the goodwill of others – We are mistaken as to the extent to which we think we are hated or feared; because, though we ourselves know very well the extent of our divergence from a person, tendency, or party, those others know us only superficially, and can, therefore, only hate us superficially. We often meet with goodwill which is inexplicable to us; but when we comprehend it, it shocks us, because it shows that we are not considered with sufficient seriousness or importance.

338

Thwarting vanities – When two persons meet whose vanity is equally great, they have afterwards a bad impression of each other; because each has been so occupied with the impression he wished to produce on the other that the other has made no impression upon him; at last it becomes clear to them both that their efforts have been in vain, and each puts the blame on the other.

339

Improper behaviour as a good sign – A superior mind takes pleasure in the tactlessness, pretentiousness, and even hostility of ambitious youths; it is the vicious habit of fiery horses which have not yet carried a rider, but, in a short time, will be so proud to carry one.

340

When it is advisable to suffer wrong – It is well to put up with accusations without refutation, even when they injure us, when the accuser would see a still greater fault on our part if we contradicted and perhaps even refuted him. In this way, certainly, a person may always be wronged and always have right on his side, and may eventually, with the best conscience in the world, become the most intolerable tyrant and tormentor; and what happens in the individual may also take place in whole classes of society.

341

Too little honoured – Very conceited persons, who have received less consideration than they expected, attempt for a long time to deceive themselves and others with regard to it, and become subtle psychologists in order to make out that they have been amply honoured. Should they not attain their aim, should the veil of deception be torn, they give way to all the greater fury.

342

Primitive conditions re-echoing in speech – By the manner in which people make assertions in their intercourse we often recognise an echo of the times when they were more conversant with weapons than anything else; sometimes they handle their assertions like sharpshooters using their arms, sometimes we think we hear the whizz and clash of swords, and with some men an assertion crashes down like a stout cudgel. Women, on the contrary, speak like beings who for thousands of years have sat at the loom, plied the needle, or played the child with children.

343

The narrator – He who gives an account of something readily betrays whether it is because the fact interests him, or because he wishes to excite interest by the narration. In the latter case he will exaggerate, employ superlatives, and such like. He then does not usually tell his story so well, because he does not think so much about his subject as about himself.

344

The reciter – He who recites dramatic works makes discoveries about his own character; he finds his voice more natural in certain moods and scenes than in others, say in the pathetic or in the scurrilous, while in ordinary life, perhaps, he has not had the opportunity to exhibit pathos or scurrility.

345

A comedy scene in real life – Some one conceives an ingenious idea on a theme in order to express it in society. Now in a comedy we should hear and see how he sets all sail for that point, and tries to land the company at the place where he can make his remark, how he continuously pushes the conversation towards the one goal, sometimes losing the way, finding it again, and finally arriving at the moment: he is almost breathless – and then one of the company takes the remark itself out of his mouth! What will he do? Oppose his own opinion?

346

Unintentionally discourteous – When a person treats another with unintentional discourtesy – for instance, not greeting him because not recognising him – he is vexed by it, although he cannot reproach his own sentiments; he is hurt by the bad opinion which he has produced in the other person, or fears the consequences of his bad humour, or is pained by the thought of having injured him – vanity, fear, or pity may therefore be aroused; perhaps all three together.

347

A masterpiece of treachery – To express a tantalising distrust of a fellow-conspirator, lest he should betray one, and this at the very moment when one is practising treachery one's self, is a masterpiece of wickedness; because it absorbs the other's attention and compels him for a time to act very unsuspiciously and openly, so that the real traitor has thus acquired a free hand.

348

To injure and to be injured – It is far pleasanter to injure and afterwards beg for forgiveness than to be injured and grant forgiveness. He who does the former gives evidence of power and afterwards of kindness of character. The person injured, however, if he does not wish to be considered inhuman, *must* forgive; his enjoyment of the other's humiliation is insignificant on account of this constraint.

349

In a dispute – When we contradict another's opinion and at the same time develop our own, the constant consideration of the other opinion usually disturbs the natural attitude of our own which appears more intentional, more distinct, and perhaps somewhat exaggerated.

350

An artifice – He who wants to get another to do something difficult must on no account treat the matter as a problem, but must set forth his plan plainly as the only one possible; and when the adversary's eye betrays objection and opposition he must understand how to break off quickly, and allow him no time to put in a word.

351

Pricks of conscience after social gatherings – Why does our conscience prick us after ordinary social gatherings? Because we have treated serious things lightly, because in talking of persons we have not spoken quite justly or have been silent when we should have spoken, because, sometimes, we have not jumped up and run away – in short, because we have behaved in society as if we belonged to it.

352

We are misjudged – He who always listens to hear how he is judged is always vexed. For we are misjudged even by those who are nearest to us ('who know us best'). Even good friends sometimes vent their ill-humour in a spiteful word; and would they be our friends if they knew us rightly? The judgments of the indifferent wound us deeply, because they sound so impartial, so objective almost. But when we see that some one hostile to us knows us in a concealed point as well as we know ourselves, how great is then our vexation!

353

The tyranny of the portrait – Artists and statesmen, who out of particular features quickly construct the whole picture of a man or an event, are mostly unjust in demanding that the event or person should afterwards be actually as they have painted it; they demand straightway that a man should be just as gifted, cunning, and unjust as he is in their representation of him.

354

Relatives as the best friends – The Greeks, who knew so well what a friend was, they alone of all peoples have a profound and largely philosophical discussion of friendship; so that it is by them firstly (and as yet lastly) that the problem of the friend has been recognised as worthy of solution – these same Greeks have designated *relatives* by an expression which is the superlative of the word 'friend'. This is inexplicable to me.

355

Misunderstood honesty – When any one quotes himself in conversation ('I then said,' 'I am accustomed to say'), it gives the impression of presumption; whereas it often proceeds from quite an opposite source; or at least from honesty, which does not wish to deck and adorn the present moment with wit which belongs to an earlier moment.

356

The parasite – It denotes entire absence of a noble disposition when a person prefers to live in dependence at the expense of others, usually with a secret bitterness against them, in order only that he may not be obliged to work. Such a disposition is far more frequent in women than in men, also far more pardonable (for historical reasons).

357

On the altar of reconciliation – There are circumstances under which one can only gain a point from a person by wounding him and becoming hostile; the feeling of having a foe torments him so much that he gladly seizes the first indication of a milder disposition to effect a reconciliation, and offers on the altar of this reconciliation what was formerly of such importance to him that he would not give it up at any price.

358

Presumption in demanding pity – There are people who, when they have been in a rage and have insulted others, demand, firstly, that it shall all be taken in good part; and, secondly, that they shall be pitied because they are subject to such violent paroxysms. So far does human presumption extend.

359

Bait – 'Every man has his price' – that is not true. But perhaps every one can be found a bait of one kind or other at which he will snap. Thus, in order to gain some supporters for a cause, it is only necessary to give it the glamour of being philanthropic, noble, charitable, and self-denying – and to what cause could this glamour not be given! It is the sweetmeat and dainty of *their* soul; others have different ones.

360

The attitude in praising – When good friends praise a gifted person he often appears to be delighted with them out of politeness and goodwill, but in reality he feels indifferent. His real nature is quite unmoved towards them, and will not budge a step on that account out of the sun or shade in which it lies; but people wish to please by praise, and it would grieve them if one did not rejoice when they praise a person.

361

The experience of Socrates – If one has become a master in one thing, one has generally remained, precisely thereby, a complete dunce in most other things; but one forms the very reverse opinion, as was already experienced by Socrates. This is the annoyance which makes association with masters disagreeable.

362

A means of defence – In warring against stupidity, the most just and gentle of men at last become brutal. They are thereby, perhaps, taking the proper course for defence; for the most appropriate argument for a stupid brain is the clenched fist. But because, as has been said, their character is just and gentle, they suffer more by this means of protection than they injure their opponents by it.

363

Curiosity – If curiosity did not exist, very little would be done for the good of our neighbour. But curiosity creeps into the houses of the unfortunate and the needy under the name of duty or of pity. Perhaps there is a good deal of curiosity even in the much-vaunted maternal love.

364

Disappointment in society – One man wishes to be interesting for his opinions, another for his likes and dislikes, a third for his acquaintances, and a fourth for his solitariness – and they all meet with disappointment. For he before whom the play is performed thinks himself the only play that is to be taken into account.

365

The duel – It may be said in favour of duels and all affairs of honour that if a man has such susceptible feelings that he does not care to live when So-and-so says or thinks this or that about him, he has a right to make it a question of the death of the one or the other. With regard to the fact that he is so susceptible, it is not at all to be remonstrated with; in that matter we are the heirs of the past, of its greatness as well as of its exaggerations, without which no greatness ever existed. So when there exists a code of honour which lets blood stand in place of death, so that the mind is relieved after a regular duel, it is a great blessing, because otherwise many human lives would be in danger. Such an institution, moreover, teaches men to be cautious in their utterances and makes intercourse with them possible.

368

The talent for friendship – Two types are distinguished amongst people who have a special faculty for friendship. The one is ever on the ascent, and for every phase of his development he finds a friend exactly suited to him. The series of friends which he thus acquires is seldom a consistent one, and is sometimes at variance and in contradiction, entirely in accordance with the fact that the later phases of his development neutralise or prejudice the earlier phases. Such a man may jestingly be called a *ladder*. The other type is represented by him who exercises an attractive influence on very different characters and endowments, so that he wins a whole circle of friends; these, however, are thereby brought voluntarily into friendly relations with one another in spite of all differences. Such a man may be called a *circle*, for this homogeneousness of such different temperaments and natures must somehow be typified in him. Furthermore, the faculty for having good friends is greater in many people than the faculty for being a good friend.

374

Tête-à-tête – Private conversation is the perfect conversation, because everything the one person says receives its particular colouring, its tone, and its accompanying gestures *out of strict consideration for the other person* engaged in the conversation; it therefore corresponds to what takes place in intercourse by letter, viz., that one and the same person exhibits ten kinds of psychical expression, according as he writes now to this individual and now to that one. In duo-logue there is only a single refraction of thought; the person conversed with produces it, as the mirror in whom we want to behold our thoughts anew in their finest form. But how is it when there are two or three, or even more persons conversing with one? Conversation then necessarily loses something of its individ-ualising subtlety, different considerations thwart and neutralise each other; the style which pleases one does not suit the taste of another. In intercourse with several individuals a person is therefore to withdraw within himself and represent facts as they are; but he has a lso to remove from the subjects the pulsating ether of humanity which makes conversation one of the pleasantest things in the world. Listen only to the tone in which those who mingle with whole groups of men are in the habit of speaking; it is as if the fundamental base of all speech were, 'It is *myself*; *I* say this, so make what you will of it!' That is the reason why clever ladies usually leave a singular, painful, and forbidding impression on those who have met them in society; it is the talking to many people, before many people, that robs them of all intellectual amiability and shows only their conscious dependence on themselves, their tactics, and their intention of gaining a public victory in full light; whilst in a private conversation the same ladies become womanly again, and recover their intellectual grace and charm.

375

Posthumous fame – There is sense in hoping for recognition in a distant future only when we take it for granted that mankind will remain essentially unchanged, and that whatever is great is not for one age only but will be looked upon as great for all time. But this is an error. In all their sentiments and judgments concerning what is good and beautiful mankind have greatly changed; it is mere fantasy to imagine one's self to be a mile ahead, and that the whole of mankind is coming *our* way. Besides, a scholar who is misjudged may at present reckon with certainty that his discovery will be made by others, and that, at best, it will be allowed to him later on by some historian that he also already knew this or that but was not in a position to secure the recognition of his knowledge. Not to be recognised is always interpreted by posterity as lack of power. In short, one should not so readily speak in favour of haughty solitude. There are, however, exceptional cases; but it is chiefly our faults, weakness, and follies that hinder the recognition of our great qualities.

Wife and Child

377

The perfect woman – The perfect woman is a higher type of humanity than the perfect man, and also something much rarer. The natural history of animals furnishes grounds in support of this theory.

378

Friendship and marriage – The best friend will probably get the best wife, because a good marriage is based on talent for friendship.

379

The survival of the parents – The undissolved dissonances in the relation of the character and sentiments of the parents survive in the nature of the child and make up the history of its inner sufferings.

380

Inherited from the mother – Every one bears within him an image of woman, inherited from his mother: it determines his attitude towards women as a whole, whether to honour, despise, or remain generally indifferent to them.

381

Correcting nature – Whoever has not got a good father should procure one.

382

Fathers and sons – Fathers have much to do to make amends for having sons.

383

The error of gentlewomen – Gentlewomen think that a thing does not really exist when it is not possible to talk of it in society.

384

A male disease – The surest remedy for the male disease of self-contempt is to be loved by a sensible woman.

385

A species of jealousy – Mothers are readily jealous of the friends of sons who are particularly successful. As a rule a mother loves *herself* in her son more than the son.

386

Rational irrationality – In the maturity of life and intelligence the feeling comes over a man that his father did wrong in begetting him.

387

Maternal excellence – Some mothers need happy and honoured children, some need unhappy ones – otherwise they cannot exhibit their maternal excellence.

388

Different sighs – Some husbands have sighed over the elopement of their wives, the greater number, however, have sighed because nobody would elope with theirs.

389

Love matches – Marriages which are contracted for love (so-called love-matches) have error for their father and need (necessity) for their mother.

390

Women's friendships – Women can enter into friendship with a man perfectly well; but in order to maintain it the aid of a little physical antipathy is perhaps required.

391

Ennui – Many people, especially women, never feel ennui because they have never learnt to work properly.

392

An element of love – In all feminine love something of maternal love also comes to light.

393

Unity of place and drama – If married couples did not live together, happy marriages would be more frequent.

399

Marriage on a good basis – A marriage in which each wishes to realise an individual aim by means of the other will stand well; for instance, when the woman wishes to become famous through the man and the man beloved through the woman.

400

Proteus-nature – Through love women actually become what they appear to be in the imagination of their lovers.

401

To love and to possess – As a rule women love a distinguished man to the extent that they wish to possess him exclusively. They would gladly keep him under lock and key, if their vanity did not forbid, but vanity demands that he should also appear distinguished before others.

402

The test of a good marriage – The goodness of a marriage is proved by the fact that it can stand an 'exception'.

406

Marriage as a long talk – In entering on a marriage one should ask one's self the question, 'Do you think you will pass your time well with this woman till your old age?' All else in marriage is transitory; talk, however, occupies most of the time of the association.

407

Girlish dreams – Inexperienced girls flatter themselves with the notion that it is in their power to make a man happy; later on they learn that it is equivalent to underrating a man to suppose that he needs only a girl to make him happy. Women's vanity requires a man to be something more than merely a happy husband.

413

Lovers as short-sighted people – A pair of powerful spectacles has sometimes sufficed to cure a person in love; and whoever has had sufficient imagination to represent a face or form twenty years older, has probably gone through life not much disturbed.

414

Women in hatred – In a state of hatred women are more dangerous than men; for one thing, because they are hampered by no regard for fairness when their hostile feelings have been aroused; but let their hatred develop unchecked to its utmost consequences; then also, because they are expert in finding sore spots (which every man and every party possess), and pouncing upon them: for which purpose their dagger-pointed intelligence is of good service (whilst men, hesitating at the sight of wounds, are often generously and conciliatorily inclined).

415

Love – The love idolatry which women practise is fundamentally and originally an intelligent device, inasmuch as they increase their power by all the idealisings of love and exhibit themselves as so much the more desirable in the eyes of men. But by being accustomed for centuries to this exaggerated appreciation of love, it has come to pass that they have been caught in their own net and have forgotten the origin of the device. They themselves are now still more deceived than the men, and on that account also suffer more from the disillusionment which, almost necessarily, enters into the life of every woman – so far, at any rate, as she has sufficient imagination and intelligence to be able to be deceived and undeceived.

420

Who suffers the more? – After a personal dissension and quarrel between a woman and a man the latter party suffers chiefly from the idea of having wounded the other, whilst the former suffers chiefly from the idea of not having wounded the other sufficiently; so she subsequently endeavours by tears, sobs, and discomposed mien, to make his heart heavier.

422

The tragedy of childhood – Perhaps it not infrequently happens that noble men with lofty aims have to fight their hardest battle in childhood; by having perchance to carry out their principles in opposition to a base-minded father addicted to feigning and falsehood, or living, like Lord Byron, in constant warfare with a childish and passionate mother. He who has had such an experience will never be able to forget all his life who has been his greatest and most dangerous enemy.

427

The happiness of marriage – Everything to which we are accustomed draws an ever-tightening cobweb-net around us; and presently we notice that the threads have become cords, and that we ourselves sit in the middle like a spider that has here got itself caught and must feed on its own blood. Hence the free spirit hates all rules and customs, all that is permanent and definitive, hence he painfully tears asunder again and again the net around him, though in consequence thereof he will suffer from numerous wounds, slight and severe; for he must break off every thread *from himself*, from his body and soul. He must learn to love where he has hitherto hated, and *vice versa*. Indeed, it must not be a thing impossible for him to sow dragon's teeth in the same field in which he formerly scattered the abundance of his bounty. From this it can be inferred whether he is suited for the happiness of marriage.

428

Too intimate – When we live on too intimate terms with a person it is as if we were again and again handling a good engraving with our fingers; the time comes when we have soiled and damaged paper in our hands, and nothing more. A man's soul also gets worn out by constant handling; at least, it eventually *appears* so to us – never again do we see its original design and beauty. We always lose through too familiar association with women and friends; and sometimes we lose the pearl of our life thereby.

A Glance at the State

438

Asking to be heard – The demagogic disposition and the intention of working upon the masses is at present common to all political parties; on this account they are all obliged to change their principles into great *al fresco* follies and thus make a show of them. In this matter there is no further alteration to be made: indeed, it is superfluous even to raise a finger against it; for here Voltaire's saying applies: '*Quand la populace se mêle de raisonner, tout est perdu.*' Since this has happened we have to accommodate ourselves to the new conditions, as we have to accommodate ourselves when an earthquake has displaced the old boundaries and the contour of the land and altered the value of property. Moreover, when it is once for all a question in the politics of all parties to make life endurable to the greatest possible majority, this majority may always decide what they understand by an endurable life; if they believe their intellect capable of finding the right means to this end why should we doubt about it? They *want*, once for all, to be the architects of their own good or ill fortune; and if their feeling of free choice and their pride in the five or six ideas that their brain conceals and brings to light, really makes life so agreeable to them that they gladly put up with the fatal consequences of their narrow-mindedness, there is little to object to, provided that their narrow-mindedness does not go so far as to demand that *everything* shall become politics in this sense, that *all* shall live and act according to this standard. For, in the first place, it must be more than ever permissible for some people to keep aloof from politics and to stand somewhat aside. To this they are also impelled by the pleasure of free choice, and connected with this there may even be some little pride in keeping silence when too many, and only the many, are speaking. Then this small group must be excused if they do not attach such great importance to the happiness of the majority (nations or strata of population may be understood thereby), and are occasionally guilty of an ironical grimace; for their seriousness lies elsewhere, their conception of happiness is quite different, and their aim cannot be encompassed by every clumsy hand that has just five fingers. Finally, there comes from time to time – what is certainly most difficult to concede to them, but must also be conceded – a moment when they emerge from their silent solitariness and try once more the strength of their lungs; they then call to each other like people lost in a wood, to make themselves known and for mutual encouragement; whereby, to be sure, much becomes audible that sounds evil to ears for which it is not intended. Soon, however, silence again prevails in the wood, such silence that the buzzing, humming, and fluttering of the countless insects that live in, above, and beneath it, are again plainly heard.

439

Culture and caste – A higher culture can only originate where there are two distinct castes of society: that of the working class, and that of the leisured class who are capable of true leisure; or, more strongly expressed, the caste of compulsory labour and the caste of free labour. The point of view of the division of happiness is not essential when it is a question of the production of a higher culture; in any case, however, the leisured caste is more susceptible to suffering and suffer more, their pleasure in existence is less and their task is greater. Now supposing there should be quite an interchange between the two castes, so that on the one hand the duller and less intelligent families and individuals are lowered from the higher caste into the lower, and, on the other hand, the freer men of the lower caste obtain access to the higher, a condition of things would be attained beyond which one can only perceive the open sea of vague wishes. Thus speaks to us the vanishing voice of the olden time; but where are there still ears to hear it?

440

Of good blood – That which men and women of good blood possess much more than others, and which gives them an undoubted right to be more highly appreciated, are two arts which are always increased by inheritance: the art of being able to command, and the art of proud obedience. Now wherever commanding is the business of the day (as in the great world of commerce and industry), there results something similar to these families of good blood, only the noble bearing in obedience is lacking which is an inheritance from feudal conditions and hardly grows any longer in the climate of our culture.

441

Subordination – The subordination which is so highly valued in military and official ranks will soon become as incredible to us as the secret tactics of the Jesuits have already become; and when this subordination is no longer possible a multitude of astonishing results will no longer be attained, and the world will be all the poorer. It must disappear, for its foundation is disappearing, the belief in unconditional authority, in ultimate truth; even in military ranks physical compulsion is not sufficient to produce it, but only the inherited adoration of the princely as of something superhuman. In *freer* circumstances people subordinate themselves only on conditions, in compliance with a mutual contract, consequently with all the provisos of self-interest.

442

The national army – The greatest disadvantage of the national army, now so much glorified, lies in the squandering of men of the highest civilisation; it is only by the favourableness of all circumstances that there are such men at all; how carefully and anxiously should we deal with them, since long periods are required to create the chance conditions for the production of such delicately organised brains! But as the Greeks wallowed in the blood of Greeks, so do Europeans now in the blood of Europeans: and indeed, taken relatively, it is mostly the highly cultivated who are sacrificed, those who promise an abundant and excellent posterity; for such stand in the front of the battle as commanders, and also expose themselves to most danger, by reason of their higher ambition. At present, when quite other and higher tasks are assigned than *patria* and *honor*, the rough Roman patriotism is either something dishonourable or a sign of being behind the times.

443

Hope as presumption – Our social order will slowly melt away, as all former orders have done, as soon as the suns of new opinions have shone upon mankind with a new glow. We can only *wish* this melting away in the hope thereof, and we are only reasonably entitled to hope when we believe that we and our equals have more strength in heart and head than the representatives of the existing state of things. As a rule, therefore, this hope will be a presumption, an *overestimation*.

444

War – Against war it may be said that it makes the victor stupid and the vanquished revengeful. In favour of war it may be said that it barbarises in both its above-named results, and thereby makes more natural; it is the sleep or the winter period of culture; man emerges from it with greater strength for good and for evil.

445

In the prince's service – To be able to act quite regardlessly it is best for a statesman to carry out his work not for himself but for a prince. The eye of the spectator is dazzled by the splendour of this general disinterestedness, so that it does not see the malignancy and severity which the work of a statesman brings with it.

446

A question of power, not of right – As regards Socialism, in the eyes of those who always consider higher utility, if it is *really* a rising against their oppressors of those who for centuries have been oppressed and downtrodden, there is no problem of *right* involved (notwithstanding the ridiculous, effeminate question, 'How far *ought* we to grant its demands?') but only a problem of *power* ('How far *can* we make use of its demands?'); the same, therefore, as in the case of a natural force – steam, for instance – which is either forced by man into his service, as a machine-god, or which, in case of defects of the machine, that is to say, defects of human calculation in its construction, destroys it and man together. In order to solve this question of power we must know how strong Socialism is, in what modification it may yet be employed as a powerful lever in the present mechanism of political forces; under certain circumstances we should do all we can to strengthen it. With every great force – be it the most dangerous – men have to think how they can make of it an instrument for their purposes. Socialism acquires a *right* only if war seems to have taken place between the two powers, the representatives of the old and the new, when, however, a wise calculation of the greatest possible preservation and advantageousness to both sides gives rise to a desire for a treaty. Without treaty no right. So far, however, there is neither war nor treaty on the ground in question, therefore no rights, no 'ought'.

447

Utilising the most trivial dishonesty – The power of the press consists in the fact that every individual who ministers to it only feels himself bound and constrained to a very small extent. He usually expresses *his* opinion, but sometimes also does *not* express it in order to serve his party or the politics of his country, or even himself. Such little faults of dishonesty, or perhaps only of a dishonest silence, are not hard to bear by the individual, but the consequences are extraordinary, because these little faults are committed by many at the same time. Each one says to himself: 'For such small concessions I live better and can make my income; by the want of such little compliances I make myself impossible'. Because it seems almost morally indifferent to write a line more (perhaps even without signature), or not to write it, a person who has money and influence can make any opinion a public one. He who knows that most people are weak in trifles, and wishes to attain his own ends thereby, is always dangerous.

448

Too loud a tone in grievances – Through the fact that an account of a bad state of things (for instance, the crimes of an administration, bribery and arbitrary favour in political or learned bodies) is greatly exaggerated, it fails in its effect on intelligent people, but has all the greater effect on the unintelligent (who would have remained indifferent to an accurate and moderate account). But as these latter are considerably in the majority, and harbour in themselves stronger will-power and more impatient desire for action, the exaggeration becomes the cause of investigations, punishments, promises, and reorganisations. In so far it is useful to exaggerate the accounts of bad states of things.

449

The apparent weather-makers of politics – Just as people tacitly assume that he who understands the weather, and foretells it about a day in advance, makes the weather, so even the educated and learned, with a display of superstitious faith, ascribe to great statesmen as their most special work all the important changes and conjunctures that have taken place during their administration, when it is only evident that they knew something thereof a little earlier than other people and made their calculations accordingly – thus they are also looked upon as weather-makers – and this belief is not the least important instrument of their power.

452

Possession and justice – When the Socialists point out that the division of property at the present day is the consequence of countless deeds of injustice and violence, and, *in summa*, repudiate obligation to anything with so unrighteous a basis, they only perceive something isolated. The entire past of ancient civilisation is built up on violence, slavery, deception, and error; we, however, cannot annul ourselves, the heirs of all these conditions, nay, the concrescences of all this past, and are not entitled to demand the withdrawal of a single fragment thereof. The unjust disposition lurks also in the souls of non-possessors; they are not better than the possessors and have no moral prerogative; for at one time or another their

ancestors have been possessors. Not forcible new dis-
tributions, but gradual transformations of opinion are
necessary; justice in all matters must become greater,
the instinct of violence weaker.

453

The helmsman of the passions – The statesman excites
public passions in order to have the advantage of the
counter-passions thereby aroused. To give an example:
a German statesman knows quite well that the Catholic
Church will never have the same plans as Russia;
indeed, that it would far rather be allied with the Turks
than with the former country; he likewise knows that
Germany is threatened with great danger from an
alliance between France and Russia. If he can succeed,
therefore, in making France the focus and fortress of
the Catholic Church, he has averted this danger for a
lengthy period. He has, accordingly, an interest in
showing hatred against the Catholics in transforming,
by all kinds of hostility, the supporters of the Pope's
authority into an impassioned political power which is
opposed to German politics, and must, as a matter of
course, coalesce with France as the adversary of
Germany; his aim is the catholicising of France, just as
necessarily as Mirabeau saw the salvation of his native
land in de-catholicising it. The one State, therefore,
desires to muddle millions of minds of another State
in order to gain advantage thereby. It is the same
disposition which supports the republican form of
government of a neighbouring State – *le désordre organisé*,
as Mérimée says – for the sole reason that it assumes
that this form of government makes the nation weaker,
more distracted, less fit for war.

463

A delusion in subversive doctrines – There are political and social dreamers who ardently and eloquently call for the overthrow of all order, in the belief that the proudest fane of beautiful humanity will then rear itself immediately, almost of its own accord. In these dangerous dreams there is still an echo of Rousseau's superstition, which believes in a marvellous primordial goodness of human nature, buried up, as it were; and lays all the blame of that burying-up on the institutions of civilisation, on society, State, and education. Unfortunately, it is well known by historical experiences that every such overthrow reawakens into new life the wildest energies, the long-buried horrors and extravagances of remotest ages; that an overthrow, therefore, may possibly be a source of strength to a deteriorated humanity, but never a regulator, architect, artist, or perfecter of human nature. It was not *Voltaire's* moderate nature, inclined towards regulating, purifying, and reconstructing, but *Rousseau's* passionate follies and half lies that aroused the optimistic spirit of the Revolution, against which I cry, '*Ecrasez l'infâme!*' Owing to this *the spirit of enlightenment and progressive development* has been long scared away; let us see – each of us individually – if it is not possible to recall it!

464

Moderation – When perfect resoluteness in thinking and investigating, that is to say, freedom of spirit, has become a feature of character, it produces moderation of conduct; for it weakens avidity, attracts much extant energy for the furtherance of intellectual aims, and shows the semi-usefulness, or uselessness and danger, of all sudden changes.

467

Public education – In large states public education will always be extremely mediocre, for the same reason that in large kitchens the cooking is at best only mediocre.

468

Innocent corruption – In all institutions into which the sharp breeze of public criticism does not penetrate an innocent corruption grows up like a fungus (for instance, in learned bodies and senates).

470

The wolf hidden behind the sheep – Almost every politician, in certain circumstances, has such need of an honest man that he breaks into the sheepfold like a famished wolf; not, however, to devour a stolen sheep, but to hide himself behind its woolly back.

473

Socialism, with regard to its means – Socialism is the fantastic younger brother of almost decrepit despotism, which it wants to succeed; its efforts are, therefore, in the deepest sense reactionary. For it desires such an amount of State power as only despotism has possessed – indeed, it outdoes all the past, in that it aims at the complete annihilation of the individual, whom it deems an unauthorised luxury of nature, which is to be improved by it into an appropriate *organ of the general community*. Owing to its relationship, it always appears in proximity to excessive developments of power, like the old typical socialist, Plato, at the court of the Sicilian tyrant; it desires (and under certain circumstances furthers) the Caesarian despotism of this century, because, as has been said, it would like to become its heir. But even this inheritance would not suffice for its objects, it requires the most submissive prostration of all citizens before the absolute State, such as has never yet been realised; and as it can no longer even count upon the old religious piety towards the State, but must rather strive involuntarily and continuously for the abolition thereof – because it strives for the abolition of all existing *States* – it can only hope for existence occasionally, here and there for short periods, by means of the extremest terrorism. It is therefore silently preparing itself for reigns of terror, and drives the word 'justice' like a nail into the heads of the half-cultured masses in order to deprive them completely of their under-standing (after they had already suffered seriously from the half-culture), and to provide them with a good conscience for the bad game they are to play. Socialism may serve to teach, very brutally and impressively, the danger of all accumulations of State power, and may serve so far to inspire distrust of the State itself. When its rough voice strikes up the war-cry '*as much State as possible,*' the shout at first becomes louder than ever – but soon the opposition cry also breaks forth, with so much greater force, '*as little State as possible.*'

477

War indispensable – It is nothing but fanaticism and beautiful-soulism to expect very much (or even, much only) from humanity when it has forgotten how to wage war. For the present we know of no other means whereby the rough energy of the camp, the deep impersonal hatred, the cold-bloodedness of murder with a good conscience, the general ardour of the system in the destruction of the enemy, the proud indifference to great losses, to one's own existence and that of one's friends, the hollow, earthquake-like convulsion of the soul, can be as forcibly and certainly communicated to enervated nations as is done by every great war: owing to the brooks and streams that here break forth, which, certainly, sweep stones and rubbish of all sorts along with them and destroy the meadows of delicate cultures, the mechanism in the workshops of the mind is afterwards, in favourable circumstances, rotated by new power. Culture can by no means dispense with passions, vices, and malignities. When the Romans, after having become Imperial, had grown rather tired of war, they attempted to gain new strength by beast-baitings, gladiatorial combats, and Christian persecutions. The English of today, who appear on the whole to have also renounced war, adopt other means in order to generate anew those vanishing forces; namely, the dangerous exploring expeditions, sea voyages and mountaineerings, nominally undertaken for scientific purposes, but in reality to bring home surplus strength from adventures and dangers of all kinds. Many other such substitutes for war will be discovered, but perhaps precisely thereby it will become more and more obvious that such a highly cultivated and therefore necessarily enfeebled humanity as that of modern Europe not only needs wars, but the greatest and most terrible wars – consequently occasional relapses into barbarism – lest, by the means of culture, it should lose its culture and its very existence.

478

Industry in the south and the north – Industry arises in two entirely different ways. The artisans of the South are not industrious because of acquisitiveness but because of the constant needs of others. The smith is industrious because some one is always coming who wants a horse shod or a carriage mended. If nobody came he would loiter about in the marketplace. In a fruitful land he has little trouble in supporting himself, for that purpose he requires only a very small amount of work, certainly no industry; eventually he would beg and be contented. The industry of English workmen, on the contrary, has acquisitiveness behind it; it is conscious of itself and its aims; with property it wants power, and with power the greatest possible liberty and individual distinction.

479

Wealth as the origin of a nobility of race – Wealth necessarily creates an aristocracy of race, for it permits the choice of the most beautiful women and the engagement of the best teachers; it allows a man cleanliness, time for physical exercises, and, above all, immunity from dulling physical labour. So far it provides all the conditions for making man, after a few generations, move and even act nobly and handsomely: greater freedom of character and absence of niggardliness, of wretchedly petty matters, and of abasement before bread-givers. It is precisely these negative qualities which are the most profitable birthday gift, that of happiness, for the young man; a person who is quite poor usually comes to grief through nobility of disposition, he does not get on, and acquires nothing, his race is not capable of living. In this connection, however, it must be remembered that wealth produces almost the same effects whether one have three hundred or thirty thousand thalers a year; there is no further essential progression of the favourable conditions afterwards. But to have less, to beg in boyhood and to abase one's self is terrible, although it may be the proper starting-point for such as seek their happiness in the splendour of courts, in subordination to the mighty and influential, or for such as wish to be heads of the Church. (It teaches how to slink crouching into the underground passages to favour.)

Man Alone by Himself

483

The enemies of truth – Convictions are more dangerous enemies of truth than lies.

484

A topsy-turvy world – We criticise a thinker more severely when he puts an unpleasant statement before us; and yet it would be more reasonable to do so when we find his statement pleasant.

485

Decided character – A man far oftener appears to have a decided character from persistently following his temperament than from persistently following his principles.

489

Not too deep – Persons who grasp a matter in all its depth seldom remain permanently true to it. They have just brought the depth up into the light, and there is always much evil to be seen there.

490

The illusion of idealists – All idealists imagine that the cause which they serve is essentially better than all other causes, and will not believe that if their cause is really to flourish it requires precisely the same evil-smelling manure which all other human under-takings have need of.

491

Self-observation – Man is exceedingly well protected from himself and guarded against his self-exploring and self-besieging; as a rule he can perceive nothing of himself but his outworks. The actual fortress is inaccessible, and even invisible, to him, unless friends and enemies become traitors and lead him inside by secret paths.

492

The right calling – Men can seldom hold on to a calling unless they believe or persuade themselves that it is really more important than any other. Women are the same with their lovers.

493

Nobility of disposition – Nobility of disposition consists largely in good-nature and absence of distrust, and therefore contains precisely that upon which money-grabbing and successful men take a pleasure in walking with superiority and scorn.

494

Goal and path – Many are obstinate with regard to the once-chosen path, few with regard to the goal.

496

The privilege of greatness – It is the privilege of greatness to confer intense happiness with insignificant gifts.

497

Unintentionally noble – A person behaves with unintentional nobleness when he has accustomed himself to seek naught from others and always to give to them.

501

Joy in itself – 'Joy in the Thing' people say; but in reality it is joy in itself by means of the thing.

502

The unassuming man – He who is unassuming towards persons manifests his presumption all the more with regard to things (town, State, society, time, humanity). That is his revenge.

503

Envy and jealousy – Envy and jealousy are the pudenda of the human soul. The comparison may perhaps be carried further.

504

The noblest hypocrite – It is a very noble hypocrisy not to talk of one's self at all.

505

Vexation – Vexation is a physical disease, which is not by any means cured when its cause is subsequently removed.

506

The champions of truth – Truth does not find fewest champions when it is dangerous to speak it, but when it is dull.

507

More troublesome even than enemies – Persons of whose sympathetic attitude we are not, in all circumstances, convinced, while for some reason or other (gratitude, for instance) we are obliged to maintain the appearance of unqualified sympathy with them, trouble our imagination far more than our enemies do.

508

Free Nature – We are so fond of being out among Nature, because it has no opinions about us.

509

Each superior in one thing – In civilised intercourse every one feels himself superior to all others in at least one thing; kindly feelings generally are based thereon, inasmuch as every one can, in certain circumstances, render help, and is therefore entitled to accept help without shame.

510

Consolatory arguments – In the case of a death we mostly use consolatory arguments not so much to alleviate the grief as to make excuses for feeling so easily consoled.

511

Persons loyal to their convictions – whoever is very busy retains his general views and opinions almost unchanged. So also does every one who labours in the service of an idea; he will nevermore examine the idea itself, he no longer has any time to do so; indeed, it is against his interests to consider it as still admitting of discussion.

514

Iron necessity – Iron necessity is a thing which has been found, in the course of history, to be neither iron nor necessary.

515

From experience – The unreasonableness of a thing is no argument against its existence, but rather a condition thereof.

516

Truth – Nobody dies nowadays of fatal truths, there are too many antidotes to them.

518

Man's lot – He who thinks most deeply knows that he is always in the wrong, however he may act and decide.

519

Truth as circle – Error has made animals into men; is truth perhaps capable of making man into an animal again?

523

Desiring to be loved – The demand to be loved is the greatest of presumptions.

526

Forgetting experiences – Whoever thinks much and to good purpose easily forgets his own experiences, but not the thoughts which these experiences have called forth.

527

Sticking to an opinion – One person sticks to an opinion because he takes pride in having acquired it himself – another sticks to it because he has learnt it with difficulty and is proud of having understood it; both of them, therefore, out of vanity.

536

The value of insipid opponents – We sometimes remain faithful to a cause merely because its opponents never cease to be insipid.

539

Youth – Youth is an unpleasant period; for then it is not possible or not prudent to be productive in any sense whatsoever.

540

Too great aims – Whoever aims publicly at great things and at length perceives secretly that he is too weak to achieve them, has usually also insufficient strength to renounce his aims publicly, and then inevitably becomes a hypocrite.

544

Seeing badly and hearing badly – The man who sees little always sees less than there is to see; the man who hears badly always hears something more than there is to hear.

545

Self-enjoyment in vanity – The vain man does not wish so much to be prominent as to feel himself prominent; he therefore disdains none of the expedients for self-deception and self-outwitting. It is not the opinion of others that he sets his heart on, but his opinion of their opinion.

551

The prophet's knack – In predicting beforehand the procedure of ordinary individuals, it must be taken for granted that they always make use of the smallest intellectual expenditure in freeing themselves from disagreeable situations.

553

Below the beast – When a man roars with laughter he surpasses all the animals by his vulgarity.

554

Partial knowledge – He who speaks a foreign language imperfectly has more enjoyment therein than he who speaks it well. The enjoyment is with the partially initiated.

555

Dangerous helpfulness – There are people who wish to make human life harder for no other reason than to be able afterwards to offer men their life-alleviating recipes – their Christianity, for example.

558

The conditions are lacking – Many people wait all their lives for the opportunity to be good in *their own way*.

562

Being a target – The bad things others say about us are often not really aimed at us, but are the manifestations of spite or ill-humour occasioned by quite different causes.

566

Love and hatred – Love and hatred are not blind, but are dazzled by the fire which they carry about with them.

567

Advantageously persecuted – people who cannot make their merits perfectly obvious to the world endeavour to awaken a strong hostility against themselves. They have then the consolation of thinking that this hostility stands between their merits and the acknowledgment thereof – and that many others think the same thing, which is very advantageous for their recognition.

568

Confession – We forget our fault when we have confessed it to another person, but he does not generally forget it.

569

Self-sufficiency – The Golden Fleece of self-sufficiency is a protection against blows, but not against needle-pricks.

570

Shadows in the flame – The flame is not so bright to itself as to those whom it illuminates – so also the wise man.

571

Our own opinions – The first opinion that occurs to us when we are suddenly asked about anything is not usually our own, but only the current opinion belonging to our caste, position, or family; our own opinions seldom float on the surface.

580

A bad memory – The advantage of a bad memory is that one enjoys several times the same good things for the *first* time.

589

The day's first thought – The best way to begin a day well is to think, on awakening, whether we cannot give pleasure during the day to at least one person. If this could become a substitute for the religious habit of prayer our fellow-men would benefit by the change.

591

The vegetation of happiness – Close beside the world's woe, and often upon its volcanic soil, man has laid out his little garden of happiness. Whether one regard life with the eyes of him who only seeks knowledge therefrom, or of him who submits and is resigned, or of him who rejoices over surmounted difficulties – everywhere one will find some happiness springing up beside the evil – and in fact always the more happiness the more volcanic the soil has been – only it would be absurd to say that suffering itself is justified by this happiness.

592

The path of our ancestors – It is sensible when a person develops still further in himself the *talent* upon which his father or grandfather spent much trouble, and does not shift to something entirely new; otherwise he deprives himself of the possibility of attaining perfection in any one craft. That is why the proverb says, 'Which road shouldst thou ride? – That of thine ancestors.'

594

Philosophical novices – Immediately we have comprehended the wisdom of a philosopher, we go through the streets with a feeling as if we had been re-created and had become great men; for we encounter only those who are ignorant of this wisdom, and have therefore to deliver new and unknown verdicts concerning everything. Because we now recognise a law-book we think we must also comport ourselves as judges.

596

Casus belli and the like – The prince who, for his determination to make war against his neighbour, invents a *casus belli*, is like a father who foists on his child a mother who is henceforth to be regarded as such. And are not almost all publicly avowed motives of action just such spurious mothers?

600

Deceptive and yet defensible – Just as in order to pass by an abyss or to cross a deep stream on a plank we require a railing, not to hold fast by – for it would instantly break down with us – but to give the notion of security to the eye, so in youth we require persons who unconsciously render us the service of that railing. It is true they would not help us if we really wished to lean upon them in great danger, but they afford the tranquillising sensation of protection close to one (for instance, fathers, teachers, friends, as all three usually are).

601

Learning to love – One must learn to love, one must learn to be kind, and this from childhood onwards; when education and chance give us no opportunity for the exercise of these feelings our soul becomes dried up, and even incapable of understanding the fine devices of loving men. In the same way hatred must be learnt and fostered, when one wants to become a proficient hater – otherwise the germ of it will gradually die out.

602

Ruin as ornament – Persons who pass through numerous mental phases retain certain sentiments and habits of their earlier states, which then project like a piece of inexplicable antiquity and grey stonework into their new thought and action, often to the embellishment of the whole surroundings.

603

Love and honour – Love desires, fear avoids. That is why one cannot be both loved and honoured by the same person, at least not at the same time. For he who honours recognises power – that is to say, he fears it, he is in a state of reverential fear (*Ehr-furcht*). But love recognises no power, nothing that divides, detaches, superordinates, or subordinates. Because it does not honour them, ambitious people secretly or openly resent being loved.

604

A prejudice in favour of cold natures – People who quickly take fire grow cold quickly, and therefore are, on the whole, unreliable. For those, therefore, who are always cold, or pretend to be so, there is the favourable prejudice that they are particularly trustworthy, reliable persons; they are confounded with those who take fire slowly and retain it long.

605

The danger in free opinions – Frivolous occupation with free opinions has a charm, like a kind of itching; if one yields to it further, one begins to chafe the places, until at last an open, painful wound results; that is to say, until the free opinion begins to disturb and torment us in our position in life and in our human relations.

608

Confusion of cause and effect – Unconsciously we seek the principles and opinions which are suited to our temperament, so that at last it seems as if these principles and opinions had formed our character and given it support and stability, whereas exactly the contrary has taken place. Our thoughts and judgments are, apparently, to be taken subsequently as the causes of our nature, but as a matter of fact *our* nature is the cause of our so thinking and judging. And what induces us to play this almost unconscious comedy? Inertness and convenience, and to a large extent also the vain desire to be regarded as thoroughly consistent and homogeneous in nature and thought; for this wins respect and gives confidence and power.

609

Age in relation to truth – Young people love what is interesting and exceptional, indifferent whether it is truth or falsehood. Riper minds love what is interesting and extraordinary when it is truth. Matured minds, finally, love truth even in those in whom it appears plain and simple and is found tiresome by ordinary people, because they have observed that truth is in the habit of giving utterance to its highest intellectual verities with all the appearance of simplicity.

610

Men as bad poets – just as bad poets seek a thought to fit the rhyme in the second half of the verse, so men in the second half of life, having become more scrupulous, are in the habit of seeking pursuits, positions, and conditions which suit those of their earlier life, so that outwardly all sounds well, but their life is no longer ruled and continuously determined anew by a powerful thought: in place thereof there is merely the intention of finding a rhyme.

613

The tone of voice of different ages – The tone in which youths speak, praise, blame, and versify, displeases an older person because it is too loud, and yet at the same time dull and confused like a sound in a vault, which acquires such a loud ring owing to the emptiness; for most of the thought of youths does not gush forth out of the fulness of their own nature, but is the accord and the echo of what has been thought, said, praised or blamed around them. As their sentiments, however (their inclinations and aversions), resound much more forcibly than the reasons thereof, there is heard, whenever they divulge these sentiments, the dull, clanging tone which is a sign of the absence or scarcity of reasons. The tone of riper age is rigorous, abruptly concise, moderately loud, but, like everything distinctly articulated, is heard very far off. Old age, finally, often brings a certain mildness and consideration into the tone of the voice, and as it were, sweetens it; in many cases, to be sure, it also sours it.

627

To live and experience – If we observe how some people can deal with their experiences – their unimportant, everyday experiences – so that these become soil which yields fruit thrice a year; whilst others – and how many! – are driven through the surf of the most exciting adventures, the most diversified movements of times and peoples, and yet always remain light, always remain on the surface, like cork; we are finally tempted to divide mankind into a minority (minimality) of those who know how to make much out of little, and a majority of those who know how to make little out of much; indeed, we even meet with the counter-sorcerers who, instead of making the world out of nothing, make a nothing out of the world.

HUMAN ALL TOO HUMAN — PART 2

15

Enthusiasts – With all that enthusiasts say in favour of their gospel or their master, they are defending themselves, however much they comport themselves as the judges and not the accused: because they are involuntarily reminded almost at every moment that they are exceptions and have to assert their legitimacy.

18

Three varieties of thinkers – There are streaming, flowing, trickling mineral springs, and three corresponding varieties of thinkers. The layman values them by the volume of the water, the expert by the contents of the water – in other words, by the elements in them that are not water.

29

On Gethsemane – The most painful thing a thinker can say to artists is: 'Could ye not *watch* with me one hour?'

30

At the loom – There are many (artists and women, for instance) who work against the few that take a pleasure in untying the knot of things and unravelling their woof. The former always want to weave the woof together again and entangle it and so turn the conceived into the unconceived and if possible inconceivable. Whatever the result may be, the woof and knot always look rather untidy, because too many hands are working and tugging at them.

31

In the desert of science – As the man of science proceeds on his modest and toilsome wanderings, which must often enough be journeys in the desert, he is confronted with those brilliant mirages known as 'philosophic systems'. With magic powers of deception they show him that the solution of all riddles and the most refreshing draught of true water of life are close at hand. His weary heart rejoices, and he well-nigh touches with his lips the goal of all scientific endurance and hardship, so that almost unconsciously he presses forward. Other natures stand still, as if spellbound by the beautiful illusion: the desert swallows them up, they become lost to science. Other natures, again, that have often experienced these subjective consolations, become very disheartened and curse the salty taste which these mirages leave behind in the mouth and from which springs a raging thirst – without one's having come one step nearer to any sort of a spring.

39

Why the stupid so often become malignant – To those arguments of our adversary against which our head feels too weak our heart replies by throwing suspicion on the motives of his arguments.

43

The conscientious – It is more convenient to follow one's conscience than one's intelligence, for at every failure conscience finds an excuse and an encouragement in itself. That is why there are so many conscientious and so few intelligent people.

46

The human 'thing in itself' – The most vulnerable and yet most unconquerable of things is human vanity: nay, through being wounded its strength increases and can grow to giant proportions.

48

The possession of joy abounding – He that has joy abounding must be a good man, but perhaps he is not the cleverest of men, although he has reached the very goal towards which the cleverest man is striving with all his cleverness.

50

Power without victory – The strongest cognition (that of the complete non-freedom of the human will) is yet the poorest in results, for it has always had the mightiest of opponents – human vanity.

51

Pleasure and error – A beneficial influence on friends is exerted by one man unconsciously, through his nature; by another consciously, through isolated actions. Although the former nature is held to be the higher, the latter alone is allied to good conscience and pleasure – the pleasure in justification by good works, which rests upon a belief in the volitional character of our good and evil doing – that is to say, upon a mistake.

52

The folly of committing injustice – The injustice we have inflicted ourselves is far harder to bear than the injustice inflicted upon us by others (not always from moral grounds, be it observed). After all, the doer is always the sufferer – that is, if he be capable of feeling the sting of conscience or of perceiving that by his action he has armed society against himself and cut himself off. For this reason we should beware still more of doing than of suffering injustice, for the sake of our own inward happiness – so as not to lose our feeling of well-being – quite apart from any consideration of the precepts of religion and morality. For in suffering injustice we have the consolation of a good conscience, of hope and of revenge, together with the sympathy and applause of the just, nay of the whole of society, which is afraid of the evil-doer. Not a few are skilled in the impure self-deception that enables them to transform every injustice of their own into an injustice inflicted upon them from without, and to reserve for their own acts the exceptional right to the plea of self-defence. Their object, of course, is to make their own burden lighter.

53

Envy with or without a mouthpiece – Ordinary envy is wont to cackle when the envied hen has laid an egg, thereby relieving itself and becoming milder. But there is a yet deeper envy that in such a case becomes dead silent, desiring that every mouth should be sealed and always more and more angry because this desire is not gratified. Silent envy grows in silence.

54

Anger as a spy – Anger exhausts the soul and brings its very dregs to light. Hence, if we know no other means of gaining certainty, we must understand how to arouse anger in our dependents and adversaries, in order to learn what is really done and thought to our detriment.

88

How one dies is indifferent – The whole way in which a man thinks of death during the prime of his life and strength is very expressive and significant for what we call his character. But the hour of death itself, his behaviour on the deathbed, is almost indifferent. The exhaustion of waning life, especially when old people die, the irregular or insufficient nourishment of the brain during this last period, the occasionally violent pain, the novel and untried nature of the whole position, and only too often the ebb and flow of superstitious impressions and fears, as if dying were of much consequence and meant the crossing of bridges of the most terrible kind – all this forbids our using death as a testimony concerning the living. Nor is it true that the dying man is generally more honest than the living. On the contrary, through the solemn attitude of the bystanders, the repressed or flowing streams of tears and emotions, every one is inveigled into a comedy of vanity, now conscious, now unconscious. The serious way in which every dying man is treated must have been to many a poor despised devil the highest joy of his whole life and a sort of compensation and repayment for many privations.

94

Judicial murder – The two greatest judicial murders in the world's history are, to speak without exaggeration, concealed and well-concealed suicide. In both cases a man *willed* to die, and in both cases he let his breast be pierced by the sword in the hand of human injustice.

95

'Love' – The finest artistic conception wherein Christianity had the advantage over other religious systems lay in one word – Love. Hence it became the *lyric* religion (whereas in its two other creations Semitism bestowed heroico-epical religions upon the world). In the word 'love' there is so much meaning, so much that stimulates and appeals to memory and hope, that even the meanest intelligence and the coldest heart feel some glimmering of its sense. The cleverest woman and the lowest man think of the comparatively unselfish moments of their whole life, even if with them Eros never soared high: and the vast number of beings who *miss* love from their parents or children or sweethearts, especially those whose sexual instincts have been refined away, have found their heart's desire in Christianity.

97

Of the future of Christianity – We may be allowed to form a conjecture as to the disappearance of Christianity and as to the places where it will be the slowest to retreat, if we consider where and for what reasons Protestantism spread with such startling rapidity. As is well known, Protestantism promised to do far more cheaply all that the old Church did, without costly masses, pilgrimages, and priestly pomp and circumstance. It spread particularly among the Northern nations, which were not so deeply rooted as those of the South in the old Church's symbolism and love of ritual. In the South the more powerful pagan religion survived in Christianity, whereas in the North Christianity meant an opposition to and a break with the old-time creed, and hence was from the first more thoughtful and less sensual, but for that very reason, in times of peril, more fanatical and more obstinate. If from the standpoint of *thought* we succeed in uprooting Christianity, we can at once know the point where it will begin to disappear – the very point at which it will be most stubborn in defence. In other places it will bend but not break, lose its leaves but burst into leaf afresh, because the senses, and not thought, have gone over to its side. But it is the senses that maintain the belief that with all its expensive outlay the Church is more cheaply and conveniently managed than under the stern conditions of work and wages. Yet what does one hold leisure (or semi-idleness) to be worth, when once one has become accustomed to it? The senses plead against a dechristianised world, saying that there would be too much work to do in it and an insufficient supply of leisure. They take the part of magic – that is, they let God work himself (*oremus nos, Deus laboret*).

107

Three-quarter strength – A work that is meant to give an impression of health should be produced with three-quarters, at the most, of the strength of its creator. If he has gone to his farthest limit, the work excites the observer and disconcerts him by its tension. All good things have something lazy about them and lie like cows in the meadow.

128

Against the short-sighted – Do you think it is piecework because it is (and must be) offered you in pieces?

129

Readers of aphorisms – The worst readers of aphorisms are the friends of the author, if they make a point of referring the general to the particular instance to which the aphorism owes its origin. This namby-pamby attitude brings all the author's trouble to naught, and instead of a philosophic lesson and a philosophic frame of mind, they deservedly gain nothing but the satisfaction of a vulgar curiosity.

137

The worst readers – The worst readers are those who act like plundering soldiers. They take out some things that they might use, cover the rest with filth and confusion, and blaspheme about the whole.

138

Signs of a good writer – Good writers have two things in common: they prefer being understood to being admired, and they do not write for the critical and over-shrewd reader.

155

The hidden barrel-organ – Genius, by virtue of its more ample drapery, knows better than talent how to hide its barrel-organ. Yet after all it too can only play its seven old pieces over and over again.

156

The name on the title-page – It is now a matter of custom and almost of duty for the author's name to appear on the book, and this is a main cause of the fact that books have so little influence. If they are good, they are worth more than the personalities of their authors, of which they are the quintessences. But as soon as the author makes himself known on the title-page, the quintessence, from the reader's point of view, becomes diluted with the personal, the most personal element, and the aim of the book is frustrated. It is the ambition of the intellect no longer to appear individual.

158

Little or no love – Every good book is written for a particular reader and men of his stamp, and for that very reason is looked upon unfavourably by all other readers, by the vast majority. Its reputation accordingly rests on a narrow basis and must be built up by degrees. The mediocre and bad book is mediocre and bad because it seeks to please, and does please, a great number.

161

Youth and criticism – To criticise a book means, for the young, not to let oneself be touched by a single productive thought therefrom, and to protect one's skin with hands and feet. The youngster lives in opposition to all novelty that he cannot love in the lump, in a position of self-defence, and in this connection he commits, as often as he can, a superfluous sin.

162

Effect of quantity – The greatest paradox in the history of poetic art lies in this: that in all that constitutes the greatness of the old poets a man may be a barbarian, faulty and deformed from top to toe, and still remain the greatest of poets. This is the case with Shakespeare, who, as compared with Sophocles, is like a mine of immeasurable wealth in gold, lead, and rubble, whereas Sophocles is not merely gold, but gold in its noblest form, one that almost makes us forget the money-value of the metal. But quantity in its highest intensity has the same effect as quality. That is a good thing for Shakespeare.

171

Music as a latecomer in every culture – Among all the arts that are accustomed to grow on a definite culture-soil and under definite social and political conditions, music is the last plant to come up, arising in the autumn and fading-season of the culture to which it belongs. At the same time, the first signs and harbingers of a new spring are usually already noticeable, and sometimes music, like the language of a forgotten age, rings out into a new, astonished world, and comes too late. In the art of the Dutch and Flemish musicians the soul of the Christian middle ages at last found its fullest tone: their sound-architecture is the posthumous but legitimate and equal sister of Gothic. Not until Handel's music was heard the note of the best in the soul of Luther and his kin, the great Judaeoheroical impulse that created the whole Reformation movement. Mozart first expressed in golden melody the age of Louis XIV and

the art of Racine and Claude Lorrain. The eighteenth
century – that century of rhapsody, of broken ideals
and transitory happiness – only sang itself out in
the music of Beethoven and Rossini. A lover of
sentimental similes might say that all really important
music was a swan-song – music is, in fact, not a
universal language for all time, as is so often said in its
praise, but responds exactly to a particular period and
warmth of emotion which involves a quite definite,
individual culture, determined by time and place, as
its inner law. The music of Palestrina would be quite
unintelligible to a Greek; and again, what would the
music of Rossini convey to Palestrina? It may be that
our most modern German music, with all its pre-
eminence and desire of pre-eminence, will soon be no
longer understood. For this music sprang from a
culture that is undergoing a rapid decay, from the soil
of that epoch of reaction and restoration in which a
certain Catholicism of feeling, as well as a delight in
all indigenous, national, primitive manners, burst into
bloom and scattered a blended perfume over Europe.
These two emotional tendencies, adopted in their
greatest strength and carried to their farthest limits,
found final expression in the music of Wagner.
Wagner's predilection for the old native sagas, his free
idealisation of their unfamiliar gods and heroes – who
are really sovereign beasts of prey with occasional fits
of thoughtfulness, magnanimity, and boredom – his
re-animation of those figures, to which he gave in
addition the mediaeval Christian thirst for ecstatic
sensuality and spiritualisation – all this Wagnerian
give-and-take with regard to materials, souls, figures,
and words – would clearly express the spirit of his
music, if it could not, like all music, speak quite

unambiguously of itself. This spirit wages the last campaign of reaction against the spirit of illumination which passed into this century from the last, and also against the supernatural ideas of French revolutionary romanticism and of English and American colourlessness in the reconstruction of state and society – But is it not evident that the spheres of thought and emotion apparently suppressed by Wagner and his school have long since acquired fresh strength, and that his late musical protest against them generally rings into ears that prefer to hear different and opposite notes; so that one day that high and wonderful art will suddenly become unintelligible and will be covered by the spider's web of oblivion? In considering this state of affairs we must not let ourselves be led astray by those transitory fluctuations which arise like a reaction within a reaction, as a temporary sinking of the mountainous wave in the midst of the general upheaval. Thus, this decade of national war, ultramontane martyrdom, and social-istic unrest may, in its remoter after-effect, even aid the Wagnerian art to acquire a sudden halo, without guaranteeing that it 'has a future' or that it has *the* future. It is in the very nature of music that the fruits of its great culture-vintage should lose their taste and wither earlier than the fruits of the plastic arts or those that grow on the tree of knowledge. Among all the products of the human artistic sense ideas are the most solid and lasting.

175

Continued existence of art – Why, really, does a creative art nowadays continue to exist? Because the majority who have hours of leisure (and such an art is for them only) think that they cannot fill up their time without music, theatres and picture-galleries, novels and poetry. Granted that one could keep them from this indulgence, either they would strive less eagerly for leisure, and the invidious sight of the rich would be less common (a great gain for the stability of society), or they would have leisure, but would learn to reflect on what can be learnt and unlearnt: on their work, for instance, their associations, the pleasure they could bestow. All the world, with the exception of the artist, would in both cases reap the advantage – Certainly, there are many vigorous, sensible readers who could take objection to this. Still, it must be said on behalf of the coarse and malignant that the author himself is concerned with this protest, and that there is in his book much to be read that is not actually written down therein.

176

The mouthpiece of the gods – The poet expresses the universal higher opinions of the nation, he is its mouthpiece and flute; but by virtue of metre and all other artistic means he so expresses them that the nation regards them as something quite new and wonderful, and believes in all seriousness that he is the mouthpiece of the gods. Yes, under the clouds of creation the poet himself forgets whence he derives all his intellectual wisdom – from father and mother, from teachers and books of all kinds, from the street and particularly from the priest. He is deceived by his own art, and really believes, in a naïve period, that a god is speaking through him, that he is creating in a state of religious inspiration. As a matter of fact, he is only saying what he has learnt, a medley of popular wisdom and popular foolishness. Hence, so far as a poet is really *vox populi* he is held to be *vox dei*.

187

The antique world and pleasure – The man of the antique world understood better how to rejoice, we understand better how to grieve less. They continually found new motives for feeling happy, for celebrating festivals, being inventive with all their wealth of shrewdness and reflection. We, on the other hand, concentrate our intellect rather on the solving of problems which have in view painlessness and the removal of sources of discomfort. With regard to suffering existence, the ancients sought to forget or in some way to convert the sensation into a pleasant one, thus trying to supply palliatives. We attack the causes of suffering, and on the whole prefer to use prophylactics – Perhaps we are only building upon a foundation whereon a later age will once more set up the temple of joy.

190

Supplementary justification of existence – Many ideas have come into the world as errors and fancies but have turned out truths, because men have afterwards given them a genuine basis to rest upon.

193

The saddest destiny of a prophet – He has worked twenty years to convince his contemporaries, and succeeds at last, but in the meantime his adversaries have also succeeded – he is no longer convinced of himself.

194

Three thinkers like one spider – In every philosophical school three thinkers follow one another in this relation: the first produces from himself sap and seed, the second draws it out in threads and spins a cunning web, the third waits in this web for the victims who are caught in it – and tries to live upon this philosophy.

196

A team of two – Vagueness of thought and outbursts of sentimentality are as often wedded to the reckless desire to have one's own way by hook or by crook, to make oneself alone of any consequence, as a genuinely helpful, gracious, and kindly spirit is wedded to the impulse towards clearness and purity of thought and towards emotional moderation and self-restraint.

197

Binding and separating forces – Surely it is in the heads of men that there arises the force that binds them – an understanding of their common interest or the reverse; and in their hearts the force that separates them – a blind choosing and groping in love and hate, a devotion to one at the expense of all, and a consequent contempt for the common utility.

198

Marksmen and thinkers – There are curious marksmen who miss their mark, but leave the shooting-gallery with secret pride in the fact that their bullet at any rate flew very far (beyond the mark, it is true), or that it did not hit the mark but hit something else. There are thinkers of the same stamp.

200

Original – Original minds are distinguished not by being the first to see a new thing, but by seeing the old, well-known thing, which is seen and overlooked by every one, as something new. The first discoverer is usually that quite ordinary and unintellectual visionary – chance.

202

Wit – Wit is the epitaph of an emotion.

203

The moment before solution – In science it occurs every day and every hour that a man, immediately before the solution, remains stuck, being convinced that his efforts have been entirely in vain – like one who, in untying a noose, hesitates at the moment when it is nearest to coming loose, because at that very moment it looks most like a knot.

205

Keen air – The best and healthiest element in science as amid the mountains is the keen air that plays about it. Intellectual molly-coddles (such as artists) dread and abuse science on account of this atmosphere.

206

Why savants are nobler than artists – Science requires nobler natures than does poetry; natures that are more simple, less ambitious, more restrained, calmer, that think less of posthumous fame and can bury themselves in studies which, in the eye of the many, scarcely seem worthy of such a sacrifice of personality.

There is another loss of which they are conscious. The nature of their occupation, its continual exaction of the greatest sobriety, weakens their will; the fire is not kept up so vigorously as on the hearths of poetic minds. As such, they often lose their strength and prime earlier than artists do – and, as has been said, they are aware of their danger. Under all circumstances they seem less gifted because they shine less, and thus they will always be rated below their value.

208

Standing on one's head – If we make truth stand on its head, we generally fail to notice that our own head, too, is not in its right position.

209

Origin and utility of fashion – The obvious satisfaction of the individual with his own form excites imitation and gradually creates the form of the many – that is, fashion. The many desire, and indeed attain, that same comforting satisfaction with their own form. Consider how many reasons every man has for anxiety and shy self-concealment, and how, on this account, three-fourths of his energy and goodwill is crippled and may become unproductive! So we must be very grateful to fashion for unfettering that three-fourths and communicating self-confidence and the power of cheerful compromise to those who feel themselves bound to each other by its law. Even foolish laws give freedom and calm of the spirit, so long as many persons have submitted to their sway.

213

Against the cultivation of music – The artistic training of the eye from childhood upwards by means of drawing, painting, landscape-sketching, figures, scenes, involves an estimable gain in life, making the eyesight keen, calm, and enduring in the observation of men and circumstances. No similar secondary advantage arises from the artistic cultivation of the ear, whence public schools will generally do well to give the art of the eye a preference over that of the ear.

220

The pagan characteristic – Perhaps there is nothing more astonishing to the observer of the Greek world than to discover that the Greeks from time to time held festivals, as it were, for all their passions and evil tendencies alike, and in fact even established a kind of series of festivals, by order of the State, for their 'all-too-human'. This is the pagan characteristic of their world, which Christianity has never understood and never can understand, and has always combated and despised – they accepted this all-too-human as unavoidable, and preferred, instead of railing at it, to give it a kind of secondary right by grafting it on to the usages of society and religion. All in man that has power they called divine, and wrote it on the walls of their heaven. They do not deny this natural instinct that expresses itself in evil characteristics, but regulate and limit it to definite cults and days, so as to turn those turbulent streams into as harmless a course as possible, after devising sufficient precautionary measures. That is the root of all the moral broad-mindedness of antiquity. To the wicked, the dubious, the backward, the animal element, as to the barbaric, pre-Hellenic and Asiatic, which still lived in the depths of Greek nature, they allowed a moderate outflow, and did not strive to destroy it utterly. The whole system was under the domain of the State, which was built up not on individuals or castes, but on common human qualities. In the structure of the State the Greeks show that wonderful sense for typical facts which later on enabled them to become investigators of Nature, historians, geographers, and philosophers. It was not a limited moral law of priests or castes, which had to decide about the constitution of the State and State worship, but the most comprehensive view of the reality of all that is human. Whence do the Greeks derive this freedom, this sense of reality? Perhaps from Homer and the poets who preceded him. For just those poets whose nature is generally not the most wise or just possess, in compensation, that delight in reality and activity of every kind, and prefer not to deny even evil. It suffices for them if evil moderates itself, does not kill or inwardly poison everything – in other words, they have similar ideas to those of the founders of Greek constitutions, and were their teachers and forerunners.

225

Faith makes holy and condemns – A Christian who happened upon forbidden paths of thought might well ask himself on some occasion whether it is really necessary that there should be a God, side by side with a representative Lamb, if faith in the existence of these beings suffices to produce the same influences? If they do exist after all, are they not superfluous beings? For all that is given by the Christian religion to the human soul, all that is beneficent, consoling, and edifying, just as much as all that depresses and crushes, emanates from that faith and not from the objects of that faith. It is here as in another well-known case – there were indeed no witches, but the terrible effects of the belief in witches were the same as if they really had existed. For all occasions where the Christian awaits the immediate intervention of a God, though in vain (for there is no God), his religion is inventive enough to find subterfuges and reasons for tranquillity. In so far Christianity is an ingenious religion – Faith, indeed, has up to the present not been able to move real mountains, although I do not know who assumed that it could. But it can put mountains where there are none.

228

Travellers and their grades – Among travellers we may distinguish five grades. The first and lowest grade is of those who travel and are seen – they become really travelled and are, as it were, blind. Next come those who really see the world. The third class experience the results of their seeing. The fourth weave their experience into their life and carry it with them henceforth. Lastly, there are some men of the highest strength who, as soon as they have returned home, must finally and necessarily work out in their lives and productions all the things seen that they have experienced and incorporated in themselves – Like these five species of travellers, all mankind goes through the whole pilgrimage of life, the lowest as purely passive, the highest as those who act and live out their lives without keeping back any residue of inner experiences.

233

For the scorners of 'herd-humanity' – He who regards human beings as a herd, and flies from them as fast as he can, will certainly be caught up by them and gored upon their horns.

235

Disappointment – When a long life of action distinguished by speeches and writings gives publicity to a man's personality, personal intercourse with him is generally disappointing on two grounds. Firstly, one expects too much from a brief period of intercourse (namely, all that the thousand and one opportunities of life can alone bring out). Secondly, no recognised person gives himself the trouble to woo recognition in individual cases. He is too careless, and we are at too high a tension.

238

With the exception of our neighbour – I admit that my head is set wrong on my neck only, for every other man, as is well known, knows better than I what I should do or leave alone. The only one who cannot help me is myself, poor beggar! Are we not all like statues on which false heads have been placed? Eh, dear neighbour? Ah no; you, just you, are the exception!

240

The wish to appear vain – In conversation with strangers or little-known acquaintances, to express only selected thoughts, to speak of one's famous acquaintances, and important experiences and travels, is a sign that one is not proud, or at least would not like to appear proud. Vanity is the polite mask of pride.

248

The way to a Christian virtue – Learning from one's enemies is the best way to love them, for it inspires us with a grateful mood towards them.

254

Honesty's miscalculation – Our newest acquaintances are sometimes the first to learn what we have hitherto kept dark. We have the foolish notion that our proof of confidence is the strongest fetter wherewith to hold them fast. But *they* do not know enough about us to feel so strongly the sacrifice involved in our speaking out, and betray our secrets to others without any idea of betrayal. Hereby we possibly lose our old friends.

260

Making friends only with the industrious – The man of leisure is dangerous to his friends, for, having nothing to do, he talks of what his friends are doing or not doing, interferes, and finally makes himself a nuisance. The clever man will only make friends with the industrious.

262

Depth and troubled waters – The public easily confounds him who fishes in troubled waters with him who pumps up from the depths.

263

Demonstrating one's vanity to friend and foe – Many a man, from vanity, maltreats even his friends, when in the presence of witnesses to whom he wishes to make his own preponderance clear. Others exaggerate the merits of their enemies, in order to point proudly to the fact that they are worthy of such foes.

266

Where danger is greatest – We seldom break our leg so long as life continues a toilsome upward climb. The danger comes when we begin to take things easily and choose the convenient paths.

271

Every philosophy is the philosophy of a period of life – The period of life in which a philosopher finds his teaching is manifested by his teaching; he cannot avoid that, however elevated above time and hour he may feel himself. Thus, Schopenhauer's philosophy remains a mirror of his hot and melancholy youth – it is no mode of thought for older men. Plato's philosophy reminds one of the middle thirties, when a warm and a cold current generally rush together, so that spray and delicate clouds and, under favourable circumstances and glimpses of sunshine, enchanting rainbow-pictures result.

272

Of the intellect of women – The intellectual strength of a woman is best proved by the fact that she offers her own intellect as a sacrifice out of love for a man and his intellect, and that nevertheless in the new domain, which was previously foreign to her nature, a second intellect at once arises as an after-growth, to which the man's mind impels her.

279

Not to distrust your emotions – The feminine phrase 'Do not distrust your emotions' does not mean much more than 'Eat what tastes good to you'. This may also, especially for moderate natures, be a good everyday rule. But other natures must live according to another maxim: 'You must eat not only with your mouth but also with your brain, in order that the greediness of your mouth may not prove your undoing.'

280

A cruel fancy of love – Every great love involves the cruel thought of killing the object of love, so that it may be removed once for all from the mischievous play of change. For love is more afraid of change than of destruction.

281

Doors – In everything that is learnt or experienced, the child, just like the man, sees doors; but for the former they are places to go *to*, for the latter to go *through*.

282

Sympathetic women – The sympathy of women, which is talkative, takes the sick-bed to market.

283

Early merit – He who acquires merit early in life tends to forget all reverence for age and old people, and accordingly, greatly to his disadvantage, excludes himself from the society of the mature, those who confer maturity. Thus in spite of his early merit he remains green, importunate, and boyish longer than others.

285

Young talents – With respect to young talents we must strictly follow Goethe's maxim, that we should often avoid harming error in order to avoid harming truth. Their condition is like the diseases of pregnancy, and involves strange appetites. These appetites should be satisfied and humoured as far as possible, for the sake of the fruit they may be expected to produce. It is true that, as nurse of these remarkable invalids, one must learn the difficult art of voluntary self-abasement.

286

Disgust with truth – Women are so constituted that all truth (in relation to men, love, children, society, aim of life) disgusts them – and that they try to be revenged on every one who opens their eyes.

287

The source of great love – Whence arises the sudden passion of a man for a woman, a passion so deep, so vital? Least of all from sensuality only: but when a man finds weakness, need of help, and high spirits united in the same creature, he suffers a sort of over-flowing of soul, and is touched and offended at the same moment. At this point arises the source of great love.

289

Of vain old men – Profundity of thought belongs to youth, clarity of thought to old age. When, in spite of this, old men sometimes speak and write in the manner of the profound, they do so from vanity, imagining that they thereby assume the charm of juvenility, enthusiasm, growth, apprehensiveness, hopefulness.

290

Enjoyment of novelty – Men use a new lesson or experience later on as a ploughshare or perhaps also as a weapon, women at once make it into an ornament.

291

How both sexes behave when in the right – If it is conceded to a woman that she is right, she cannot deny herself the triumph of setting her heel on the neck of the vanquished; she must taste her victory to the full. On the other hand, man towards man in such a case is ashamed of being right. But then man is accustomed to victory; with woman it is an exception.

303

When it is necessary to remain stationary – When the masses begin to rage, and reason is under a cloud, it is a good thing, if the health of one's soul is not quite assured, to go under a doorway and look out to see what the weather is like.

305

Party tactics – When a party observes that a previous member has changed from an unqualified to a qualified adherent, it endures it so ill that it irritates and mortifies him in every possible way with the object of forcing him to a decisive break and making him an opponent. For the party suspects that the intention of finding a relative value in its faith, a value which admits of pro and con, of weighing and discarding, is more dangerous than downright opposition.

306

For the strengthening of parties – Whoever wishes to strengthen a party internally should give it an opportunity of being forcibly treated with obvious injustice. The party thus acquires a capital of good conscience, which hitherto it perhaps lacked.

307

To provide for one's past – As men after all only respect the old-established and slowly developed, he who would survive after his death must not only provide for posterity but still more for the past. Hence tyrants of every sort (including tyrannical artists and politicians) like to do violence to history, so that history may seem a preparation for and a ladder up to them.

308

Party writers – The beating of drums, which delights young writers who serve a party, sounds to him who does not belong to the party like a rattling of chains, and excites sympathy rather than admiration.

311

Joy in commanding and obeying – Commanding is a joy, like obeying; the former when it has not yet become a habit, the latter just when it has become a habit. Old servants under new masters advance each other mutually in giving pleasure.

317

Possession possesses – Only up to a certain point does possession make men feel freer and more independent; one step farther, and possession becomes lord, the possessor a slave. The latter must sacrifice his time, his thoughts to the former, and feels himself compelled to an intercourse, nailed to a spot, incorporated with the State – perhaps quite in conflict with his real and essential needs.

326

Two kinds of sobriety – In order not to confound the sobriety arising from mental exhaustion with that arising from moderation, one must remark that the former is peevish, the latter cheerful.

340

To one who is praised – So long as you are praised, believe that you are not yet on your own course but on that of another.

348

From cannibal country – In solitude the lonely man is eaten up by himself, among crowds by the many. Choose which you prefer.

358

Never in vain – In the mountains of truth you never climb in vain. Either you already reach a higher point today, or you exercise your strength in order to be able to climb higher tomorrow.

361

Medicine of the soul – To lie still and think little is the cheapest medicine for all diseases of the soul, and, with the aid of good-will, becomes pleasanter every hour that it is used.

362

Intellectual order of precedence – You rank far below others when you try to establish the exception and they the rule.

364

The reason for much fretfulness – He that prefers the beautiful to the useful in life will undoubtedly, like children who prefer sweetmeats to bread, destroy his digestion and acquire a very fretful outlook on the world.

373

After death – It is only long after the death of a man that we find it inconceivable that he should be missed – in the case of really great men, only after decades. Those who are honest usually think when any one dies that he is not much missed, and that the pompous funeral oration is a piece of hypocrisy. Necessity first teaches the necessariness of an individual, and the proper epitaph is a belated sigh.

376

Chain-thinkers – To him who has thought a great deal, every new thought that he hears or reads at once assumes the form of a chain.

377

Pity – In the gilded sheath of pity is sometimes hidden the dagger of envy.

378

What is genius? – To aspire to a lofty aim and to will the means to that aim.

394

A mistake of biographers – The small force that is required to launch a boat into the stream must not be confounded with the force of the stream that carries the boat along. Yet this mistake is made in nearly all biographies.

399

Being satisfied – We show that we have attained maturity of understanding when we no longer go where rare flowers lurk under the thorniest hedges of knowledge, but are satisfied with gardens, forests, meadows, and ploughlands, remembering that life is too short for the rare and uncommon.

404

How duty acquires a glamour – You can change a brazen duty into gold in the eyes of all by always performing something more than you have promised.

THUS SPAKE ZARATHUSTRA
PART I

Zarathustra's Prologue

When Zarathustra was thirty years old, he left his home and the lake of his home, and went into the mountains. There he enjoyed his spirit and his solitude, and for ten years did not weary of it. But at last his heart changed – and rising one morning with the rosy dawn, he went before the sun, and spake thus unto it:

Thou great star! What would be thy happiness if thou hadst not those for whom thou shinest!

For ten years hast thou climbed hither unto my cave: thou wouldst have wearied of thy light and of the journey, had it not been for me, mine eagle, and my serpent.

But we awaited thee every morning, took from thee thine overflow, and blessed thee for it.

Lo! I am weary of my wisdom, like the bee that hath gathered too much honey; I need hands outstretched to take it.

I would fain bestow and distribute, until the wise have once more become joyous in their folly, and the poor happy in their riches.

Therefore must I descend into the deep: as thou doest in the evening, when thou goest behind the sea, and givest light also to the nether-world, thou exuberant star!

Like thee must I *go down*, as men say, to whom I shall descend.

Bless me, then, thou tranquil eye, that canst behold even the greatest happiness without envy!

Bless the cup that is about to overflow, that the water may flow golden out of it, and carry everywhere the reflection of thy bliss!

Lo! This cup is again going to empty itself, and Zarathustra is again going to be a man.

Thus began Zarathustra's down-going.

2

Zarathustra went down the mountain alone, no one meeting him. When he entered the forest, however, there suddenly stood before him an old man, who had left his holy cot to seek roots. And thus spake the old man to Zarathustra:

'No stranger to me is this wanderer: many years ago passed he by. Zarathustra he was called; but he hath altered.

'Then thou carriedst thine ashes into the mountains: wilt thou now carry thy fire into the valleys? Fearest thou not the incendiary's doom?

'Yea, I recognise Zarathustra. Pure is his eye, and no loathing lurketh about his mouth. Goeth he not along like a dancer?

'Altered is Zarathustra; a child hath Zarathustra become; an awakened one is Zarathustra: what wilt thou do in the land of the sleepers?

'As in the sea hast thou lived in solitude, and it hath borne thee up. Alas, wilt thou now go ashore? Alas, wilt thou again drag thy body thyself?'

Zarathustra answered: 'I love mankind.'

'Why,' said the saint, 'did I go into the forest and the desert? Was it not because I loved men far too well?

170

'Now I love God: men, I do not love. Man is a thing too imperfect for me. Love to man would be fatal to me.'

Zarathustra answered: 'What spake I of love? I am bringing gifts unto men.'

'Give them nothing,' said the saint. 'Take rather part of their load, and carry it along with them – that will be most agreeable unto them: if only it be agreeable unto thee!

'If, however, thou wilt give unto them, give them no more than an alms, and let them also beg for it!'

'No,' replied Zarathustra, 'I give no alms. I am not poor enough for that.'

The saint laughed at Zarathustra, and spake thus: 'Then see to it that they accept thy treasures! They are distrustful of anchorites, and do not believe that we come with gifts.

'The fall of our footsteps ringeth too hollow through their streets. And just as at night, when they are in bed and hear a man abroad long before sunrise, so they ask themselves concerning us: Where goeth the thief?

'Go not to men, but stay in the forest! Go rather to the animals! Why not be like me – a bear amongst bears, a bird amongst birds?'

'And what doeth the saint in the forest?' asked Zarathustra.

The saint answered: 'I make hymns and sing them; and in making hymns I laugh and weep and mumble: thus do I praise God.

'With singing, weeping, laughing, and mumbling do I praise the God who is my God. But what dost thou bring us as a gift?'

When Zarathustra had heard these words, he bowed to the saint and said: 'What should I have to give thee!

Let me rather hurry hence lest I take aught away from thee!' – And thus they parted from one another, the old man and Zarathustra, laughing like schoolboys.

When Zarathustra was alone, however, he said to his heart: 'Could it be possible? This old saint in the forest hath not yet heard of it, that *God is dead*?'

3

When Zarathustra arrived at the nearest town which adjoineth the forest, he found many people assembled in the marketplace; for it had been announced that a rope-dancer would give a performance. And Zarathustra spake thus unto the people:

I teach you the Superman. Man is something that is to be surpassed. What have ye done to surpass man?

All beings hitherto have created something beyond themselves: and ye want to be the ebb of that great tide, and would rather go back to the beast than surpass man?

What is the ape to man? A laughing-stock, a thing of shame. And just the same shall man be to the Superman: a laughing-stock, a thing of shame.

Ye have made your way from the worm to man, and much within you is still worm. Once were ye apes, and even yet man is more of an ape than any of the apes.

Even the wisest among you is only a disharmony and hybrid of plant and phantom. But do I bid you become phantoms or plants?

Lo, I teach you the Superman!

The Superman is the meaning of the earth. Let your will say: The Superman *shall be* the meaning of the earth!

I conjure you, my brethren, *remain true to the earth*, and believe not those who speak unto you of super-earthly hopes! Poisoners are they, whether they know it or not.

Despisers of life are they, decaying ones and poisoned ones themselves, of whom the earth is weary: so away with them!

Once blasphemy against God was the greatest blasphemy; but God died, and therewith also those blasphemers. To blaspheme the earth is now the dreadfulest sin, and to rate the heart of the unknowable higher than the meaning of the earth!

Once the soul looked contemptuously on the body, and then that contempt was the supreme thing: – the soul wished the body meagre, ghastly, and famished. Thus it thought to escape from the body and the earth.

Oh, that soul was itself meagre, ghastly, and famished; and cruelty was the delight of that soul!

But ye also, my brethren, tell me: what doth your body say about your soul? Is your soul not poverty and pollution and wretched self-complacency?

Verily, a polluted stream is man. One must be a sea, to receive a polluted stream without becoming impure.

Lo, I teach you the Superman: he is that sea; in him can your great contempt be submerged.

What is the greatest thing ye can experience? It is the hour of great contempt. The hour in which even your happiness becometh loathsome unto you, and so also your reason and virtue.

The hour when ye say: 'What good is my happiness! It is poverty and pollution and wretched self-complacency. But my happiness should justify existence itself!'

The hour when ye say: 'What good is my reason! Doth it long for knowledge as the lion for his food? It is poverty and pollution and wretched self-com-placency!'

The hour when ye say: 'What good is my virtue! As yet it hath not made me passionate. How weary I am of my good and my bad! It is all poverty and pollution and wretched self-complacency!'

The hour when ye say: 'What good is my justice! I do not see that I am fervour and fuel. The just, however, are fervour and fuel!'

The hour when we say: 'What good is my pity! Is not pity the cross on which he is nailed who loveth man? But my pity is not a crucifixion.'

Have ye ever spoken thus? Have ye ever cried thus? Ah! Would that I had heard you crying thus!

It is not your sin – it is your self-satisfaction that crieth unto heaven; your very sparingness in sin crieth unto heaven!

Where is the lightning to lick you with its tongue? Where is the frenzy with which ye should be inoc-ulated?

Lo, I teach you the Superman: he is that lightning, he is that frenzy!

When Zarathustra had thus spoken, one of the people called out: 'We have now heard enough of the rope-dancer; it is time now for us to see him!' And all the people laughed at Zarathustra. But the rope-dancer, who thought the words applied to him, began his performance.

4

Zarathustra, however, looked at the people and wondered. Then he spake thus:

Man is a rope stretched between the animal and the Superman – a rope over an abyss.

A dangerous crossing, a dangerous wayfaring, a dangerous looking-back, a dangerous trembling and halting.

What is great in man is that he is a bridge and not a goal: what is lovable in man is that he is an *over-going* and a *down-going*.

I love those that know not how to live except as down-goers, for they are the over-goers.

I love the great despisers, because they are the great adorers, and arrows of longing for the other shore.

I love those who do not first seek a reason beyond the stars for going down and being sacrifices, but sacrifice themselves to the earth, that the earth of the Superman may hereafter arrive.

I love him who liveth in order to know, and seeketh to know in order that the Superman may hereafter live. Thus seeketh he his own down-going.

I love him who laboureth and inventeth, that he may build the house for the Superman, and prepare for him earth, animal, and plant: for thus seeketh he his own down-going.

I love him who loveth his virtue: for virtue is the will to down-going, and an arrow of longing.

I love him who reserveth no share of spirit for himself, but wanteth to be wholly the spirit of his virtue: thus walketh he as spirit over the bridge.

I love him who maketh his virtue his inclination and destiny: thus, for the sake of his virtue, he is willing to live on, or live no more.

I love him who desireth not too many virtues. One virtue is more of a virtue than two, because it is more of a knot for one's destiny to cling to.

I love him whose soul is lavish, who wanteth no thanks and doth not give back: for he always bestoweth, and desireth not to keep for himself.

I love him who is ashamed when the dice fall in his favour, and who then asketh: 'Am I a dishonest player?' – for he is willing to succumb.

I love him who scattereth golden words in advance of his deeds, and always doeth more than he promiseth: for he seeketh his own down-going.

I love him who justifieth the future ones, and redeemeth the past ones: for he is willing to succcumb through the present ones

I love him who chasteneth his God, because he loveth his God: for he must succumb through the wrath of his God.

I love him whose soul is deep even in the wounding, and may succumb through a small matter: thus goeth he willingly over the bridge.

I love him whose soul is so overfull that he forgetteth himself, and all things are in him: thus all things become his down-going.

I love him who is of a free spirit and a free heart: thus is his head only the bowels of his heart; his heart, however, causeth his down-going.

I love all who are like heavy drops falling one by one out of the dark cloud that lowereth over man: they herald the coming of the lightning, and succumb as heralds.

Lo, I am a herald of the lightning, and a heavy drop out of the cloud: the lightning, however, is the *Superman*.

5

When Zarathustra had spoken these words, he again looked at the people, and was silent. 'There they stand,' said he to his heart; 'there they laugh: they understand me not; I am not the mouth for these ears.

Must one first batter their ears, that they may learn to hear with their eyes? Must one clatter like kettle-drums and penitential preachers? Or do they only believe the stammerer?

They have something whereof they are proud. What do they call it, that which maketh them proud? Culture, they call it; it distinguisheth them from the goatherds.

They dislike, therefore, to hear of 'contempt' of themselves. So I will appeal to their pride.

I will speak unto them of the most contemptible thing: that, however, is *the last man!*'

And thus spake Zarathustra unto the people:

It is time for man to fix his goal. It is time for man to plant the germ of his highest hope.

Still is his soil rich enough for it. But that soil will one day be poor and exhausted, and no lofty tree will any longer be able to grow thereon.

Alas! There cometh the time when man will no longer launch the arrow of his longing beyond man – and the string of his bow will have unlearned to whizz!

I tell you: one must still have chaos in one, to give birth to a dancing star. I tell you: ye have still chaos in you.

Alas! There cometh the time when man will no longer give birth to any star. Alas! There cometh the time of the most despicable man, who can no longer despise himself.

Lo! I show you *the last man.*

'What is love? What is creation? What is longing? What is a star?' – so asketh the last man and blinketh.

The earth hath then become small, and on it there hoppeth the last man who maketh everything small.

His species is ineradicable like that of the ground-flea; the last man liveth longest.

'We have discovered happiness' – say the last men, and blink thereby.

They have left the regions where it is hard to live; for they need warmth. One still loveth one's neighbour and rubbeth against him; for one needeth warmth.

Turning ill and being distrustful, they consider sinful: they walk warily. He is a fool who still stumbleth over stones or men!

A little poison now and then: that maketh pleasant dreams. And much poison at last for a pleasant death.

One still worketh, for work is a pastime. But one is careful lest the pastime should hurt one.

One no longer becometh poor or rich; both are too burdensome. Who still wanteth to rule? Who still wanteth to obey? Both are too burdensome.

No shepherd, and one herd! Every one wanteth the same; every one is equal: he who hath other sentiments goeth voluntarily into the madhouse.

'Formerly all the world was insane,' say the subtlest of them, and blink thereby.

They are clever and know all that hath happened: so there is no end to their raillery. People still fall out, but are soon reconciled – otherwise it spoileth their stomachs.

They have their little pleasures for the day, and their little pleasures for the night: but they have a regard for health.

'We have discovered happiness,' say the last men, and blink thereby.

And here ended the first discourse of Zarathustra, which is also called 'The Prologue': for at this point the shouting and mirth of the multitude interrupted him. 'Give us this last man, O Zarathustra' – they called out – 'make us into these last men! Then will we make thee a present of the Superman!' And all the people exulted and smacked their lips. Zarathustra, however, turned sad, and said to his heart:

'They understand me not: I am not the mouth for these ears.

Too long, perhaps, have I lived in the mountains; too much have I hearkened unto the brooks and trees: now do I speak unto them as unto the goatherds.

Calm is my soul, and clear, like the mountains in the morning. But they think me cold, and a mocker with terrible jests.

And now do they look at me and laugh: and while they laugh they hate me too. There is ice in their laughter.'

6

Then, however, something happened which made every mouth mute and every eye fixed. In the meantime, of course, the rope-dancer had commenced his performance: he had come out at a little door, and was going along the rope which was stretched between two towers, so that it hung above the market-place and the people. When he was just midway across, the little door opened once more, and a gaudily-dressed fellow like a buffoon sprang out, and went rapidly after the first one. 'Go on, halt-foot,' cried his frightful voice, 'go on, lazy-bones, interloper, sallow-face! – lest I tickle thee with my heel! What dost thou here between the towers? In the tower is the place for thee, thou shouldst be locked up; to one better than thyself thou blockest the way!' – And with every word he came nearer and nearer the first one.

When, however, he was but a step behind, there happened the frightful thing which made every mouth mute and every eye fixed: – he uttered a yell like a devil, and jumped over the other who was in his way. The latter, however, when he thus saw his rival triumph, lost at the same time his head and his footing on the rope; he threw his pole away, and shot downwards faster than it, like an eddy of arms and legs, into the depth. The marketplace and the people were like the sea when the storm cometh on: they all flew apart and in disorder, especially where the body was about to fall.

Zarathustra, however, remained standing, and just beside him fell the body, badly injured and disfigured, but not yet dead. After a while consciousness returned to the shattered man, and he saw Zarathustra kneeling beside him. 'What art thou doing there?' said he at last, 'I knew long ago that the devil would trip me up. Now he draggeth me to hell: wilt thou prevent him?'

'On mine honour, my friend,' answered Zarathustra, 'there is nothing of all that whereof thou speakest: there is no devil and no hell. Thy soul will be dead even sooner than thy body: fear, therefore, nothing any more!'

The man looked up distrustfully. 'If thou speakest the truth,' said he, 'I lose nothing when I lose my life. I am not much more than an animal which hath been taught to dance by blows and scanty fare.'

'Not at all,' said Zarathustra, 'thou hast made danger thy calling; therein there is nothing contemptible. Now thou perishest by thy calling: therefore will I bury thee with mine own hands.'

When Zarathustra had said this the dying one did

not reply further; but he moved his hand as if he sought the hand of Zarathustra in gratitude.

7

Meanwhile the evening came on, and the marketplace veiled itself in gloom. Then the people dispersed, for even curiosity and terror become fatigued. Zarathustra, however, still sat beside the dead man on the ground, absorbed in thought: so he forgot the time. But at last it became night, and a cold wind blew upon the lonely one. Then arose Zarathustra and said to his heart:

Verily, a fine catch of fish hath Zarathustra made today! It is not a man he hath caught, but a corpse.

Sombre is human life, and as yet without meaning: a buffoon may be fateful to it.

I want to teach men the sense of their existence, which is the Superman, the lightning out of the dark cloud – man.

But still am I far from them, and my sense speaketh not unto their sense. To men I am still something between a fool and a corpse.

Gloomy is the night, gloomy are the ways of Zarathustra. Come, thou cold and stiff companion!

I carry thee to the place where I shall bury thee with mine own hands.

8

When Zarathustra had said this to his heart, he put the corpse upon his shoulders and set out on his way. Yet had he not gone a hundred steps, when there stole a man up to him and whispered in his ear – and lo! he that spake was the buffoon from the tower. 'Leave this town, O Zarathustra,' said he, 'there are too many here who hate thee. The good and just hate thee, and call thee their enemy and despiser; the believers in the orthodox belief hate thee, and call thee a danger to the multitude. It was thy good fortune to be laughed at: and verily thou spakest like a buffoon. It was thy good fortune to associate with the dead dog; by so humiliating thyself thou hast saved thy life today. Depart, however, from this town – or tomorrow I shall jump over thee, a living man over a dead one.' And when he had said this, the buffoon vanished; Zarathustra, however, went on through the dark streets.

At the gate of the town the grave-diggers met him: they shone their torch on his face, and, recognising Zarathustra, they sorely derided him. 'Zarathustra is carrying away the dead dog: a fine thing that Zarathustra hath turned a grave-digger! For our hands are too cleanly for that roast. Will Zarathustra steal the bite from the devil? Well then, good luck to the repast! If only the devil is not a better thief than Zarathustra! He will steal them both, he will eat them both!' And they laughed among themselves, and put their heads together.

Zarathustra made no answer thereto, but went on his way. When he had gone on for two hours, past forests and swamps, he had heard too much of the hungry howling of the wolves, and he himself became a-hungry. So he halted at a lonely house in which a light was burning.

'Hunger attacketh me,' said Zarathustra, 'like a robber. Among forests and swamps my hunger attacketh me, and late in the night.

'Strange humours hath my hunger. Often it cometh to me only after a repast, and all day it hath failed to come: where hath it been?'

And thereupon Zarathustra knocked at the door of

the house. An old man appeared, who carried a light, and asked: 'Who cometh unto me and my bad sleep?'

'A living man and a dead one,' said Zarathustra. 'Give me something to eat and drink, I forgot it during the day. He that feedeth the hungry refresheth his own soul, saith wisdom.'

The old man withdrew, but came back immediately and offered Zarathustra bread and wine. 'A bad country for the hungry,' said he; 'that is why I live here. Animal and man come unto me, the anchorite. But bid thy companion eat and drink also, he is wearier than thou.' Zarathustra answered: 'My companion is dead; I shall hardly be able to persuade him to eat.' 'That doth not concern me,' said the old man sullenly; 'he that knocketh at my door must take what I offer him. Eat, and fare ye well!'

Thereafter Zarathustra again went on for two hours, trusting to the path and the light of the stars: for he was an experienced night-walker, and liked to look into the face of all that slept. When the morning dawned, however, Zarathustra found himself in a thick forest, and no path was any longer visible. He then put the dead man in a hollow tree at his head – for he wanted to protect him from the wolves – and laid himself down on the ground and moss. And immediately he fell asleep, tired in body, but with a tranquil soul.

9

Long slept Zarathustra; and not only the rosy dawn passed over his head, but also the morning. At last, however, his eyes opened, and amazedly he gazed into the forest and the stillness, amazedly he gazed into himself. Then he arose quickly, like a seafarer who all at once seeth the land; and he shouted for joy: for he saw a new truth. And he spake thus to his heart:

A light hath dawned upon me: I need companions – living ones; not dead companions and corpses, which I carry with me where I will.

But I need living companions, who will follow me because they want to follow themselves – and to the place where I will.

A light hath dawned upon me. Not to the people is Zarathustra to speak, but to companions! Zarathustra shall not be the herd's herdsman and hound!

To allure many from the herd – for that purpose have I come. The people and the herd must be angry with me: a robber shall Zarathustra be called by the herdsmen.

Herdsmen, I say, but they call themselves the good and just. Herdsmen, I say, but they call themselves the believers in the orthodox belief.

Behold the good and just! Whom do they hate most? Him who breaketh up their tables of values, the breaker, the law-breaker – he, however, is the creator.

Behold the believers of all beliefs! Whom do they hate most? Him who breaketh up their tables of values, the breaker, the law-breaker – he, however, is the creator.

Companions, the creator seeketh, not corpses – and not herds or believers either. Fellow-creators the creator seeketh – those who grave new values on new tables.

Companions, the creator seeketh, and fellow-reapers: for everything is ripe for the harvest with him. But he lacketh the hundred sickles: so he plucketh the ears of corn and is vexed.

Companions, the creator seeketh, and such as know how to whet their sickles. Destroyers, will they be called, and despisers of good and evil. But they are the reapers and rejoicers.

Fellow-creators, Zarathustra seeketh; fellow-reapers and fellow-rejoicers, Zarathustra seeketh: what hath he to do with herds and herdsmen and corpses!

And thou, my first companion, rest in peace! Well have I buried thee in thy hollow tree; well have I hid thee from the wolves.

But I part from thee; the time hath arrived. 'Twixt rosy dawn and rosy dawn there came unto me a new truth.

I am not to be a herdsman, I am not to be a grave-digger. Not any more will I discourse unto the people; for the last time have I spoken unto the dead.

With the creators, the reapers, and the rejoicers will I associate: the rainbow will I show them, and all the stairs to the Superman.

To the lone-dwellers will I sing my song, and to the twain-dwellers; and unto him who hath still ears for the unheard, will I make the heart heavy with my happiness.

I make for my goal, I follow my course; over the loitering and tardy will I leap. Thus let my on-going be their down-going!

10

This had Zarathustra said to his heart when the sun stood at noontide. Then he looked inquiringly aloft – for he heard above him the sharp call of a bird. And behold! An eagle swept through the air in wide circles, and on it hung a serpent, not like a prey, but like a friend: for it kept itself coiled round the eagle's neck.

'They are mine animals,' said Zarathustra, and rejoiced in his heart.

'The proudest animal under the sun, and the wisest animal under the sun – they have come out to reconnoitre.

They want to know whether Zarathustra still liveth. Verily, do I still live?

More dangerous have I found it among men than among animals; in dangerous paths goeth Zarathustra. Let mine animals lead me!'

When Zarathustra had said this, he remembered the words of the saint in the forest. Then he sighed and spake thus to his heart:

'Would that I were wiser! Would that I were wise from the very heart, like my serpent!

But I am asking the impossible. Therefore do I ask my pride to go always with my wisdom!

And if my wisdom should some day forsake me – alas, it loveth to fly away – may my pride then fly with my folly!'

Thus began Zarathustra's down-going.

The Three Metamorphoses

Three metamorphoses of the spirit do I designate to you: how the spirit becometh a camel, the camel a lion, and the lion at last a child.

Many heavy things are there for the spirit, the strong load-bearing spirit in which reverence dwelleth: for the heavy and the heaviest longeth its strength.

What is heavy? So asketh the load-bearing spirit; then kneeleth it down like the camel, and wanteth to be well laden.

What is the heaviest thing, ye heroes? asketh the load-bearing spirit, that I may take it upon me and rejoice in my strength.

Is it not this: to humiliate oneself in order to mortify one's pride? To exhibit one's folly in order to mock at one's wisdom?

Or is it this: to desert our cause when it celebrateth its triumph? To ascend high mountains to tempt the tempter?

Or is it this: to feed on the acorns and grass of knowledge, and for the sake of truth to suffer hunger of soul?

Or is it this: to be sick and dismiss comforters, and make friends of the deaf, who never hear thy requests?

Or is it this: to go into foul water when it is the water of truth, and not disclaim cold frogs and hot toads?

Or is it this: to love those who despise us, and give one's hand to the phantom when it is going to frighten us?

All these heaviest things the load-bearing spirit taketh upon itself: and like the camel, which, when laden, hasteneth into the wilderness, so hasteneth the spirit into its wilderness.

But in the loneliest wilderness happeneth the second metamorphosis: here the spirit becometh a lion; freedom will it capture, and lordship in its own wilderness.

Its last Lord it here seeketh: hostile will it be to him, and to its last God; for victory will it struggle with the great dragon.

What is the great dragon which the spirit is no longer inclined to call Lord and God? 'Thou-shalt' is the great dragon called. But the spirit of the lion saith, 'I will.'

'Thou-shalt' lieth in its path, sparkling with gold – a scale-covered beast; and on every scale glittereth golden, 'Thou shalt!'

The values of a thousand years glitter on those scales, and thus speaketh the mightiest of all dragons: 'All the values of things – glitter on me.

'All values have already been created, and all created values – do I represent. Verily, there shall be no "I will" any more.' Thus speaketh the dragon.

My brethren, wherefore is there need of the lion in the spirit? Why sufficeth not the beast of burden, which renounceth and is reverent?

To create new values – that, even the lion cannot yet accomplish: but to create itself freedom for new creating – that can the might of the lion do.

To create itself freedom, and give a holy Nay even unto duty: for that, my brethren, there is need of the lion.

To assume the right to new values – that is the most

formidable assumption for a load-bearing and reverent spirit. Verily, unto such a spirit it is preying, and the work of a beast of prey.

As its holiest, it once loved 'Thou-shalt': now is it forced to find illusion and arbitrariness even in the holiest things, that it may capture freedom from its love: the lion is needed for this capture.

But tell me, my brethren, what the child can do, which even the lion could not do? Why hath the preying lion still to become a child?

Innocence is the child, and forgetfulness, a new beginning, a game, a self-rolling wheel, a first movement, a holy Yea.

Aye, for the game of creating, my brethren, there is needed a holy Yea unto life: *its own* will, willeth now the spirit; *his own* world winneth the world's outcast.

Three metamorphoses of the spirit have I designated to you: how the spirit became a camel, the camel a lion, and the lion at last a child.

Thus spake Zarathustra. And at that time he abode in the town which is called The Pied Cow.

The Academic Chairs of Virtue

People commended unto Zarathustra a wise man, as one who could discourse well about sleep and virtue: greatly was he honoured and rewarded for it, and all the youths sat before his chair. To him went Zarathustra, and sat among the youths before his chair. And thus spake the wise man:

Respect and modesty in presence of sleep! That is the first thing! And to go out of the way of all who sleep badly and keep awake at night!

Modest is even the thief in presence of sleep: he always stealeth softly through the night. Immodest, however, is the night-watchman; immodestly he carrieth his horn.

No small art is it to sleep: it is necessary for that purpose to keep awake all day.

Ten times a day must thou overcome thyself: that causeth wholesome weariness, and is poppy to the soul.

Ten times must thou reconcile again with thyself; for overcoming is bitterness, and badly sleep the unreconciled.

Ten truths must thou find during the day; otherwise wilt thou seek truth during the night, and thy soul will have been hungry.

Ten times must thou laugh during the day, and be cheerful; otherwise thy stomach, the father of affliction, will disturb thee in the night.

Few people know it, but one must have all the virtues in order to sleep well. Shall I bear false witness? Shall I commit adultery?

Shall I covet my neighbour's maidservant? All that would ill accord with good sleep.

And even if one have all the virtues, there is still one thing needful: to send the virtues themselves to sleep at the right time.

That they may not quarrel with one another, the good females! And about thee, thou unhappy one!

Peace with God and thy neighbour: so desireth good sleep. And peace also with thy neighbour's devil! Otherwise it will haunt thee in the night.

Honour to the government, and obedience, and also to the crooked government! So desireth good sleep. How can I help it, if power like to walk on crooked legs?

He who leadeth his sheep to the greenest pasture, shall always be for me the best shepherd: so doth it accord with good sleep.

Many honours I want not, nor great treasures: they excite the spleen. But it is bad sleeping without a good name and a little treasure.

A small company is more welcome to me than a bad one: but they must come and go at the right time. So doth it accord with good sleep.

Well, also, do the poor in spirit please me: they promote sleep. Blessed are they, especially if one always give in to them.

Thus passeth the day unto the virtuous. When night cometh, then take I good care not to summon sleep. It disliketh to be summoned – sleep, the lord of the virtues!

But I think of what I have done and thought during the day. Thus ruminating, patient as a cow, I ask myself: What were thy ten overcomings?

And what were the ten reconciliations, and the ten truths, and the ten laughters with which my heart enjoyed itself?

Thus pondering, and cradled by forty thoughts, it overtaketh me all at once – sleep, the unsummoned, the lord of the virtues.

Sleep tappeth on mine eye, and it turneth heavy. Sleep toucheth my mouth, and it remaineth open.

Verily, on soft soles doth it come to me, the dearest of thieves, and stealeth from me my thoughts: stupid do I then stand, like this academic chair.

But not much longer do I then stand: I already lie.

When Zarathustra heard the wise man thus speak, he laughed in his heart: for thereby had a light dawned upon him. And thus spake he to his heart:

A fool seemeth this wise man with his forty thoughts: but I believe he knoweth well how to sleep.

Happy even is he who liveth near this wise man! Such sleep is contagious – even through a thick wall it is contagious.

A magic resideth even in his academic chair. And not in vain did the youths sit before the preacher of virtue.

His wisdom is to keep awake in order to sleep well. And verily, if life had no sense, and had I to choose nonsense, this would be the desirablest nonsense for me also.

Now know I well what people sought formerly above all else when they sought teachers of virtue. Good sleep they sought for themselves, and poppy-head virtues to promote it!

To all those belauded sages of the academic chairs, wisdom was sleep without dreams: they knew no higher significance of life.

Even at present, to be sure, there are some like this preacher of virtue, and not always so honourable: but their time is past. And not much longer do they stand: there they already lie.

Blessed are those drowsy ones: for they shall soon nod to sleep.

Thus spake Zarathustra.

The Despisers of the Body

To the despisers of the body will I speak my word. I wish them neither to learn afresh, nor teach anew, but only to bid farewell to their own bodies – and thus be dumb.

'Body am I, and soul' – so saith the child. And why should one not speak like children?

But the awakened one, the knowing one, saith: 'Body am I entirely, and nothing more; and soul is only the name of something in the body.'

The body is a big sagacity, a plurality with one sense, a war and a peace, a flock and a shepherd.

An instrument of thy body is also thy little sagacity, my brother, which thou callest 'spirit' – a little instrument and plaything of thy big sagacity.

'Ego,' sayest thou, and art proud of that word. But the greater thing – in which thou art unwilling to believe – is thy body with its big sagacity; it saith not 'ego,' but doeth it.

What the sense feeleth, what the spirit discerneth, hath never its end in itself. But sense and spirit would fain persuade thee that they are the end of all things: so vain are they.

Instruments and playthings are sense and spirit: behind them there is still the Self. The Self seeketh with the eyes of the senses, it hearkeneth also with the ears of the spirit.

Ever hearkeneth the Self, and seeketh; it compareth, mastereth, conquereth, and destroyeth. It ruleth, and is also the ego's ruler.

Behind thy thoughts and feelings, my brother, there is a mighty lord, an unknown sage – it is called Self; it dwelleth in thy body, it is thy body.

There is more sagacity in thy body than in thy best wisdom. And who then knoweth why thy body requireth just thy best wisdom?

Thy Self laugheth at thine ego, and its proud prancings. 'What are these prancings and flights of thought unto me?' it saith to itself. 'A by-way to my purpose. I am the leading-string of the ego, and the prompter of its notions.'

The Self saith unto the ego: 'Feel pain!' And thereupon it suffereth, and thinketh how it may put an end thereto – and for that very purpose it *is meant* to think.

The Self saith unto the ego: 'Feel pleasure!' Thereupon it rejoiceth, and thinketh how it may oft-times rejoice – and for that very purpose it *is meant* to think.

To the despisers of the body will I speak a word. That they despise is caused by their esteem. What is it that created esteeming and despising and worth and will?

The creating Self created for itself esteeming and despising, it created for itself joy and woe. The creating body created for itself spirit, as a hand to its will.

Even in your folly and despising ye each serve your Self, ye despisers of the body. I tell you, your very Self wanteth to die, and turneth away from life.

No longer can your Self do that which it desireth most – create beyond itself. That is what it desireth most; that is all its fervour.

But it is now too late to do so – so your Self wisheth

to succumb, ye despisers of the body.

To succumb – so wisheth your Self; and therefore have ye become despisers of the body. For ye can no longer create beyond yourselves.

And therefore are ye now angry with life and with the earth. And unconscious envy is in the sidelong look of your contempt.

I go not your way, ye despisers of the body! Ye are no bridges for me to the Superman!

Thus spake Zarathustra.

5

Joys and Passions

My brother, when thou hast a virtue, and it is thine own virtue, thou hast it in common with no one.

To be sure, thou wouldst call it by name and caress it; thou wouldst pull its ears and amuse thyself with it.

And lo! Then hast thou its name in common with the people, and hast become one of the people and the herd with thy virtue!

Better for thee to say: 'Ineffable is it, and nameless, that which is pain and sweetness to my soul, and also the hunger of my bowels.'

Let thy virtue be too high for the familiarity of names, and if thou must speak of it, be not ashamed to stammer about it.

Thus speak and stammer: 'That is *my* good, that do I love, thus doth it please me entirely, thus only do *I* desire the good.

Not as the law of a God do I desire it, not as a human law or a human need do I desire it; it is not to be a guide-post for me to super-earths and paradises.

An earthly virtue is it which I love: little prudence is therein, and the least everyday wisdom.

But that bird built its nest beside me: therefore, I love and cherish it – now sitteth it beside me on its golden eggs.'

Thus shouldst thou stammer, and praise thy virtue.

Once hadst thou passions and calledst them evil.

But now hast thou only thy virtues: they grew out of thy passions.

Thou implantedst thy highest aim into the heart of those passions: then became they thy virtues and joys.

And though thou wert of the race of the hot-tempered, or of the voluptuous, or of the fanatical, or the vindictive;

All thy passions in the end became virtues, and all thy devils angels.

Once hadst thou wild dogs in thy cellar: but they changed at last into birds and charming songstresses.

Out of thy poisons brewedst thou balsam for thyself; thy cow, affliction, milkedst thou – now drinkest thou the sweet milk of her udder.

And nothing evil groweth in thee any longer, unless it be the evil that groweth out of the conflict of thy virtues.

My brother, if thou be fortunate, then wilt thou have one virtue and no more: thus goest thou easier over the bridge.

Illustrious is it to have many virtues, but a hard lot; and many a one hath gone into the wilderness and killed himself, because he was weary of being the battle and battlefield of virtues.

My brother, are war and battle evil? Necessary, however, is the evil; necessary are the envy and the distrust and the backbiting among the virtues.

Lo! how each of thy virtues is covetous of the highest place; it wanteth thy whole spirit to be *its* herald, it wanteth thy whole power, in wrath, hatred, and love.

Jealous is every virtue of the others, and a dreadful thing is jealousy. Even virtues may succumb by jealousy.

He whom the flame of jealousy encompasseth, turneth at last, like the scorpion, the poisoned sting against himself.

Ah! my brother, hast thou never seen a virtue backbite and stab itself?

Man is something that hath to be surpassed: and therefore shalt thou love thy virtues – for thou wilt succumb by them.

Thus spake Zarathustra.

6

The Pale Criminal

Ye do not mean to slay, ye judges and sacrificers, until the animal hath bowed its head? Lo! the pale criminal hath bowed his head: out of his eye speaketh the great contempt.

'Mine ego is something which is to be surpassed: mine ego is to me the great contempt of man': so speaketh it out of that eye.

When he judged himself – that was his supreme moment; let not the exalted one relapse again into his low estate!

There is no salvation for him who thus suffereth from himself, unless it be speedy death.

Your slaying, ye judges, shall be pity, and not revenge; and in that ye slay, see to it that ye yourselves justify life!

It is not enough that ye should reconcile with him whom ye slay. Let your sorrow be love to the Superman: thus will ye justify your own survival!

'Enemy' shall ye say but not 'villain,' 'invalid' shall ye say but not 'wretch', 'fool' shall ye say but not 'sinner'.

And thou, red judge, if thou would say audibly all thou hast done in thought, then would every one cry: 'Away with the nastiness and the virulent reptile!'

But one thing is the thought, another thing is the deed, and another thing is the idea of the deed. The wheel of causality doth not roll between them.

An idea made this pale man pale. Adequate was he

for his deed when he did it, but the idea of it, he could not endure when it was done.

Evermore did he now see himself as the doer of one deed. Madness, I call this: the exception reversed itself to the rule in him.

The streak of chalk bewitcheth the hen; the stroke he struck bewitched his weak reason. Madness *after* the deed, I call this.

Hearken, ye judges! There is another madness besides, and it is *before* the deed. Ah! ye have not gone deep enough into this soul!

Thus speaketh the red judge: 'Why did this criminal commit murder? He meant to rob.' I tell you, however, that his soul wanted blood, not booty: he thirsted for the happiness of the knife!

But his weak reason understood not this madness, and it persuaded him. 'What matter about blood!' it said; 'wishest thou not, at least, to make booty thereby? Or take revenge?'

And he hearkened unto his weak reason: like lead lay its words upon him – thereupon he robbed when he murdered. He did not mean to be ashamed of his madness.

And now once more lieth the lead of his guilt upon him, and once more is his weak reason so benumbed, so paralysed, and so dull.

Could he only shake his head, then would his burden roll off; but who shaketh that head?

What is this man? A mass of diseases that reach out into the world through the spirit; there they want to get their prey.

What is this man? A coil of wild serpents that are seldom at peace among themselves – so they go forth apart and seek prey in the world.

Look at that poor body! What it suffered and craved, the poor soul interpreted to itself – it interpreted it as murderous desire, and eagerness for the happiness of the knife.

Him who now turneth sick, the evil overtaketh which is now the evil: he seeketh to cause pain with that which causeth him pain. But there have been other ages, and another evil and good.

Once was doubt evil, and the will to Self. Then the invalid became a heretic or sorcerer; as heretic or sorcerer he suffered, and sought to cause suffering.

But this will not enter your ears; it hurteth your good people, ye tell me. But what doth it matter to me about your good people?

Many things in your good people cause me disgust, and verily, not their evil. I would that they had a madness by which they succumbed, like this pale criminal!

Verily, I would that their madness were called truth, or fidelity, or justice: but they have their virtue in order to live long, and in wretched self-complacency.

I am a railing alongside the torrent; whoever is able to grasp me may grasp me! Your crutch, however, I am not.

Thus spake Zarathustra.

Reading and Writing

Of all that is written, I love only what a person hath written with his blood. Write with blood, and thou wilt find that blood is spirit.

It is no easy task to understand unfamiliar blood; I hate the reading idlers.

He who knoweth the reader, doeth nothing more for the reader. Another century of readers – and spirit itself will stink.

Every one being allowed to learn to read, ruineth in the long run not only writing but also thinking.

Once spirit was God, then it became man, and now it even becometh populace.

He that writeth in blood and proverbs doth not want to be read, but learnt by heart.

In the mountains the shortest way is from peak to peak, but for that route thou must have long legs. Proverbs should be peaks, and those spoken to should be big and tall.

The atmosphere rare and pure, danger near and the spirit full of a joyful wickedness: thus are things well matched.

I want to have goblins about me, for I am courageous. The courage which scareth away ghosts, createth for itself goblins – it wanteth to laugh.

I no longer feel in common with you; the very cloud which I see beneath me, the blackness and heaviness at which I laugh – that is your thundercloud.

Ye look aloft when ye long for exaltation; and I look

downward because I am exalted.

Who among you can at the same time laugh and be exalted?

He who climbeth on the highest mountains, laugheth at all tragic plays and tragic realities.

Courageous, unconcerned, scornful, coercive – so wisdom wisheth us; she is a woman, and ever loveth only a warrior.

Ye tell me, 'Life is hard to bear.' But for what purpose should ye have your pride in the morning and your resignation in the evening?

Life is hard to bear: but do not affect to be so delicate! We are all of us fine sumpter asses and assesses.

What have we in common with the rosebud, which trembleth because a drop of dew hath formed upon it?

It is true we love life; not because we are wont to live, but because we are wont to love.

There is always some madness in love. But there is always, also, some method in madness.

And to me also, who appreciate life, the butterflies, and soap-bubbles, and whatever is like them amongst us, seem most to enjoy happiness.

To see these light, foolish, pretty, lively little sprites flit about – that moveth Zarathustra to tears and songs.

I should only believe in a god that would know how to dance.

And when I saw my devil, I found him serious, thorough, profound, solemn: he was the spirit of gravity – through him all things fall.

Not by wrath, but by laughter, do we slay. Come, let us slay the spirit of gravity!

I learned to walk; since then have I let myself run. I

learned to fly; since then I do not need pushing in order to move from a spot.

Now am I light, now do I fly; now do I see myself under myself. Now there danceth a god in me.

Thus spake Zarathustra.

10

War and Warriors

By our best enemies we do not want to be spared, nor by those either whom we love from the very heart. So let me tell you the truth!

My brethren in war! I love you from the very heart. I am, and was ever, your counterpart. And I am also your best enemy. So let me tell you the truth!

I know the hatred and envy of your hearts. Ye are not great enough not to know of hatred and envy. Then be great enough not to be ashamed of them!

And if ye cannot be saints of knowledge, then, I pray you, be at least its warriors. They are the companions and forerunners of such saintship.

I see many soldiers; could I but see many warriors! 'Uniform' one calleth what they wear; may it not be uniform what they therewith hide!

Ye shall be those whose eyes ever seek for an enemy – for *your* enemy. And with some of you there is hatred at first sight.

Your enemy shall ye seek; your war shall ye wage, and for the sake of your thoughts! And if your thoughts succumb, your uprightness shall still shout triumph thereby!

Ye shall love peace as a means to new wars – and the short peace more than the long.

You I advise not to work, but to fight. You I advise not to peace, but to victory. Let your work be a fight, let your peace be a victory!

One can only be silent and sit peacefully when one

hath arrow and bow; otherwise one prateth and quarrelleth. Let your peace be a victory!

Ye say it is the good cause which halloweth even war? I say unto you: it is the good war which halloweth every cause.

War and courage have done more great things than charity. Not your sympathy, but your bravery hath hitherto saved the victims.

'What is good?' ye ask. To be brave is good. Let the little girls say: 'To be good is what is pretty, and at the same time touching.'

They call you heartless: but your heart is true, and I love the bashfulness of your goodwill. Ye are ashamed of your flow, and others are ashamed of their ebb.

Ye are ugly? Well then, my brethren, take the sublime about you, the mantle of the ugly!

And when your soul becometh great, then doth it become haughty, and in your sublimity there is wickedness. I know you.

In wickedness the haughty man and the weakling meet. But they misunderstand one another. I know you.

Ye shall only have enemies to be hated, but not enemies to be despised. Ye must be proud of your enemies; then, the successes of your enemies are also your successes.

Resistance – that is the distinction of the slave. Let your distinction be obedience. Let your commanding itself be obeying!

To the good warrior soundeth 'thou shalt' pleasanter than 'I will.' And all that is dear unto you, ye shall first have it commanded unto you.

Let your love to life be love to your highest hope; and let your highest hope be the highest thought of life!

Your highest thought, however, ye shall have it commanded unto you by me – and it is this: man is something that is to be surpassed.

So live your life of obedience and of war! What matter about long life? What warrior wisheth to be spared?

I spare you not, I love you from my very heart, my brethren in war!

Thus spake Zarathustra.

11

The New Idol

Somewhere there are still peoples and herds, but not with us, my brethren: here there are states.

A state? What is that? Well! open now your ears unto me, for now will I say unto you my word concerning the death of peoples.

A state, is called the coldest of all cold monsters. Coldly lieth it also; and this lie creepeth from its mouth: 'I, the state, am the people.'

It is a lie! Creators were they who created peoples, and hung a faith and a love over them: thus they served life.

Destroyers, are they who lay snares for many, and call it the state: they hang a sword and a hundred cravings over them.

Where there is still a people, there the state is not understood, but hated as the evil eye, and as sin against laws and customs.

This sign I give unto you: every people speaketh its language of good and evil: this its neighbour understandeth not. Its language hath it devised for itself in laws and customs.

But the state lieth in all languages of good and evil; and whatever it saith it lieth; and whatever it hath it hath stolen.

False is everything in it; with stolen teeth it biteth, the biting one. False are even its bowels.

Confusion of language of good and evil; this sign I give unto you as the sign of the state. Verily, the will to death, indicateth this sign! Verily, it beckoneth unto the preachers of death!

Many too many are born: for the superfluous ones was the state devised!

See just how it enticeth them to it, the many-too-many! How it swalloweth and cheweth and recheweth them!

'On earth there is nothing greater than I: it is I who am the regulating finger of God' – thus roareth the monster. And not only the long-eared and short-sighted fall upon their knees!

Ah! even in your ears, ye great souls, it whispereth its gloomy lies! Ah! it findeth out the rich hearts which willingly lavish themselves!

Yea, it findeth you out too, ye conquerors of the old God! Weary ye became of the conflict, and now your weariness serveth the new idol!

Heroes and honourable ones, it would fain set up around it, the new idol! Gladly it basketh in the sunshine of good consciences – the cold monster!

Everything will it give *you*, if *ye* worship it, the new idol: thus it purchaseth the lustre of your virtue, and the glance of your proud eyes.

It seeketh to allure by means of you, the many-too-many! Yea, a hellish artifice hath here been devised, a death-horse jingling with the trappings of divine honours!

Yea, a dying for many hath here been devised, which glorifieth itself as life: verily, a hearty service unto all preachers of death!

The state, I call it, where all are poison-drinkers, the good and the bad: the state, where all lose themselves, the good and the bad: the state, where the slow suicide of all – is called 'life'.

Just see these superfluous ones! They steal the works of the inventors and the treasures of the wise. Culture, they call their theft – and everything becometh sickness and trouble unto them!

Just see these superfluous ones! Sick are they always; they vomit their bile and call it a newspaper. They devour one another, and cannot even digest themselves.

Just see these superfluous ones! Wealth they acquire and become poorer thereby. Power they seek for, and above all, the lever of power, much money – these impotent ones!

See them clamber, these nimble apes! They clamber over one another, and thus scuffle into the mud and the abyss.

Towards the throne they all strive: it is their madness – as if happiness sat on the throne! Ofttimes sitteth filth on the throne – and ofttimes also the throne on filth.

Madmen they all seem to me, and clambering apes, and too eager. Badly smelleth their idol to me, the cold monster: badly they all smell to me, these idolaters.

My brethren, will ye suffocate in the fumes of their maws and appetites! Better break the windows and jump into the open air!

Do go out of the way of the bad odour! Withdraw from the idolatry of the superfluous!

Do go out of the way of the bad odour! Withdraw from the steam of these human sacrifices!

Open still remaineth the earth for great souls. Empty are still many sites for lone ones and twain ones, around which floateth the odour of tranquil seas.

Open still remaineth a free life for great souls. Verily, he who possesseth little is so much the less possessed: blessed be moderate poverty!

There, where the state ceaseth – there only commenceth the man who is not superfluous: there commenceth the song of the necessary ones, the single and irreplaceable melody.

There, where the state *ceaseth* – pray look thither, my brethren! Do ye not see it, the rainbow and the bridges of the Superman?

Thus spake Zarathustra.

Chastity

I love the forest. It is bad to live in cities: there, there are too many of the lustful.

Is it not better to fall into the hands of a murderer, than into the dreams of a lustful woman?

And just look at these men: their eye saith it – they know nothing better on earth than to lie with a woman.

Filth is at the bottom of their souls; and alas! if their filth hath still spirit in it!

Would that ye were perfect – at least as animals! But to animals belongeth innocence.

Do I counsel you to slay your instincts? I counsel you to innocence in your instincts.

Do I counsel you to chastity? Chastity is a virtue with some, but with many almost a vice.

These are continent, to be sure: but doggish lust looketh enviously out of all that they do.

Even into the heights of their virtue and into their cold spirit doth this creature follow them, with its discord.

And how nicely can doggish lust beg for a piece of spirit, when a piece of flesh is denied it!

Ye love tragedies and all that breaketh the heart? But I am distrustful of your doggish lust.

Ye have too cruel eyes, and ye look wantonly towards the sufferers. Hath not your lust just disguised itself and taken the name of fellow-suffering?

And also this parable give I unto you: Not a few who meant to cast out their devil, went thereby into the swine themselves.

To whom chastity is difficult, it is to be dissuaded: lest it become the road to hell – to filth and lust of soul.

Do I speak of filthy things? That is not the worst thing for me to do.

Not when the truth is filthy, but when it is shallow, doth the discerning one go unwillingly into its waters.

Verily, there are chaste ones from their very nature; they are gentler of heart, and laugh better and oftener than you.

They laugh also at chastity, and ask: 'What is chastity?

Is chastity not folly? But the folly came unto us, and not we unto it.

We offered that guest harbour and heart: now it dwelleth with us – let it stay as long as it will!'

Thus spake Zarathustra.

18

Old and Young Women

'Why stealest thou along so furtively in the twilight, Zarathustra? And what hidest thou so carefully under thy mantle?

Is it a treasure that hath been given thee? Or a child that hath been born thee? Or goest thou thyself on a thief's errand, thou friend of the evil?'

Verily, my brother, said Zarathustra, it is a treasure that hath been given me: it is a little truth which I carry.

But it is naughty, like a young child; and if I hold not its mouth, it screameth too loudly.

As I went on my way alone today, at the hour when the sun declineth, there met me an old woman, and she spake thus unto my soul:

'Much hath Zarathustra spoken also to us women, but never spake he unto us concerning woman.'

And I answered her: 'Concerning woman, one should only talk unto men.'

'Talk also unto me of woman,' said she; 'I am old enough to forget it presently.'

And I obliged the old woman and spake thus unto her;

Everything in woman is a riddle, and everything in woman hath one solution – it is called pregnancy.

Man is for woman, a means: the purpose is always the child. But what is woman for man?

Two different things wanteth the true man: danger and diversion. Therefore wanteth he woman, as the most dangerous plaything.

Man shall be trained for war, and woman for the recreation of the warrior: all else is folly.

Too sweet fruits – these the warrior liketh not. Therefore liketh he woman; bitter is even the sweetest woman.

Better than man doth woman understand children, but man is more childish than woman.

In the true man there is a child hidden: it wanteth to play. Up then, ye women, and discover the child in man!

A plaything let woman be, pure and fine like the precious stone, illumined with the virtues of a world not yet come.

Let the beam of a star shine in your love! Let your hope say: 'May I bear the Superman!'

In your love let there be valour! With your love shall ye assail him who inspireth you with fear!

In your love be your honour! Little doth woman understand otherwise about honour. But let this be your honour: always to love more than ye are loved, and never be the second.

Let man fear woman when she loveth: then maketh she every sacrifice, and everything else she regardeth as worthless.

Let man fear woman when she hateth: for man in his innermost soul is merely evil; woman, however, is mean.

Whom hateth woman most? Thus spake the iron to the loadstone: 'I hate thee most, because thou attractest, but art too weak to draw unto thee.'

The happiness of man is, 'I will.' The happiness of woman is, 'He will.'

'Lo! now hath the world become perfect!' – thus

thinketh every woman when she obeyeth with all her love.

Obey, must the woman, and find a depth for her surface. Surface, is woman's soul, a mobile, stormy film on shallow water.

Man's soul, however, is deep, its current gusheth in subterranean caverns: woman surmiseth its force, but comprehendeth it not.

Then answered me the old woman: 'Many fine things hath Zarathustra said, especially for those who are young enough for them.

Strange! Zarathustra knoweth little about woman, and yet he is right about them! Doth this happen, because with women nothing is impossible?

And now accept a little truth by way of thanks! I am old enough for it!

Swaddle it up and hold its mouth: otherwise it will scream too loudly, the little truth.'

'Give me, woman, thy little truth!' said I. And thus spake the old woman:

'Thou goest to women? Do not forget thy whip!'

Thus spake Zarathustra.

The Bite of the Adder

One day had Zarathustra fallen asleep under a fig-tree, owing to the heat, with his arms over his face. And there came an adder and bit him in the neck, so that Zarathustra screamed with pain. When he had taken his arm from his face he looked at the serpent; and then did it recognise the eyes of Zarathustra, wriggled awkwardly, and tried to get away. 'Not at all,' said Zarathustra, 'as yet hast thou not received my thanks! Thou hast awakened me in time; my journey is yet long.' 'Thy journey is short,' said the adder, sadly; 'my poison is fatal.' Zarathustra smiled. 'When did ever a dragon die of a serpent's poison?' said he. 'But take thy poison back! Thou art not rich enough to present it to me.' Then fell the adder again on his neck, and licked his wound.

When Zarathustra once told this to his disciples they asked him: 'And what, O Zarathustra, is the moral of thy story?' And Zarathustra answered them thus:

The destroyer of morality, the good and just call me: my story is immoral.

When, however, ye have an enemy, then return him not good for evil: for that would abash him. But prove that he hath done something good to you.

And rather be angry than abash any one! And when ye are cursed, it pleaseth me not that ye should then desire to bless. Rather curse a little also!

And should a great injustice befall you, then do quickly five small ones besides. Hideous to behold is he on whom injustice presseth alone.

Did ye ever know this? Shared injustice is half justice. And he who can bear it, shall take the injustice upon himself!

A small revenge is humaner than no revenge at all. And if the punishment be not also a right and an honour to the transgressor, I do not like your punishing.

Nobler is it to own oneself in the wrong than to establish one's right, especially if one be in the right. Only, one must be rich enough to do so.

I do not like your cold justice; out of the eye of your judges there always glanceth the executioner and his cold steel.

Tell me: where find we justice, which is love with seeing eyes?

Devise me, then, the love which not only beareth all punishment, but also all guilt!

Devise me, then, the justice which acquitteth every one, except the judge!

And would ye hear this likewise? To him who seeketh to be just from the heart, even the lie becometh philanthropy.

But how could I be just from the heart! How can I give every one his own! Let this be enough for me: I give unto every one mine own.

Finally, my brethren, guard against doing wrong to any anchorite. How could an anchorite forget! How could he requite!

Like a deep well is an anchorite. Easy is it to throw in a stone: if it should sink to the bottom, however, tell me, who will bring it out again?

Guard against injuring the anchorite! If ye have done so, however, well then, kill him also!

Thus spake Zarathustra.

22

The Bestowing Virtue

I

When Zarathustra had taken leave of the town to which his heart was attached, the name of which is 'The Pied Cow,' there followed him many people who called themselves his disciples, and kept him company. Thus came they to a cross-road. Then Zarathustra told them that he now wanted to go alone; for he was fond of going alone. His disciples, however, presented him at his departure with a staff, on the golden handle of which a serpent twined round the sun. Zarathustra rejoiced on account of the staff, and supported himself thereon; then spake he thus to his disciples:

Tell me, pray: how came gold to the highest value? Because it is uncommon, and unprofiting, and beaming, and soft in lustre; it always bestoweth itself.

Only as image of the highest virtue came gold to the highest value. Goldlike, beameth the glance of the bestower. Gold-lustre maketh peace between moon and sun.

Uncommon is the highest virtue, and unprofiting, beaming is it, and soft of lustre: a bestowing virtue is the highest virtue.

Verily, I divine you well, my disciples: ye strive like me for the bestowing virtue. What should ye have in common with cats and wolves?

It is your thirst to become sacrifices and gifts yourselves: and therefore have ye the thirst to accumulate all riches in your soul.

Insatiably striveth your soul for treasures and jewels, because your virtue is insatiable in desiring to bestow.

Ye constrain all things to flow towards you and into you, so that they shall flow back again out of your fountain as the gifts of your love.

Verily, an appropriator of all values must such bestowing love become; but healthy and holy, call I this selfishness. –

Another selfishness is there, an all-too-poor and hungry kind, which would always steal – the selfishness of the sick, the sickly selfishness.

With the eye of the thief it looketh upon all that is lustrous; with the craving of hunger it measureth him who hath abundance; and ever doth it prowl round the tables of bestowers.

Sickness speaketh in such craving, and invisible degeneration; of a sickly body, speaketh the larcenous craving of this selfishness.

Tell me, my brother, what do we think bad, and worst of all? Is it not *degeneration*? – And we always suspect degeneration when the bestowing soul is lacking.

Upward goeth our course from genera on to supergenera. But a horror to us is the degenerating sense, which saith: 'All for myself.'

Upward soareth our sense: thus is it a simile of our body, a simile of an elevation. Such similes of elevations are the names of the virtues.

Thus goeth the body through history, a becomer and fighter. And the spirit – what is it to the body? Its fights' and victories' herald, its companion and echo.

Similes, are all names of good and evil; they do not speak out, they only hint. A fool who seeketh knowledge from them!

Give heed, my brethren, to every hour when your spirit would speak in similes: there is the origin of your virtue.

Elevated is then your body, and raised up; with its delight, enraptureth it the spirit; so that it becometh creator, and valuer, and lover, and everything's benefactor.

When your heart overfloweth broad and full like the river, a blessing and a danger to the lowlanders: there is the origin of your virtue.

When ye are exalted above praise and blame, and your will would command all things, as a loving one's will: there is the origin of your virtue.

When ye despise pleasant things, and the effeminate couch, and cannot couch far enough from the effeminate: there is the origin of your virtue.

When ye are willers of one will, and when that change of every need is needful to you: there is the origin of your virtue.

Verily, a new good and evil is it! Verily, a new deep murmuring, and the voice of a new fountain!

Power is it, this new virtue; a ruling thought is it, and around it a subtle soul: a golden sun, with the serpent of knowledge around it.

2

Here paused Zarathustra awhile, and looked lovingly on his disciples. Then he continued to speak thus – and his voice had changed:

Remain true to the earth, my brethren, with the power of your virtue! Let your bestowing love and your knowledge be devoted to be the meaning of the earth! Thus do I pray and conjure you.

Let it not fly away from the earthly and beat against eternal walls with its wings! Ah, there hath always been so much flown-away virtue!

Lead, like me, the flown-away virtue back to the earth – yea, back to body and life: that it may give to the earth its meaning, a human meaning!

A hundred times hitherto hath spirit as well as virtue flown away and blundered. Alas! in our body dwelleth still all this delusion and blundering: body and will hath it there become.

A hundred times hitherto hath spirit as well as virtue attempted and erred. Yea, an attempt hath man been. Alas, much ignorance and error hath become embodied in us!

Not only the rationality of millenniums – also their madness, breaketh out in us. Dangerous is it to be an heir.

Still fight we step by step with the giant Chance, and over all mankind hath hitherto ruled nonsense, the lack-of-sense.

Let your spirit and your virtue be devoted to the sense of the earth, my brethren: let the value of everything be determined anew by you! Therefore shall ye be fighters! Therefore shall ye be creators!

Intelligently doth the body purify itself; attempting with intelligence it exalteth itself; to the discerners all impulses sanctify themselves; to the exalted the soul becometh joyful.

Physician, heal thyself: then wilt thou also heal thy patient. Let it be his best cure to see with his eyes him who maketh himself whole.

A thousand paths are there which have never yet

been trodden; a thousand salubrities and hidden islands of life. Unexhausted and undiscovered is still man and man's world.

Awake and hearken, ye lonesome ones! From the future come winds with stealthy pinions, and to fine ears good tidings are proclaimed.

Ye lonesome ones of today, ye seceding ones, ye shall one day be a people: out of you who have chosen yourselves, shall a chosen people arise: – and out of it the Superman.

Verily, a place of healing shall the earth become! and already is a new odour diffused around it, a salvation-bringing odour – and a new hope!

3

When Zarathustra had spoken these words, he paused, like one who had not said his last word; and long did he balance the staff doubtfully in his hand. At last he spake thus – and his voice had changed:

I now go alone, my disciples! Ye also now go away, and alone! So will I have it.

Verily, I advise you: depart from me, and guard yourselves against Zarathustra! And better still: be ashamed of him! Perhaps he hath deceived you.

The man of knowledge must be able not only to love his enemies, but also to hate his friends.

One requiteth a teacher badly if one remain merely a scholar. And why will ye not pluck at my wreath?

Ye venerate me; but what if your veneration should some day collapse? Take heed lest a statue crush you!

Ye say, ye believe in Zarathustra? But of what account is Zarathustra! Ye are my believers: but of what account are all believers!

Ye had not yet sought yourselves: then did ye find

me. So do all believers; therefore all belief is of so little account.

Now do I bid you lose me and find yourselves; and only when ye have all denied me, will I return unto you.

Verily, with other eyes, my brethren, shall I then seek my lost ones; with another love shall I then love you.

And once again shall ye have become friends unto me, and children of one hope: then will I be with you for the third time, to celebrate the great noontide with you.

And it is the great noontide, when man is in the middle of his course between animal and Superman, and celebrateth his advance to the evening as his highest hope: for it is the advance to a new morning.

At such time will the down-goer bless himself, that he should be an over-goer; and the sun of his knowledge will be at noontide.

'*Dead are all the gods: now do we desire the Superman to live.*' Let this be our final will at the great noontide!

Thus spake Zarathustra.

BEYOND GOOD AND EVIL

Prejudices of Philosophers

I

The Will to Truth, which is to tempt us to many a hazardous enterprise, the famous Truthfulness of which all philosophers have hitherto spoken with respect, what questions has this Will to Truth not laid before us! What strange, perplexing, questionable questions! It is already a long story; yet it seems as if it were hardly commenced. Is it any wonder if we at last grow distrustful, lose patience, and turn impatiently away? That this Sphinx teaches us at last to ask questions ourselves? *Who* is it really that puts questions to us here? *What* really is this 'Will to Truth' in us? In fact we made a long halt at the question as to the origin of this Will – until at last we came to an absolute standstill before a yet more fundamental question. We inquired about the *value* of this Will. Granted that we want the truth: *why not rather* untruth? And uncertainty? Even ignorance? The problem of the value of truth presented itself before us – or was it we who presented ourselves before the problem? Which of us is the Oedipus here? Which the Sphinx? It would seem to be a rendezvous of questions and notes of interrogation. And could it be believed that it at last seems to us as if the problem had never been propounded before, as if we were the first to discern it, get a sight of it, and *risk raising* it? For there is risk in raising it, perhaps there is no greater risk.

2

'*How could* anything originate out of its opposite? For example, truth out of error? Or the Will to Truth out of the will to deception? Or the generous deed out of selfishness? Or the pure sun-bright vision of the wise man out of covetousness? Such genesis is impossible; whoever dreams of it is a fool, nay, worse than a fool; things of the highest value must have a different origin, an origin of *their own* – in this transitory, seductive, illusory, paltry world, in this turmoil of delusion and cupidity, they cannot have their source. But rather in the lap of Being, in the intransitory, in the concealed God, in the "Thing-in-itself" – *there* must be their source, and nowhere else!' – This mode of reasoning discloses the typical prejudice by which metaphysicians of all times can be recognised, this mode of valuation is at the back of all their logical procedure; through this 'belief' of theirs, they exert themselves for their 'knowledge', for something that is in the end solemnly christened 'the Truth'. The fundamental belief of metaphysicians is *the belief in antitheses of values*. It never occurred even to the wariest of them to doubt here on the very threshold (where doubt, however, was most necessary); though they had made a solemn vow, '*de omnibus dubitandum*'. For it may be doubted, firstly, whether antitheses exist at all; and secondly, whether the popular valuations and antitheses of value upon which metaphysicians have set their seal, are not perhaps merely superficial estimates, merely provisional perspectives, besides being probably made from some corner, perhaps from below – 'frog perspectives', as it were, to borrow an expression current among painters. In spite of all the value which may belong to the true, the positive, and the unselfish, it might be possible that a higher and more fundamental value for life generally should be assigned to pretence, to the will to delusion, to selfishness, and cupidity. It might even be possible that *what* constitutes the value of those good and respected things, consists precisely in their being insidiously related, knotted, and crocheted to these evil and apparently opposed things – perhaps even in being essentially identical with them. Perhaps! But who wishes to concern himself with such dangerous 'Perhapses'? For that investigation one must await the advent of a new order of philosophers, such as will have other tastes and inclinations, the reverse of those hitherto prevalent – philosophers of the dangerous 'Perhaps' in every sense of the term. And to speak in all seriousness, I see such new philosophers beginning to appear.

3

Having kept a sharp eye on philosophers, and having read between their lines long enough, I now say to myself that the greater part of conscious thinking must be counted amongst the instinctive functions, and it is so even in the case of philosophical thinking; one has here to learn anew, as one learned anew about heredity and 'innateness'. As little as the act of birth comes into consideration in the whole process and procedure of heredity, just as little is 'being-conscious' *opposed* to the instinctive in any decisive sense; the greater part of the conscious thinking of a philosopher is secretly influenced by his instincts, and forced into definite channels. And behind all logic and its seeming sovereignty of movement, there are valuations, or to speak more plainly, physiological demands, for the maintenance of a definite mode of life. For example, that the certain is worth more than the uncertain, that illusion is less valuable than 'truth': such valuations, in spite of their regulative importance for *us*, might notwithstanding be only superficial valuations, special kinds of *niaiserie*, such as may be necessary for the maintenance of beings such as ourselves. Supposing, in effect, that man is not just the 'measure of things . . . '

4

The falseness of an opinion is not for us any objection to it: it is here, perhaps, that our new language sounds most strangely. The question is, how far an opinion is life-furthering, life-preserving, species-preserving, perhaps species-rearing; and we are fundamentally inclined to maintain that the falsest opinions (to which the synthetic judgments *a priori* belong), are the most indispensable to us; that without a recognition of logical fictions, without a comparison of reality with the purely *imagined* world of the absolute and immutable, without a constant counterfeiting of the world by means of numbers, man could not live – that the renunciation of false opinions would be a renunciation of life, a negation of life. *To recognise untruth as a condition of life*: that is certainly to impugn the traditional ideas of value in a dangerous manner, and a philosophy which ventures to do so, has thereby alone placed itself beyond good and evil.

5

That which causes philosophers to be regarded half-distrustfully and half-mockingly, is not the oft-repeated discovery how innocent they are – how often and easily they make mistakes and lose their way, in short, how childish and childlike they are – but that there is not enough honest dealing with them, whereas they all raise a loud and virtuous outcry when the problem of truthfulness is even hinted at in the remotest manner. They all pose as though their real opinions had been discovered and attained through the self-evolving of a cold, pure, divinely indifferent dialectic (in contrast to all sorts of mystics, who, fairer and foolisher, talk of 'inspiration'); whereas, in fact, a prejudiced proposition, idea, or 'suggestion', which is generally their heart's desire abstracted and refined, is defended by them with arguments sought out after the event. They are all advocates who do not wish to be regarded as such, generally astute defenders, also, of their prejudices, which they dub 'truths' – and *very* far from having the conscience which bravely admits this to itself; very far from having the good taste of the courage which goes so far as to let this be understood, perhaps to warn friend or foe, or in cheerful confidence and self-ridicule. The spectacle of the Tartuffery of old Kant, equally stiff and decent, with which he entices us into the dialectic by-ways that lead (more correctly mislead) to his 'categorical imperative' – makes us fastidious ones smile, we who find no small amusement in spying out the subtle tricks of old moralists and ethical preachers. Or, still more so, the hocus-pocus in mathematical form, by means of which Spinoza has as it were clad his philosophy in mail and mask – in fact, the 'love of *his* wisdom', to translate the term fairly and squarely – in order thereby to strike terror at once into the heart of the assailant who should dare to cast a glance on that invincible maiden, that Pallas Athene: – how much of personal timidity and vulnerability does this masquerade of a sickly recluse betray!

6

It has gradually become clear to me what every great philosophy up till now has consisted of – namely, the confession of its originator, and a species of involuntary and unconscious autobiography; and moreover that the moral (or immoral) purpose in every philosophy has constituted the true vital germ out of which the entire plant has always grown. Indeed, to understand how the abstrusest metaphysical assertions of a philosopher have been arrived at, it is always well (and wise) to first ask oneself: 'What morality do they (or does he) aim at?' Accordingly, I do not believe that an 'impulse to knowledge' is the father of philosophy; but that another impulse, here as elsewhere, has only made use of knowledge (and mistaken knowledge!) as an instrument. But whoever considers the fundamental impulses of man with a view to determining how far they may have here acted as *inspiring* genii (or as demons and cobolds), will find that they have all practised philosophy at one time or another, and that each one of them would have been only too glad to look upon itself as the ultimate end of existence and the legitimate *lord* over all the other impulses. For every impulse is imperious, and as *such*, attempts to philosophise. To be sure, in the case of scholars, in the case of really scientific men, it may be otherwise – 'better', if you will; there there may really be such a thing as an 'impulse to knowledge', some kind of small, independent clockwork, which, when well wound up, works away industriously to that end, *without* the rest of the scholarly impulses taking any material part therein. The actual 'interests' of the scholar, therefore, are generally in quite another direction – in the family, perhaps, or in money-making, or in politics; it is, in fact, almost indifferent at what point of research his little machine is placed, and whether the hopeful young worker becomes a good philologist, a mushroom specialist, or a chemist; he is not *characterized* by becoming this or that. In the philosopher, on the contrary, there is absolutely nothing impersonal; and above all, his morality furnishes a decided and decisive testimony as to *who he is* – that is to say, in what order the deepest impulses of his nature stand to each other.

7

How malicious philosophers can be! I know of nothing more stinging than the joke Epicurus took the liberty of making on Plato and the Platonists: he called them *Dionysiokolakes*. In its original sense, and on the face of it, the word signifies 'Flatterers of Dionysius' – consequently, tyrants' accessories and lick-spittles; besides this, however, it is as much as to say, 'They are all *actors*, there is nothing genuine about them' (for *Dionysiokolax* was a popular name for an actor). And the latter is really the malignant reproach that Epicurus cast upon Plato: he was annoyed by the grandiose manner, the *mise en scène* style of which Plato and his scholars were masters – of which Epicurus was not a master! He, the old schoolteacher of Samos, who sat concealed in his little garden at Athens and wrote three hundred books, perhaps out of rage and ambitious envy of Plato, who knows! Greece took a hundred years to find out who the garden-god Epicurus really was. Did she ever find out?

8

There is a point in every philosophy at which the 'conviction' of the philosopher appears on the scene; or, to put it in the words of an ancient mystery:

> Adventavit asinus,
> Pulcher et fortissimus.

9

You desire to *live* 'according to Nature'? Oh, you noble Stoics, what fraud of words! Imagine to yourselves a being like Nature, boundlessly extravagant, boundlessly indifferent, without purpose or consideration, without pity or justice, at once fruitful and barren and uncertain: imagine to yourselves *indifference* as a power – how *could* you live in accordance with such indifference? To live – is not that just endeavouring to be otherwise than this Nature? Is not living valuing, preferring, being unjust, being limited, endeavouring to be different? And granted that your imperative, 'living according to Nature', means actually the same as 'living according to life' – how could you do *differently*? Why should you make a principle out of what you yourselves are, and must be? In reality, however, it is quite otherwise with you: while you pretend to read with rapture the canon of your law in Nature, you want something quite the contrary, you extraordinary stage-players and self-deluders! In your pride you wish to dictate your morals and ideals to Nature, to Nature herself, and to incorporate them therein; you insist that it shall be Nature 'according to the Stoa', and would like everything to be made after your own image, as a vast, eternal glorification and generalisation of Stoicism! With all your love for truth, you have forced yourselves so long, so persistently, and with such hypnotic rigidity to see Nature *falsely*, that is to say, Stoically, that you are no longer able to see it otherwise – and to crown all, some unfathomable superciliousness gives you the Bedlamite hope that *because* you are able to tyrannise over yourselves – Stoicism is self-tyranny – Nature will also allow herself to be tyrannised over: is not the Stoic a *part* of Nature? . . . But this is an old and everlasting story: what happened in old times with the Stoics still happens today, as soon as ever a philosophy begins to believe in itself. It always creates the world in its own image; it cannot do otherwise; philosophy is this tyrannical impulse itself, the most spiritual Will to Power, the will to 'creation of the world', the will to the *causa prima*.

10

The eagerness and subtlety, I should even say craftiness, with which the problem of 'the real and the apparent world' is dealt with at present throughout Europe, furnishes food for thought and attention; and he who hears only a 'Will to Truth' in the background, and nothing else, cannot certainly boast of the sharpest ears. In rare and isolated cases, it may really have happened that such a Will to Truth – a certain extravagant and adventurous pluck, a metaphysician's ambition of the forlorn hope – has participated therein: that which in the end always prefers a handful of 'certainty' to a whole cartload of beautiful possibilities; there may even be puritanical fanatics of conscience, who prefer to put their last trust in a sure nothing, rather than in an uncertain something. But that is Nihilism, and the sign of a despairing, mortally wearied soul, notwithstanding the courageous bearing such a virtue may display. It seems, however, to be otherwise with stronger and livelier thinkers who are still eager for life. In that they side *against* appearance, and speak superciliously of 'perspective', in that they rank the credibility of their own bodies about as low as the credibility of the ocular evidence that 'the earth stands still', and thus, apparently, allowing with complacency their securest possession to escape (for what does one at present believe in more firmly than in one's body?) – who knows if they are not really trying to win back something which was formerly an even *securer* possession, something of the old domain of the faith of former times, perhaps the 'immortal soul', perhaps 'the old God', in short, ideas by which they could live better, that is to say, more vigorously and more joyously, than by 'modern ideas'? There is *distrust* of these modern ideas in this mode of looking at things, a disbelief in all that has been constructed yesterday and today; there is perhaps some slight admixture of satiety and scorn, which can no longer endure the *bric-à-brac* of ideas of the most varied origin, such as so-called Positivism at present throws on the market; a disgust of the more refined taste at the village-fair motleyness and patchiness of all these reality-philoso-phasters, in whom there is nothing either new or true, except this motleyness. Therein it seems to me that we should agree with those sceptical anti-realists and knowledge microscopists of the present day; their

instinct, which repels them from *modern* reality, is
unrefuted . . . what do their retrograde by-paths
concern us! The main thing about them is *not* that
they wish to go 'back', but that they wish to get *away*
therefrom. A little *more* strength, swing, courage, and
artistic power, and they would be *off* – and not back!

11

It seems to me that there is everywhere an attempt at
present to divert attention from the actual influence
which Kant exercised on German philosophy, and
especially to ignore prudently the value which he set
upon himself. Kant was first and foremost proud of
his Table of Categories; with it in his hand he said:
'This is the most difficult thing that could ever be
undertaken on behalf of metaphysics.' Let us only
understand this 'could be'! He was proud of having
discovered a new faculty in man, the faculty of synthetic
judgment *a priori*. Granting that he deceived himself
in this matter, the development and rapid flourishing
of German philosophy depended nevertheless on his
pride, and on the eager rivalry of the younger
generation to discover if possible something – at all
events 'new faculties' – of which to be still prouder!' –
But let us reflect for a moment – it is high time to do
so. 'How are synthetic judgments *a priori possible*?'
Kant asks himself – and what is really his answer? '*By
means of a means* (faculty)' – but unfortunately not in
five words, but so circumstantially, imposingly, and
with such display of German proundity and verbal
flourishes, that one altogether loses sight of the
comical *niaiserie allemande* involved in such an
answer. People were beside themselves with delight
over this new faculty, and the jubilation reached its

climax when Kant further discovered a moral faculty in man – for at that time Germans were still moral, not yet dabbling in the 'Politics of hard fact'. Then came the honeymoon of German philosophy. All the young theologians of the Tübingen institution went immediately into the groves – all seeking for 'faculties'. And what did they not find – in that innocent, rich, and still youthful period of the German spirit, to which Romanticism, the malicious fairy, piped and sang, when one could not yet distinguish between 'finding' and 'inventing'! Above all a faculty for the 'transcendental'; Schelling christened it, intellectual intuition, and thereby gratified the most earnest longings of the naturally pious-inclined Germans. One can do no greater wrong to the whole of this exuberant and eccentric movement (which was really youthfulness, notwithstanding that it disguised itself so boldly in hoary and senile conceptions), than to take it seriously, or even treat it with moral indignation. Enough, however – the world grew older, and the dream vanished. A time came when people rubbed their foreheads, and they still rub them today. People had been dreaming, and first and foremost – old Kant. 'By means of a means (faculty)' – he had said, or at least meant to say. But, is that – an answer? An explanation? Or is it not rather merely a repetition of the question? How does opium induce sleep? 'By means of a means (faculty),' namely the *virtus dormitiva*, replies the doctor in Molière,

> Quia est in eo virtus dormitiva,
> Cujus est natura sensus assoupire.

But such replies belong to the realm of comedy, and it is high time to replace the Kantian question, 'How are synthetic judgments *a priori* possible?' by another question, 'Why is belief in such judgments *necessary*?' – in effect, it is high time that we should understand that such judgments must be *believed* to be true, for the sake of the preservation of creatures like ourselves; though they still might naturally be *false* judgments! Or, more plainly spoken, and roughly and readily – synthetic judgments *a priori* should not 'be possible' at all; we have no right to them; in our mouths they are nothing but false judgments. Only, of course, the belief in their truth is necessary, as plausible belief and ocular evidence belonging to the perspective view of life. And finally, to call to mind the enormous influence which 'German philosophy' – I hope you understand its right to inverted commas (goosefeet)? – has exercised throughout the whole of Europe, there is no doubt that a certain *virtus dormitiva* had a share in it; thanks to German philosophy, it was a delight to the noble idlers, the virtuous, the mystics, the artists, the three-fourths Christians, and the political obscurantists of all nations, to find an antidote to the still overwhelming sensualism which overflowed from the last century into this, in short – '*sensus assoupire*' . . .

12

As regards materialistic atomism, it is one of the best refuted theories that have been advanced, and in Europe there is now perhaps no one in the learned world so unscholarly as to attach serious signification to it, except for convenient everyday use (as an abbreviation of the means of expression) – thanks chiefly to the Pole Boscovich: he and the Pole Copernicus have hitherto been the greatest and most successful opponents of ocular evidence. For whilst Copernicus has persuaded us to believe, contrary to all the senses, that the earth does *not* stand fast, Boscovich has taught us to abjure the belief in the last thing that 'stood fast' of the earth – the belief in 'substance', in 'matter', in the earth-residuum, and particle-atom: it is the greatest triumph over the senses that has hitherto been gained on earth. One must, however, go still further, and also declare war, relentless war to the knife, against the 'atomistic requirements' which still lead a dangerous afterlife in places where no one suspects them, like the more celebrated 'metaphysical requirements': one must also above all give the finishing stroke to that other and more portentous atomism which Christianity has taught best and longest, the *soul-atomism*. Let it be permitted to designate by this expression the belief which regards the soul as something indestructible, eternal, indivisible, as a monad, as an *atomon*: *this* belief ought to be expelled from science! Between ourselves, it is not at all necessary to get rid of 'the soul' thereby, and thus renounce one of the oldest and most venerated hypotheses – as happens frequently to the clumsiness of naturalists, who can hardly touch on the soul without immediately losing it. But the way is open for new acceptations and refinements of the soul-hypothesis; and such conceptions as 'mortal soul', and 'soul as subjective multiplicity', and 'soul as social structure of the instincts and passions', want henceforth to have legitimate rights in science. In that the *new* psychologist is about to put an end to the superstitions which have hitherto flourished with almost tropical luxuriance around the idea of the soul, he is really, as it were, thrusting himself into a new desert and a new distrust – it is possible that the older psychologists had a merrier and more comfortable time of it; eventually, however, he finds that precisely thereby he is also condemned to *invent* – and, who knows, perhaps to *discover* the new.

13

Psychologists should bethink themselves before putting down the instinct of self-preservation as the cardinal instinct of an organic being. A living thing seeks above all to *discharge* its strength – life itself is *Will to Power*; self-preservation is only one of the indirect and most frequent *results* thereof. In short, here, as everywhere else, let us beware of *superfluous* teleological principles! – one of which is the instinct of self-preservation (we owe it to Spinoza's inconsistency). It is thus, in effect, that method ordains, which must be essentially economy of principles.

14

It is perhaps just dawning on five or six minds that natural philosophy is only a world-exposition and world-arrangement (according to us, if I may say so!) and *not* a world-explanation; but in so far as it is based on belief in the senses, it is regarded as more, and for a long time to come must be regarded as more – namely, as an explanation. It has eyes and fingers of its own, it has ocular evidence and palpableness of its own: this operates fascinatingly, persuasively, and *convincingly* upon an age with fundamentally plebeian tastes – in fact, it follows instinctively the canon of truth of eternal popular sensualism. What is clear, what is 'explained'? Only that which can be seen and felt – one must pursue every problem thus far.

Obversely, however, the charm of the Platonic mode of thought, which was an *aristocratic* mode, consisted precisely in *resistance to* obvious sense-evidence – perhaps among men who enjoyed even stronger and more fastidious senses than our contemporaries, but who knew how to find a higher triumph in remaining masters of them: and this by means of pale, cold, grey conceptional networks which they threw over the motley whirl of the senses – the mob of the senses, as Plato said. In this overcoming of the world, and interpreting of the world in the manner of Plato, there was an *enjoyment* different from that which the physicists of today offer us – and likewise the Darwinists and antiteleologists among the physiological workers, with their principle of the 'smallest possible effort', and the greatest possible blunder. 'Where there is nothing more to see or to grasp, there is also nothing more for men to do' – that is certainly an imperative different from the Platonic one, but it may notwithstanding be the right imperative for a hardy, laborious race of machinists and bridge-builders of the future, who have nothing but *rough* work to perform.

15

To study physiology with a clear conscience, one must insist on the fact that the sense-organs are *not* phenomena in the sense of the idealistic philosophy; as such they certainly could not be causes! Sensualism, therefore, at least as regulative hypothesis, if not as heuristic principle. What? And others say even that the external world is the work of our organs? But then our body, as a part of this external world, would be the work of our organs! But then our organs themselves would be the work of our organs! It seems to me that this is a complete *reductio ad absurdum*, if the conception *causa sui* is something fundamentally absurd. Consequently, the external world is *not* the work of our organs?

16

There are still harmless self-observers who believe that there are 'immediate certainties'; for instance, 'I think', or as the superstition of Schopenhauer puts it, 'I will'; as though cognition here got hold of its object purely and simply as 'the thing in itself', without any falsification taking place either on the part of the subject or the object. I would repeat it, however, a hundred times, that 'immediate certainty', as well as 'absolute knowledge' and the 'thing in itself', involve a *contradictio in adjecto*; we really ought to free ourselves from the misleading significance of words! The people on their part may think that cognition is knowing all about things, but the philosopher must say to himself: 'When I analyse the process that is expressed in the sentence, "I think", I find a whole series of daring assertions, the argumentative proof of which would be difficult, perhaps impossible: for instance, that it is *I* who think, that there must necessarily be something that thinks, that thinking is an activity and operation on the part of a being who is thought of as a cause, that there is an 'ego', and finally, that it is already determined what is to be designated by thinking – that I *know* what thinking is. For if I had not already decided within myself what it is, by what standard could I determine whether that which is just happening is not perhaps "willing" or "feeling"? In short, the assertion "I think", assumes that I *compare* my state at the present moment with other states of myself which

I know, in order to determine what it is; on account of this retrospective connection with further "knowledge", it has at any rate no immediate certainty for me.' – In place of the 'immediate certainty' in which the people may believe in the special case, the philosopher thus finds a series of metaphysical questions presented to him, veritable conscience questions of the intellect, to wit: 'From whence did I get the notion of "thinking"? Why do I believe in cause and effect? What gives me the right to speak of an "ego", and even of an "ego" as cause, and finally of an "ego" as cause of thought?' He who ventures to answer these metaphysical questions at once by an appeal to a sort of *intuitive* perception, like the person who says, 'I think, and know that this, at least, is true, actual, and certain' – will encounter a smile and two notes of interrogation in a philosopher nowadays. 'Sir,' the philosopher will perhaps give him to understand, 'it is improbable that you are not mistaken, but why should it be the truth?'

17

With regard to the superstitions of logicians, I shall never tire of emphasising a small, terse fact, which is unwillingly recognised by these credulous minds – namely, that a thought comes when 'it' wishes, and not when 'I' wish; so that it is a *perversion* of the facts of the case to say that the subject 'I' is the condition of the predicate 'think'. *One* thinks; but that this 'one' is precisely the famous old 'ego', is, to put it mildly, only a supposition, an assertion, and assuredly not an 'immediate certainty'. After all, one has even gone too far with this 'one thinks' – even the 'one' contains an *interpretation* of the process, and does not belong to the process itself. One infers here according to the usual grammatical formula – 'To think is an activity; every activity requires an agency that is active; consequently . . . ' It was pretty much on the same lines that the older atomism sought, besides the operating 'power', the material particle wherein it resides and out of which it operates – the atom. More rigorous minds, however, learnt at last to get along without this 'earth-residuum', and perhaps some day we shall accustom ourselves, even from the logician's point of view, to get along without the little 'one' (to which the worthy old 'ego' has refined itself).

18

It is certainly not the least charm of a theory that it is refutable; it is precisely thereby that it attracts the more subtle minds. It seems that the hundred-times-refuted theory of the 'free will' owes its persistence to this charm alone; some one is always appearing who feels himself strong enough to refute it.

19

Philosophers are accustomed to speak of the will as though it were the best-known thing in the world; indeed, Schopenhauer has given us to understand that the will alone is really known to us, absolutely and completely known, without deduction or addition. But it again and again seems to me that in this case Schopenhauer also only did what philosophers are in the habit of doing – he seems to have adopted a *popular prejudice* and exaggerated it. Willing – seems to me to be above all something *complicated*, something that is a unity only in name – and it is precisely in a name that popular prejudice lurks, which has got the mastery over the inadequate precautions of philosophers in all ages. So let us for once be more cautious, let us be 'unphilosophical': let us say that in all willing there is firstly a plurality of sensations, namely, the sensation of the condition *'away from which* we go', the sensation of the condition *'towards which* we go,' the sensation of this *'from'* and *'towards'* itself, and then besides, an accompanying muscular sensation, which, even without our putting in motion 'arms and legs,' commences its action by force of habit, directly we 'will' anything. Therefore, just as sensations (and indeed many kinds of sensations) are to be recognised as ingredients of the will, so, in the second place, thinking is also to be recognised; in every act of the will there is a ruling thought – and let us not imagine it possible to sever this thought from the 'willing,' as if the will would then remain over! In the third place, the will is not only a complex of sensation and thinking, but it is above all an *emotion*, and in fact the emotion of the command. That which is termed 'freedom of the will' is essentially the emotion of supremacy in respect to him who must obey: 'I am free, "he" must obey' – this consciousness is inherent in every will; and equally so the straining of the attention, the straight look which fixes itself exclusively on one thing, the unconditional judgment that 'this and nothing else is necessary now,' the inward certainty that obedience will be rendered – and whatever else pertains to the position of the commander. A man who *wills* commands something within himself which renders obedience, or which he believes renders obedience. But now let us notice what is the strangest thing about the will – this affair so extremely complex, for which the people have only one name. Inasmuch

as in the given circumstances we are at the same time
the commanding *and* the obeying parties, and as the
obeying party we know the sensations of constraint,
impulsion, pressure, resistance, and motion, which
usually commence immediately after the act of will;
inasmuch as, on the other hand, we are accustomed
to disregard this duality, and to deceive ourselves
about it by means of the synthetic term 'I': a whole
series of erroneous conclusions, and consequently of
false judgments about the will itself, has become
attached to the act of willing – to such a degree that he
who wills believes firmly that willing *suffices* for action.
Since in the majority of cases there has only been
exercise of will when the effect of the command –
consequently obedience, and therefore action – was to
be *expected*, the *appearance* has translated itself into the
sentiment, as if there were there a *necessity of effect*; in a
word, he who wills believes with a fair amount of
certainty that will and action are somehow one; he
ascribes the success, the carrying out of the willing, to
the will itself, and thereby enjoys an increase of the
sensation of power which accompanies all success.
'Freedom of Will' – that is the expression for the complex state of delight of the person exercising volition,
who commands and at the same time identifies
himself with the executor of the order – who, as such,
enjoys also the triumph over obstacles, but thinks
within himself that it was really his own will that
overcame them. In this way the person exercising
volition adds the feelings of delight of his successful
executive instruments, the useful 'underwills' or
under-souls – indeed, our body is but a social
structure composed of many souls – to his feelings of
delight as commander. *L'effet c'est moi*: what happens

here is what happens in every well-constructed and happy commonwealth, namely, that the governing class identifies itself with the successes of the commonwealth. In all willing it is absolutely a question of commanding and obeying, on the basis, as already said, of a social structure composed of many 'souls'; on which account a philosopher should claim the right to include willing-as-such within the sphere of morals – regarded as the doctrine of the relations of supremacy under which the phenomenon of 'life' manifests itself.

20

That the separate philosophical ideas are not anything optional or autonomously evolving, but grow up in connection and relationship with each other; that, however suddenly and arbitrarily they seem to appear in the history of thought, they nevertheless belong just as much to a system as the collective members of the fauna of a continent – is betrayed in the end by the circumstance: how unfailingly the most diverse philosophers always fill in again a definite fundamental scheme of *possible* philosophies. Under an invisible spell, they always revolve once more in the same orbit; however independent of each other they may feel themselves with their critical or systematic wills, something within them leads them, something impels them in definite order the one after the other – to wit, the innate methodology and relationship of their ideas. Their thinking is in fact far less a discovery than a re-recognising, a remembering, a return and a homecoming to a far-off, ancient common-household of the soul, out of which those ideas formerly grew: philosophising is so far a kind of atavism of the highest order. The wonderful family resemblance of all

Indian, Greek, and German philosophising is easily enough explained. In fact, where there is affinity of language, owing to the common philosophy of grammar – I mean owing to the unconscious domination and guidance of similar grammatical functions – it cannot but be that everything is prepared at the outset for a similar development and succession of philosophical systems; just as the way seems barred against certain other possibilities of world-interpretation. It is highly probable that philosophers within the domain of the Ural-Altaic languages (where the conception of the subject is least developed) look otherwise 'into the world', and will be found on paths of thought different from those of the Indo-Germans and Mussulmans, the spell of certain grammatical functions is ultimately also the spell of *physiological* valuations and racial conditions. So much by way of rejecting Locke's superficiality with regard to the origin of ideas.

21

The *causa sui* is the best self-contradiction that has yet been conceived, it is a sort of logical violation and unnaturalness; but the extravagant pride of man has managed to entangle itself profoundly and frightfully with this very folly. The desire for 'freedom of will' in the superlative, metaphysical sense, such as still holds sway, unfortunately, in the minds of the half-educated, the desire to bear the entire and ultimate responsibility for one's actions oneself, and to absolve God, the world, ancestors, chance, and society there-from, involves nothing less than to be precisely this *causa sui*, and, with more than Munchausen daring, to pull oneself up into existence by the hair, out of the slough of nothingness. If any one should find out in

251

this manner the crass stupidity of the celebrated conception of 'free will' and put it out of his head altogether, I beg of him to carry his 'enlightenment' a step further, and also put out of his head the contrary of this monstrous conception of 'free will': I mean 'non-free will', which is tantamount to a misuse of cause and effect. One should not wrongly *materialise* 'cause' and 'effect', as the natural philosophers do (and whoever like them naturalise in thinking at present), according to the prevailing mechanical doltishness which makes the cause press and push until it 'effects' its end; one should use 'cause' and 'effect' only as pure *conceptions*, that is to say, as conventional fictions for the purpose of designation and mutual understanding – *not* for explanation. In 'being-in-itself' there is nothing of 'causal-connection', of 'necessity,' or of 'psychological non-freedom'; there the effect does *not* follow the cause, there 'law' does not obtain. It is *we* alone who have devised cause, sequence, reciprocity, relativity, constraint, number, law, freedom, motive, and purpose; and when we interpret and intermix this symbol-world, as 'being in itself', with things, we act once more as we have always acted – *mythologically*. The 'non-free will' is mythology; in real life it is only a question of *strong* and *weak* wills. It is almost always a symptom of what is lacking in himself, when a thinker, in every 'causal-connection' and 'psychological necessity', manifests something of compulsion, indigence, obsequiousness, oppression, and non-freedom; it is suspicious to have such feelings – the person betrays himself. And in general, if I have observed correctly, the 'non-freedom of the will' is regarded as a problem from two entirely opposite standpoints, but always in a profoundly *personal* manner: some will not give up their 'responsibility', their belief in *themselves*, the personal right to *their* merits, at any price (the vain races belong to this class); others on the contrary, do not wish to be answerable for anything, or blamed for anything, and owing to an inward self-contempt, seek *to get out of the business*, no matter how. The latter, when they write books, are in the habit at present of taking the side of criminals; a sort of socialistic sympathy is their favourite disguise. And as a matter of fact, the fatalism of the weak-willed embellishes itself surprisingly when it can pose as '*la religion de la souffrance humaine*'; that is *its* 'good taste'.

22

Let me be pardoned, as an old philologist who cannot desist from the mischief of putting his finger on bad modes of interpretation, but 'Nature's conformity to law,' of which you physicists talk so proudly, as though – why, it exists only owing to your interpretation and bad 'philology'. It is no matter of fact, no 'text,' but rather just a naïvely humanitarian adjustment and perversion of meaning, with which you make abundant concessions to the democratic instincts of the modern soul! 'Everywhere equality before the law – Nature is not different in that respect, nor better than we:' a fine instance of secret motive, in which the vulgar antagonism to everything privileged and autocratic – likewise a second and more refined atheism – is once more disguised. '*Ni dieu, ni maître*' – that, also, is what you want; and therefore 'Cheers for natural law!' – is it not so? But, as has been said, that is interpretation, not text; and somebody might come along, who, with opposite intentions and modes of interpretation, could read out of the same 'Nature', and with regard to the same phenomena, just the tyrannically inconsiderate and relentless enforcement of the claims of power – an interpreter who should so place the unexceptionalness and unconditionalness of all 'Will to Power' before your eyes, that almost every word, and the word 'tyranny' itself, would eventually seem unsuitable, or like a weakening and softening metaphor – as being too human; and who should, nevertheless, end by asserting the same about this world as you do, namely, that it has a 'necessary' and 'calculable' course, *not*, however, because laws obtain in it, but because they are absolutely *lacking*, and every power effects its ultimate consequences every moment. Granted that this also is only interpretation – and you will be eager enough to make this objection? – well, so much the better.

23

All psychology hitherto has run aground on moral prejudices and timidities, it has not dared to launch out into the depths. In so far as it is allowable to recognise in that which has hitherto been written, evidence of that which has hitherto been kept silent, it seems as if nobody had yet harboured the notion of psychology as the Morphology and *Development-doctrine of the Will to Power*, as I conceive of it. The power of moral prejudices has penetrated deeply into the most intellectual world, the world apparently most indifferent and unprejudiced, and has obviously operated in an injurious, obstructive, blinding, and distorting manner. A proper physio-psychology has to contend with unconscious antagonism in the heart of the investigator, it has 'the heart' against it: even a doctrine of the reciprocal conditionalness of the 'good' and the 'bad' impulses, causes (as refined immorality) distress and aversion in a still strong and manly conscience – still more so, a doctrine of the derivation of all good impulses from bad ones. If, however, a person should regard even the emotions of hatred, envy, covetousness, and imperiousness as life-conditioning emotions, as factors which must be present, fundamentally and essentially, in the general economy of life (which must, therefore, be further developed if life is to be further developed), he will suffer from such a view of things as from seasickness. And yet this hypothesis is far from being the strangest and most painful in this immense and almost new domain of dangerous knowledge; and there are in fact a hundred good reasons why every one should keep away from it who *can* do so! On the other hand, if one has once drifted hither with one's bark – well, very good! – now let us set our teeth firmly! Let us open our eyes and keep our hand fast on the helm! We sail away right *over* morality, we crush out, we destroy perhaps the remains of our own morality by daring to make our voyage thither – but what do *we* matter! Never yet did a *profounder* world of insight reveal itself to daring travellers and adventurers, and the psychologist who thus 'makes a sacrifice' – it is *not* the *sacrifizio dell' intelletto*, on the contrary! – will at least be entitled to demand in return that psychology shall once more be recognised as the queen of the sciences, for whose service and equipment the other sciences exist. For psychology is once more the path to the fundamental problems.

The Free Spirit

32

Throughout the longest period of human history – one calls it the prehistoric period – the value or non-value of an action was inferred from its *consequences*; the action in itself was not taken into consideration, any more than its origin; but pretty much as in China at present, where the distinction or disgrace of a child redounds to its parents, the retro-operating power of success or failure was what induced men to think well or ill of an action. Let us call this period the *pre-moral* period of mankind; the imperative, 'know thyself!' was then still unknown. – In the last ten thousand years, on the other hand, on certain large portions of the earth, one has gradually got so far, that one no longer lets the consequences of an action, but its origin, decide with regard to its worth: a great achievement as a whole, an important refinement of vision and of criterion, the unconscious effect of the supremacy of aristocratic values and of the belief in 'origin', the mark of a period which may be designated in the narrower sense as the *moral* one: the first attempt at self-knowledge is thereby made. Instead of the consequences, the origin – what an inversion of perspective! And assuredly an inversion effected only after long struggle and wavering! To be sure, an ominous new superstition, a peculiar narrowness of interpretation, attained supremacy precisely thereby: the origin of an action was interpreted in the most definite sense possible, as origin out of an *intention*; people were agreed in the belief that the value of an action lay in the value of its intention. The intention as the sole origin and antecedent history of an action: under the influence of this prejudice moral praise and blame have been bestowed, and men have judged and even philosophised almost up to the present day. Is it not possible, however, that the necessity may now have arisen of again making up our minds with regard to the reversing and fundamental shifting of values, owing to a new self-consciousness and acuteness in man – is it not possible that we may be standing on the threshold of a period which to begin with, would be distinguished negatively as *ultra-moral*: nowadays when, at least amongst us immoralists, the suspicion arises that the decisive value of an action lies precisely in that which is *not intentional*, and that all its intentionalness, all that is seen, sensible, or 'sensed' in it, belongs to its surface or skin – which, like every skin, betrays something, but *conceals* still more? In short, we believe that the intention is only a sign or symptom, which first requires an explanation – a sign, moreover, which has too many interpretations, and consequently hardly any meaning in itself alone: that morality, in the sense in which it has been understood hitherto, as intention-morality, has been a prejudice, perhaps a prematureness or preliminariness, probably something of the same rank as astrology and alchemy, but in any case something which must be surmounted. The surmounting of morality, in a certain sense even the self-surmounting of morality – let that be the name for the long secret labour which has been reserved for the most refined, the most upright, and also the most wicked consciences of today, as the living touchstones of the soul.

33

It cannot be helped: the sentiment of surrender, of sacrifice for one's neighbour, and all self-renunciation – morality, must be mercilessly called to account, and brought to judgment; just as the aesthetics of 'disinterested contemplation', under which the emasculation of art nowadays seeks insidiously enough to create itself a good conscience. There is far too much witchery and sugar in the sentiments 'for others' and '*not* for myself', for one not needing to be doubly distrustful here, and for one asking promptly: 'Are they not perhaps – *deceptions*?' That they *please* – him who has them, and him who enjoys their fruit, and also the mere spectator – that is still no argument in their *favour*, but just calls for caution. Let us therefore be cautious!

34

At whatever standpoint of philosophy one may place oneself nowadays, seen from every position, the *erroneousness* of the world in which we think we live is the surest and most certain thing our eyes can light upon: we find proof after proof thereof, which would fain allure us into surmises concerning a deceptive principle in the 'nature of things'. He, however, who makes thinking itself, and consequently 'the spirit', responsible for the falseness of the world – an honourable exit, which every conscious or unconscious *advocatus dei* avails himself of – he who regards this world, including space, time, form, and movement, as falsely *deduced*, would have at least good reason in the end to become distrustful also of all thinking; has it not hitherto been playing upon us the worst of scurvy tricks? And what guarantee would it give that it would not continue to do what it has always been doing? In all seriousness, the innocence of thinkers has something touching and respect-inspiring in it, which even nowadays permits them to wait upon consciousness with the request that it will give them *honest* answers: for example, whether it be 'real' or not, and why it keeps the outer world so resolutely at a distance, and other questions of the same description. The belief in 'immediate certainties' is a *moral naïveté* which does honour to us philo-sophers; but – we have now to cease being '*merely* moral' men! Apart from morality, such belief is a folly which does little honour to us! If in middle-class life an ever-ready distrust is regarded as the sign of a 'bad character,' and consequently as an imprudence, here amongst us, beyond the middle-class world and its Yeas and Nays, what should prevent us being im-prudent and saying: the philosopher has at length a *right* to 'bad character', as the being who has hitherto been most befooled on earth – he is now under *obligation* to distrustfulness, to the wickedest squinting out of every abyss of suspicion. Forgive me the joke of this gloomy grimace and turn of expression; for I myself have long ago learned to think and estimate differently with regard to deceiving and being deceived, and I keep at least a couple of pokes in the ribs ready for the blind rage with which philosophers struggle against being deceived. Why *not*? It is nothing more than a moral prejudice that truth is worth more than semblance; it is, in fact, the worst proved supposition in the world. *So* much must be conceded:

there could have been no life at all except upon the basis of perspective estimates and semblances; and if, with the virtuous enthusiasm and stupidity of many philosophers, one wished to do away altogether with the 'seeming world' – well, granted that *you* could do that, at least nothing of your 'truth' would thereby remain! Indeed, what is it that forces us in general to the supposition that there is an essential opposition of 'true' and 'false'? Is it not enough to suppose degrees of seemingness, and as it were lighter and darker shades and tones of semblance – different *valeurs*, as the painters say? Why might not the world *which concerns us* – be a fiction? And to any one who suggested: 'But to a fiction belongs an originator?' – might it not be bluntly replied: *Why*? May not this 'belong' also belong to the fiction? Is it not at length permitted to be a little ironical towards the subject, just as towards the predicate and object? Might not the philosopher elevate himself above faith in grammar? All respect to governesses, but is it not time that philosophy should renounce governess-faith?

35

O Voltaire! O humanity! O idiocy! There is something ticklish in 'the truth', and in the *search* for the truth; and if man goes about it too humanely – '*il ne cherche le vrai que pour faire le bien*' – I wager he finds nothing!

36

Supposing that nothing else is 'given' as real but our world of desires and passions, that we cannot sink or rise to any other 'reality' but just that of our impulses – for thinking is only a relation of these impulses to one another – are we not permitted to make the attempt and to ask the question whether this which is 'given' does not *suffice*, by means of our counterparts, for the understanding even of the so-called mechanical (or 'material') world? I do not mean as an illusion, a 'semblance', a 'representation' (in the Berkeleyan and Schopenhauerian sense), but as possessing the same degree of reality as our emotions themselves – as a more primitive form of the world of emotions, in which everything still lies locked in a mighty unity, which afterwards branches off and develops itself in organic processes (naturally also, refines and debilitates) – as a kind of instinctive life in which all organic functions, including self-regulation, assimilation, nutrition, secretion, and change of matter, are still synthetically united with one another – as a *primary form* of life? In the end, it is not only permitted to make this attempt, it is commanded by the conscience of *logical method*. Not to assume several kinds of causality, so long as the attempt to get along with a single one has not been pushed to its furthest extent (to absurdity, if I may be allowed to say so): that is a morality of method which one may not repudiate nowadays – it follows 'from its definition', as mathematicians say. The question is ultimately whether we really recognise the will as *operating*, whether we believe in the causality of the will; if we do so – and fundamentally our belief *in this* is just our belief in causality itself – we *must* make the attempt to posit hypothetically the causality of the will as the only causality. 'Will' can naturally only operate on 'will' – and not on 'matter' (not on 'nerves', for instance): in short, the hypothesis must be hazarded, whether will does not operate on will wherever 'effects' are recognised – and whether all mechanical action, inasmuch as a power operates therein, is not just the power of will, the effect of will. Granted, finally, that we succeeded in explaining our entire instinctive life as the development and ramification of one fundamental form of will – namely, the Will to Power, as *my* thesis puts it; granted that all organic functions could be traced back to this Will to Power, and that the solution of the problem of generation and nutrition – it is one problem – could also be found therein: one would thus have acquired the right to define *all* active force unequivocally as *Will to Power*. The world seen from within, the world defined and designated according to its 'intelligible character' – it would simply be 'Will to Power,' and nothing else.

37

'What? Does not that mean in popular language: God is disproved, but not the devil?' – On the contrary! On the contrary, my friends! And who the devil also compels you to speak popularly!

38

As happened finally in all the enlightenment of modern times with the French Revolution (that terrible farce, quite superfluous when judged close at hand, into which, however, the noble and visionary spectators of all Europe have interpreted from a distance their own indignation and enthusiasm so long and passionately, *until the text has disappeared under the interpretation*), so a noble posterity might once more misunderstand the whole of the past, and perhaps only thereby make *its* aspect endurable. Or rather, has not this already happened? Have not we ourselves been – that 'noble posterity'? And, in so far as we now comprehend this, is it not – thereby already past?

39

Nobody will very readily regard a doctrine as true merely because it makes people happy or virtuous – excepting perhaps the amiable 'Idealists', who are enthusiastic about the good, true, and beautiful, and let all kinds of motley, coarse, and good-natured desirabilities swim about promiscuously in their pond. Happiness and virtue are no arguments. It is willingly forgotten, however, even on the part of thoughtful minds, that to make unhappy and to make bad are just as little counter-arguments. A thing could be *true*, although it were in the highest degree injurious and dangerous; indeed, the fundamental constitution of existence might be such that one succumbed by a full knowledge of it – so that the strength of a mind might be measured by the amount of 'truth' it could endure – or to speak more plainly, by the extent to which it *required* truth attenuated, veiled, sweetened, damped, and falsified. But there is no doubt that for the discovery of certain *portions* of truth the wicked and unfortunate are more favourably situated and have a greater likelihood of success; not to speak of the wicked who are happy – a species about whom moralists are silent. Perhaps severity and craft are more favourable conditions for the development of strong, independent spirits and philosophers than the gentle, refined, yielding good-nature, and habit of taking things easily, which are prized, and rightly prized, in a learned man. Pre-supposing always, to begin with, that the term 'philo-sopher' be not confined to the philosopher who writes books, or even introduces *his* philosophy into books! Stendhal furnishes a last feature of the portrait of the free-spirited philosopher, which for the sake of German taste I will not omit to underline – for it is *opposed* to German taste. '*Pour être bon philosophe,*' says this last great psychologist, '*il faut être sec, clair, sans illusion. Un banquier, qui a fait fortune, a une partie du caractère requis pour faire des découvertes en philosophie, c'est-à-dire pour voir clair dans ce qui est.*'

42

A new order of philosophers is appearing; I shall venture to baptize them by a name not without danger. As far as I understand them, as far as they allow themselves to be understood – for it is their nature to *wish* to remain something of a puzzle – these philosophers of the future might rightly, perhaps also wrongly, claim to be designated as '*tempters*'. This name itself is after all only an attempt, or, if it be preferred, a temptation.

43

Will they be new friends of 'truth,' these coming philosophers? Very probably, for all philosophers hitherto have loved their truths. But assuredly they will not be dogmatists. It must be contrary to their pride, and also contrary to their taste, that their truth should still be truth for every one – that which has hitherto been the secret wish and ultimate purpose of all dogmatic efforts. 'My opinion is *my* opinion: another person has not easily a right to it' – such a philosopher of the future will say, perhaps. One must renounce the bad taste of wishing to agree with many people. 'Good' is no longer good when one's neighbour takes it into his mouth. And how could there be a 'common good'! The expression contradicts itself; that which can be common is always of small value. In the end things must be as they are and have always been – the great things remain for the great, the abysses for the profound, the delicacies and thrills for the refined, and, to sum up shortly, everything rare for the rare.

44

Need I say expressly after all this that they will be free, *very* free spirits, these philosophers of the future – as certainly also they will not be merely free spirits, but something more, higher, greater, and fundamentally different, which does not wish to be misunderstood and mistaken? But while I say this, I feel under *obligation* almost as much to them as to ourselves (we free spirits who are their heralds and forerunners), to sweep away from ourselves altogether a stupid old prejudice and misunderstanding, which, like a fog, has too long made the conception of 'free spirit' obscure. In every country of Europe, and the same in America, there is at present something which makes an abuse of this name: a very narrow, prepossessed, enchained class of spirits, who desire almost the opposite of what our intentions and instincts prompt – not to mention that in respect to the *new* philosophers who are appearing, they must still more be closed windows and bolted doors. Briefly and regrettably, they belong to the *levellers*, these wrongly named 'free spirits' – as glib-tongued and scribe-fingered slaves of the democratic taste and its 'modern ideas': all of them men without solitude, without personal solitude, blunt honest fellows to whom neither courage nor honourable conduct ought to be denied; only, they are not free, and are ludicrously superficial, especially in their innate partiality for seeing the cause of almost *all* human misery and failure in the old forms in which society has hitherto existed – a notion which happily inverts the truth entirely! What they would fain attain with all their strength, is the universal, green-meadow happiness of the herd, together with security, safety, comfort, and alleviation of life for every one; their two most frequently chanted songs and doctrines are called 'Equality of Rights' and 'Sympathy with all Sufferers' – and suffering itself is looked upon by them as something which must be *done away with*. We opposite ones, however, who have opened our eye and conscience to the question how and where the plant 'man' has hitherto grown most vigorously, believe that this has always taken place under the opposite conditions, that for this end the dangerousness of his situation had to be increased enormously, his inventive faculty and dissembling power (his 'spirit') had to develop into subtlety and daring under long oppression and compulsion, and his Will to Life had to be increased to the unconditioned Will to Power: we believe that severity, violence, slavery, danger in the street and in the heart, secrecy, stoicism, tempter's art and devilry of every kind – that everything wicked, terrible, tyrannical, predatory, and serpentine in man, serves as well for the elevation of the human species as its opposite: we do not even say enough when we only say *this much*; and in any case we find ourselves here, both with our speech and our silence, at the *other* extreme of all modern ideology and gregarious desirability, as their antipodes perhaps? What wonder that we 'free spirits' are not exactly the most communicative spirits? That we do not wish to betray in every respect *what* a spirit can free itself from, and *where* perhaps it will then be driven? And as to the import of the dangerous formula, 'Beyond Good and Evil', with which we at least avoid confusion, we *are* something else than '*libres-penseurs*', '*liberi pensatori*', 'free-thinkers', and whatever these honest advocates of 'modern ideas' like to call themselves. Having been at home, or at least guests, in many realms of the spirit; having escaped again and again from the gloomy, agreeable nooks in which preferences and prejudices, youth, origin, the accident of men and books, or even the weariness of travel seemed to confine us; full of malice against the seductions of dependency which lie concealed in honours, money, positions, or exaltation of the senses; grateful even for distress and the vicissitudes of illness, because they always free us from some rule, and its 'prejudice', grateful to the god, devil, sheep, and worm in us; inquisitive to a fault, investigators to the point of cruelty, with unhesitating fingers for the intangible, with teeth and stomachs for the most indigestible, ready for any business that requires sagacity and acute senses, ready for every adventure, owing to an excess of 'free will'; with anterior and posterior souls, into the ultimate intentions of which it is difficult to pry, with foregrounds and backgrounds to the end of which no foot may run; hidden ones under the mantles of light, appropriators, although we resemble heirs and spendthrifts, arrangers and collectors from morning till night, misers of our wealth and our full-crammed drawers, economical in learning and forgetting, inventive in scheming; sometimes proud of tables of categories, sometimes pedants, sometimes night-owls of work even in full day; yea, if necessary, even scarecrows – and it is necessary nowadays, that is to say, inasmuch as we are the born, sworn, jealous friends of *solitude*, of our own profoundest midnight and midday solitude: such kind of men are we, we free spirits! And perhaps *ye* are also something of the same kind, ye coming ones, ye *new* philosophers?

Apophthegms and Interludes

63

He who is a thorough teacher takes things seriously –
and even himself – only in relation to his pupils.

64

'Knowledge for its own sake' – that is the last snare
laid by morality: we are thereby completely entangled
in morals once more.

65

The charm of knowledge would be small, were it not
that so much shame has to be overcome on the way
to it.

65A

We are most dishonourable towards our God: he is
not *permitted* to sin.

66

The tendency of a person to allow himself to be
degraded, robbed, deceived, and exploited might be
the diffidence of a god amongst men.

67

Love to one only is a barbarity, for it is exercised at the
expense of all others. Love to God also!

68

'I did that,' says my memory. 'I could not have done that,' says my pride, and remains inexorable. Eventually – the memory yields.

69

One has regarded life carelessly, if one has failed to see the hand that – kills with leniency.

70

If a man has character, he has also his typical experience, which always recurs.

71

The Sage as Astronomer. – So long as thou feelest the stars as an 'above thee', thou lackest the eye of the discerning one.

72

It is not the strength, but the duration of great sentiments that makes great men.

73

He who attains his ideal, precisely thereby surpasses it.

73A

Many a peacock hides his tail from every eye – and calls it his pride.

74

A man of genius is unbearable, unless he possess at least two things besides: gratitude and purity.

75

The degree and nature of a man's sensuality extends to the highest altitudes of his spirit.

76

Under peaceful conditions the militant man attacks himself.

77

With his principles a man seeks either to dominate, or justify, or honour, or reproach, or conceal his habits: two men with the same principles probably seek fundamentally different ends therewith.

78

He who despises himself, nevertheless esteems himself thereby, as a despiser.

79

A soul which knows that it is loved, but does not itself love, betrays its sediment: its dregs come up.

80

A thing that is explained ceases to concern us. What did the god mean who gave the advice, 'Know thyself!' Did it perhaps imply: 'Cease to be concerned about thyself! become objective!' And Socrates? – and the 'scientific man'?

81

It is terrible to die of thirst at sea. Is it necessary that you should so salt your truth that it will no longer – quench thirst?

82

'Sympathy for all' – would be harshness and tyranny for *thee*, my good neighbour!

83

Instinct – When the house is on fire one forgets even the dinner – Yes, but one recovers it from amongst the ashes.

84

Woman learns how to hate in proportion as she – forgets how to charm.

85

The same emotions are in man and woman, but in different *tempo*; on that account man and woman never cease to misunderstand each other.

86

In the background of all their personal vanity, women themselves have still their impersonal scorn – for 'woman'.

87

Fettered Heart, Free Spirit – When one firmly fetters one's heart and keeps it prisoner, one can allow one's spirit many liberties: I said this once before. But people do not believe it when I say so, unless they know it already.

88

One begins to distrust very clever persons when they become embarrassed.

89

Dreadful experiences raise the question whether he who experiences them is not something dreadful also.

90

Heavy, melancholy men turn lighter, and come temporarily to their surface, precisely by that which makes others heavy – by hatred and love.

91

So cold, so icy, that one burns one's finger at the touch of him! Every hand that lays hold of him shrinks back! And for that very reason many think him red-hot.

92

Who has not, at one time or another – sacrificed himself for the sake of his good name?

93

In affability there is no hatred of men, but precisely on that account a great deal too much contempt of men.

94

The maturity of man – that means, to have re-acquired the seriousness that one had as a child at play.

95

To be ashamed of one's immorality is a step on the ladder at the end of which one is ashamed also of one's morality.

96

One should part from life as Ulysses parted from Nausicaa – blessing it rather than in love with it.

97

What? A great man? I always see merely the play-actor of his own ideal.

98

When one trains one's conscience, it kisses one while it bites.

99

The Disappointed One Speaks – 'I listened for the echo and I heard only praise'.

100

We all feign to ourselves that we are simpler than we are; we thus relax ourselves away from our fellows.

101

A discerning one might easily regard himself at present as the animalisation of God.

102

Discovering reciprocal love should really disenchant the lover with regard to the beloved. 'What! *She* is modest enough to love even you? Or stupid enough? Or – or – '

103

The Danger in Happiness – 'Everything now turns out best for me, I now love every fate: – who would like to be my fate?'

104

Not their love of humanity, but the impotence of their love, prevents the Christians of today – burning us.

105

The *pia fraus* is still more repugnant to the taste (*the 'piety'*) of the free spirit (the 'pious man of knowledge') than the *impia fraus*. Hence the profound lack of judgment, in comparison with the church, characteristic of the type 'free spirit' – as *its* non-freedom.

106

By means of music the very passions enjoy themselves.

107

A sign of strong character, when once the resolution has been taken, to shut the ear even to the best counter-arguments. Occasionally, therefore, a will to stupidity.

108

There is no such thing as moral phenomena, but only a moral interpretation of phenomena.

109

The criminal is often enough not equal to his deed: he extenuates and maligns it.

110

The advocates of a criminal are seldom artists enough to turn the beautiful terribleness of the deed to the advantage of the doer.

III

Our vanity is most difficult to wound just when our pride has been wounded.

112

To him who feels himself preordained to contemplation and not to belief, all believers are too noisy and obtrusive; he guards against them.

113

'You want to prepossess him in your favour? Then you must be embarrassed before him.'

114

The immense expectation with regard to sexual love, and the coyness in this expectation, spoils all the perspectives of women at the outset.

115

Where there is neither love nor hatred in the game, woman's play is mediocre.

116

The great epochs of our life are at the points when we gain courage to rebaptize our badness as the best in us.

117

The will to overcome an emotion, is ultimately only the will of another, or of several other, emotions.

118

There is an innocence of admiration: it is possessed by

him to whom it has not yet occurred that he himself may be admired some day.

119

Our loathing of dirt may be so great as to prevent us cleaning ourselves – 'justifying' ourselves.

120

Sensuality often forces the growth of love too much, so that its root remains weak, and is easily torn up.

121

It is a curious thing that God learned Greek when he wished to turn author – and that he did not learn it better.

122

To rejoice on account of praise is in many cases merely politeness of heart – and the very opposite of vanity of spirit.

123

Even concubinage has been corrupted – by marriage.

124

He who exults at the stake, does not triumph over pain, but because of the fact that he does not feel pain where he expected it. A parable.

125

When we have to change an opinion about any one, we charge heavily to his account the inconvenience he thereby causes us.

126

A nation is a detour of nature to arrive at six or seven great men – Yes, and then to get round them.

127

In the eyes of all true women science is hostile to the sense of shame. They feel as if one wished to peep under their skin with it – or worse still! under their dress and finery.

128

The more abstract the truth you wish to teach, the more must you allure the senses to it.

129

The devil has the most extensive perspectives for God; on that account he keeps so far away from him: the devil, in effect, as the oldest friend of knowledge.

130

What a person *is* begins to betray itself when his talent decreases – when he ceases to show what he *can do*. Talent is also an adornment; an adornment is also a concealment.

131

The sexes deceive themselves about each other: the reason is that in reality they honour and love only themselves (or their own ideal, to express it more agreeably). Thus man wishes woman to be peaceable: but in fact woman is *essentially* unpeaceable, like the cat, however well she may have assumed the peaceable demeanour.

132

One is punished best for one's virtues.

133

He who cannot find the way to *his* ideal, lives more frivolously and shamelessly than the man without an ideal.

134

From the senses originate all trustworthiness, all good conscience, all evidence of truth.

135

Pharisaism is not a deterioration of the good man; a considerable part of it is rather an essential condition of being good.

136

The one seeks an accoucheur for his thoughts, the other seeks some one whom he can assist: a good conversation thus originates.

137

In intercourse with scholars and artists one readily makes mistakes of opposite kinds: in a remarkable scholar one not infrequently finds a mediocre man; and often even in a mediocre artist, one finds a very remarkable man.

138

We do the same when awake as when dreaming: we only invent and imagine him with whom we have intercourse – and forget it immediately.

139

In revenge and in love woman is more barbarous than man.

140

Advice as a Riddle – 'If the band is not to break, bite it first – secure to make!'

141

The belly is the reason why man does not so readily take himself for a god.

142

The chastest utterance I ever heard: '*Dans le véritable amour c'est l'âme qui enveloppe le corps.*'

143

Our vanity would like what we do best to pass precisely for what is most difficult to us – concerning the origin of many systems of morals.

144

When a woman has scholarly inclinations there is generally something wrong with her sexual nature. Barrenness itself conduces to a certain virility of taste; man, indeed, if I may say so, is 'the barren animal'.

145

Comparing man and woman generally, one may say that woman would not have the genius for adornment, if she had not the instinct for the *secondary* rôle.

146

He who fights with monsters should be careful lest he thereby become a monster. And if thou gaze long into an abyss, the abyss will also gaze into thee.

147

From old Florentine novels – moreover, from life: *Buona femmina e mala femmina vuol bastone* – Sacchetti, November 86

148

To seduce their neighbour to a favourable opinion, and afterwards to believe implicitly in this opinion of their neighbour – who can do this conjuring trick so well as women?

149

That which an age considers evil is usually an un-seasonable echo of what was formerly considered good – the atavism of an old ideal.

150

Around the hero everything becomes a tragedy; around the demigod everything becomes a satyrplay; and around God everything becomes – what? perhaps a 'world'?

151

It is not enough to possess a talent: one must also have your permission to possess it – eh, my friends?

152

'Where there is the tree of knowledge, there is always Paradise:' so say the most ancient and the most modern serpents.

153

What is done out of love always takes place beyond good and evil.

154

Objection, evasion, joyous distrust, and love of irony are signs of health; everything absolute belongs to pathology.

155

The sense of the tragic increases and declines with sensuousness.

156

Insanity in individuals is something rare – but in groups, parties, nations, and epochs it is the rule.

157

The thought of suicide is a great consolation: by means of it one gets successfully through many a bad night.

158

Not only our reason, but also our conscience, truckles to our strongest impulse – the tyrant in us.

159

One *must* repay good and ill; but why just to the person who did us good or ill?

160

One no longer loves one's knowledge sufficiently after one has communicated it.

161

Poets act shamelessly towards their experiences: they exploit them.

162

'Our fellow-creature is not our neighbour, but our neighbour's neighbour' – so thinks every nation.

163

Love brings to light the noble and hidden qualities of a lover – his rare and exceptional traits: it is thus liable to be deceptive as to his normal character.

164

Jesus said to his Jews: 'The law was for servants – love God as I love him, as his Son! What have we Sons of God to do with morals!'

165

In Sight of every Party. – A shepherd has always need of a bell-wether – or he has himself to be a wether occasionally.

166

One may indeed lie with the mouth; but with the accompanying grimace one nevertheless tells the truth.

167

To vigorous men intimacy is a matter of shame – and something precious.

168

Christianity gave Eros poison to drink; he did not die of it, certainly, but degenerated to Vice.

The Natural History of Morals

186

In contrast to *laisser-aller*, every system of morals is a sort of tyranny against 'nature' and also against 'reason'; that is, however, no objection, unless one should again decree by some system of morals, that all kinds of tyranny and unreasonableness are unlawful. What is essential and invaluable in every system of morals, is that it is a long constraint. In order to understand Stoicism, or Port-Royal, or Puritanism, one should remember the constraint under which every language has attained to strength and freedom – the metrical constraint, the tyranny of rhyme and rhythm. How much trouble have the poets and orators of every nation given themselves – not excepting some of the prose writers of today, in whose ear dwells an inexorable conscientiousness – 'for sake of a folly', as utilitarian bunglers say, and thereby deem themselves wise – 'from submission to arbitrary laws', as the anarchists say, and thereby fancy themselves 'free', even free-spirited. The singular fact remains, however, that everything of the nature of freedom, elegance, boldness, dance, and masterly certainty, which exists or has existed, whether it be in thought itself, or in administration, or in speaking and persuading, in art just as in conduct, has only developed by means of the tyranny of such arbitrary law; and in all seriousness, it is not at all improbable that precisely this is 'nature' and 'natural' – and *not laisser-aller*! Every artist knows how different from the state of letting himself go, is his 'most natural' condition, the free arranging, locating, disposing, and constructing in the moments of 'inspiration' – and how strictly and delicately he then obeys a thousand laws, which, by their very rigidness and precision, defy all formulation by means of ideas (even the most stable idea has, in comparison therewith, something floating, manifold, and ambiguous in it). The essential thing 'in heaven and in earth' is, apparently (to repeat it once more), that there should be long *obedience* in the same direction; there thereby results, and has always resulted in the long run, something which has made life worth living; for instance, virtue, art, music, dancing, reason, spirituality – anything whatever that is transfiguring, refined, foolish, or divine. The long bondage of the spirit, the distrustful constraint in the communicability of ideas, the discipline which the thinker imposed on himself to think in accordance with the rules of a church or a court, or conformable to Aristotelian premises, the persistent spiritual will to interpret everything that happened according to a Christian scheme, and in every occurrence to rediscover and justify the Christian God – all this violence, arbitrariness, severity, dreadfulness, and unreasonableness, has proved itself the disciplinary means whereby the European spirit has attained its strength, its remorseless curiosity and subtle mobility; granted also that much irrecoverable strength and spirit had to be stifled, suffocated, and spoilt in the process (for here, as everywhere, 'nature' shows herself as she is, in all her extravagant and *indifferent* magnificence, which is shocking, but nevertheless noble). That for centuries European thinkers only thought in order to prove something – nowadays, on the contrary, we are suspicious of every thinker who 'wishes to prove something' – that it was always settled beforehand what *was to be* the result of their strictest thinking, as it was perhaps in the Asiatic astrology of former times, or as it still is at the present day in the innocent, Christian-moral explanation of immediate personal events 'for the glory of God', or 'for the good of the soul': this tyranny, this arbitrariness, this severe and magnificent stupidity, has *educated* the spirit; slavery, both in the coarser and the finer sense, is apparently an indispensable means even of spiritual education and discipline. One may look at every system of morals in this light: it is 'nature' therein which teaches to hate the *laisser aller*, the too great freedom, and implants the need for limited horizons, for immediate duties – it teaches the *narrowing of perspectives*, and thus, in a certain sense, that stupidity is a condition of life and development. 'Thou must obey some one, and for a long time; *otherwise* thou wilt come to grief, and lose all respect for thyself' – this seems to me to be the moral imperative of nature, which is certainly neither 'categorical', as old Kant wished (consequently the 'otherwise'), nor does it address itself to the individual (what does nature care for the individual), but to nations, races, ages, and ranks, above all, however, to the animal 'man' generally, to *mankind*.

189

Industrious races find it a great hardship to be idle: it was a master stroke of *English* instinct to hallow and begloom Sunday to such an extent that the Englishman unconsciously hankers for his week and workday again – as a kind of cleverly devised, cleverly intercalated *fast*, such as is also frequently found in the ancient world (although, as is appropriate in southern nations, not precisely with respect to work). Many kinds of fasts are necessary; and wherever powerful impulses and habits prevail, legislators have to see that intercalary days are appointed, on which such impulses are fettered, and learn to hunger anew. Viewed from a higher standpoint, whole generations and epochs, when they show themselves infected with any moral fanaticism, seem like those intercalated periods of restraint and fasting, during which an impulse learns to humble and submit itself – at the same time also to *purify* and *sharpen* itself; certain philosophical sects likewise admit of a similar interpretation (for instance, the Stoa, in the midst of Hellenic culture, with the atmosphere rank and overcharged with Aphrodisiacal odours). Here also is a hint for the explanation of the paradox, why it was precisely in the most Christian period of European history, and in general only under the pressure of Christian sentiments, that the sexual impulse sublimated into love (*amour-passion*).

190

There is something in the morality of Plato which does not really belong to Plato, but which only appears in his philosophy, one might say, in spite of him: namely, Socratism, for which he himself was too noble. 'No one desires to injure himself, hence all evil is done unwittingly. The evil man inflicts injury on himself; he would not do so, however, if he knew that evil is evil. The evil man, therefore, is only evil through error; if one free him from error one will necessarily make him – good.' This mode of reasoning savours of the *populace*, who perceive only the unpleasant consequences of evil-doing, and practically judge that 'it is *stupid* to do wrong'; while they accept 'good' as identical with 'useful and pleasant', without further thought. As regards every system of utilitarianism, one may at once assume that it has the same origin, and follow the scent: one will seldom err. Plato did all he could to interpret something refined and noble into the tenets of his teacher, and above all to interpret himself into them – he, the most daring of all interpreters, who lifted the entire Socrates out of the street, as a popular theme and song, to exhibit him in endless and impossible modifications – namely, in all his own disguises and multiplicities. In jest, and in Homeric language as well, what is the Platonic Socrates, if not –

πρόσθε Πλάτων ὄπιθέν τε Πλάτων μέσση τε Χίμαιρα.

191

The old theological problem of 'Faith' and 'Knowledge', or more plainly, of instinct and reason – the question whether, in respect to the valuation of things, instinct deserves more authority than rationality, which wants to appreciate and act according to motives, according to a 'Why', that is to say, in conformity to purpose and utility – it is always the old moral problem that first appeared in the person of Socrates, and had divided men's minds long before Christianity. Socrates himself, following, of course, the taste of his talent – that of a surpassing dialectician – took first the side of reason; and, in fact, what did he do all his life but laugh at the awkward incapacity of the noble Athenians, who were men of instinct, like all noble men, and could never give satisfactory answers concerning the motives of their actions? In the end, however, though silently and secretly, he laughed also at himself: with his finer conscience and introspection, he found in himself the same difficulty and incapacity. 'But why' – he said to himself – 'should one on that account separate oneself from the instincts? One must set them right, and the reason *also* – one must follow the instincts, but at the same time persuade the reason to support them with good arguments.' This was the real *falseness* of that great and mysterious ironist; he brought his conscience up to the point that he was satisfied with a kind of self-outwitting: in fact, he perceived the irrationality in the moral judgment. Plato, more innocent in such matters, and without the craftiness of the plebeian, wished to prove to himself, at the expenditure of all his strength – the greatest strength a philosopher had ever expended – that reason and instinct lead spontaneously to one goal, to the good, to 'God'; and since Plato, all theologians and philosophers have followed the same path – which means that in matters of morality, instinct (or as Christians call it, 'Faith', or as I call it, 'the herd') has hitherto triumphed. Unless one should make an exception in the case of Descartes, the father of rationalism (and consequently the grandfather of the Revolution), who recognised only the authority of reason: but reason is only a tool, and Descartes was superficial.

192

Whoever has followed the history of a single science, finds in its development a clue to the understanding of the oldest and commonest processes of all 'knowledge and cognisance': there, as here, the premature hypotheses, the fictions, the good stupid will to 'belief', and the lack of distrust and patience are first developed – our senses learn late, and never learn completely, to be subtle, reliable, and cautious organs of knowledge. Our eyes find it easier on a given occasion to produce a picture already often produced, than to seize upon the divergence and novelty of an impression: the latter requires more force, more 'morality'. It is difficult and painful for the ear to listen to anything new; we hear strange music badly. When we hear another language spoken, we involuntarily attempt to form the sounds into words with which we are more familiar and conversant – it was thus, for example, that the Germans modified the spoken word *arcubalista* into *armbrust* (crossbow). Our senses are also hostile and averse to the new; and generally, even in the 'simplest' processes of sensation, the emotions *dominate* – such as fear, love, hatred, and the passive emotion of indolence. As little as a reader nowadays reads all the single words (not to speak of syllables) of a page – he rather takes about five out of every twenty words at random, and 'guesses' the probably appropriate sense to them – just as little do we see a tree correctly and completely in respect to its leaves, branches, colour, and shape; we find it so much easier to fancy the chance of a tree. Even in the midst of the most remarkable experiences, we still do just the same; we fabricate the greater part of the experience, and can hardly be made to contemplate any event, *except* as 'inventors' thereof.

All this goes to prove that from our fundamental nature and from remote ages we have been – *accustomed to lying*. Or, to express it more politely and hypocritically, in short, more pleasantly – one is much more of an artist than one is aware of. In an animated conversation, I often see the face of the person with whom I am speaking so clearly and sharply defined before me, according to the thought he expresses, or which I believe to be evoked in his mind, that the degree of distinctness far exceeds the *strength* of my visual faculty – the delicacy of the play of the muscles and of the expression of the eyes *must* therefore be imagined by me. Probably the person put on quite a different expression, or none at all.

193

Quidquid luce fuit, tenebris agit: but also contrariwise. What we experience in dreams, provided we experience it often, pertains at last just as much to the general belongings of our soul as anything 'actually' experienced; by virtue thereof we are richer or poorer, we have a requirement more or less, and finally, in broad daylight, and even in the brightest moments of our waking life, we are ruled to some extent by the nature of our dreams. Supposing that some one has often flown in his dreams, and that at last, as soon as he dreams, he is conscious of the power and art of flying as his privilege and his peculiarly enviable happiness; such a person, who believes that on the slightest impulse, he can actualise all sorts of curves and angles, who knows the sensation of a certain divine levity, an 'upwards' without effort or constraint, a 'downwards' without descending or lowering – without *trouble*! – how could the man with such dream-experiences and dream-habits fail to find 'happiness' differently coloured and defined, even in his waking hours! How could he fail – to long *differently* for happiness? 'Flight', such as is described by poets, must, when compared with his own 'flying', be far too earthly, muscular, violent, far too 'troublesome' for him.

194

The difference among men does not manifest itself only in the difference of their lists of desirable things – in their regarding different good things as worth striving for, and being disagreed as to the greater or less value, the order of rank, of the commonly recognised desirable things – it manifests itself much more in what they regard as actually *having* and *possessing* a desirable thing. As regards a woman, for instance, the control over her body and her sexual gratification serves as an amply sufficient sign of ownership and possession to the more modest man; another with a more suspicious and ambitious thirst for possession, sees the 'questionableness', the mere apparentness of such ownership, and wishes to have finer tests in order to know especially whether the woman not only gives herself to him, but also gives up for his sake what she has or would like to have – only *then* does he look upon her as 'possessed'. A third, however, has not even here got to the limit of his distrust and his desire for possession: he asks himself whether the woman, when she gives up everything for him, does not perhaps do so for a phantom of him; he wishes first to be thoroughly, indeed, profoundly well known; in order to be loved at all he ventures to let himself be found out. Only then does he feel the beloved one fully in his possession, when she no longer deceives herself about him, when she loves him just as much for the sake of his devilry and concealed insatiability, as for his goodness, patience, and spirituality. One man would like to possess a nation, and he finds all the higher arts of Cagliostro and Catalina suitable for his purpose. Another, with a more refined thirst for possession, says to himself: 'One may not deceive where one desires to possess' – he is irritated and impatient at the idea that a mask of him should rule in the hearts of the people: 'I must, therefore, *make* myself known, and first of all learn to know myself!' Amongst helpful and charitable people, one almost always finds the awkward craftiness which first gets up suitably him who has to be helped, as though, for instance, he should 'merit' help, seek just *their* help, and would show himself deeply grateful, attached, and subservient to them for all help. With these conceits, they take control of the needy as a property, just as in general they are charitable and helpful out of a desire for property. One finds them jealous when they are crossed or forestalled in their charity. Parents involuntarily make something like themselves out of their children – they call that 'education'; no mother doubts at the bottom of her heart that the child she has born is thereby her property, no father hesitates about his right to subject it to *his own* ideas and notions of worth. Indeed, in former times fathers deemed it right to use their discretion concerning the life or death of the newly born (as amongst the ancient Germans). And like the father, so also do the teacher, the class, the priest, and the prince still see in every new individual an unobjectionable opportunity for a new possession. The consequence is . . .

195

The Jews – a people 'born for slavery', as Tacitus and the whole ancient world say of them; 'the chosen people among the nations', as they themselves say and believe – the Jews performed the miracle of the inversion of valuations, by means of which life on earth obtained a new and dangerous charm for a couple of millenniums. Their prophets fused into one the expressions 'rich', 'godless', 'wicked', 'violent', 'sensual', and for the first time coined the word 'world' as a term of reproach. In this inversion of valuations (in which is also included the use of the word 'poor' as synonymous with 'saint' and 'friend') the significance of the Jewish people is to be found; it is with *them* that the *slave-insurrection in morals* commences.

196

It is to be *inferred* that there are countless dark bodies near the sun – such as we shall never see. Amongst ourselves, this is an allegory; and the psychologist of morals reads the whole star-writing merely as an allegorical and symbolic language in which much may be unexpressed.

197

The beast of prey and the man of prey (for instance, Caesar Borgia) are fundamentally misunderstood, 'nature' is misunderstood, so long as one seeks a 'morbidness' in the constitution of these healthiest of all tropical monsters and growths, or even an innate 'hell' in them – as almost all moralists have done hitherto. Does it not seem that there is a hatred of the virgin forest and of the tropics among moralists? And that the 'tropical man' must be discredited at all costs, whether as disease and deterioration of mankind, or as his own hell and self-torture? And why? In favour of the 'temperate zones'? In favour of the temperate men? The 'moral'? The mediocre? – This for the chapter: 'Morals as Timidity'.

198

All the systems of morals which address themselves to individuals with a view to their 'happiness', as it is called – what else are they but suggestions for behaviour adapted to the degree of *danger* from themselves in which the individuals live; recipes for their passions, their good and bad propensities, in so far as such have the Will to Power and would like to play the master; small and great expediencies and elaborations, permeated with the musty odour of old family medicines and old-wife wisdom; all of them grotesque and absurd in their form – because they address themselves to 'all', because they generalize where generalisation is not authorised; all of them speaking unconditionally, and taking themselves unconditionally; all of them flavoured not merely with one grain of salt, but rather endurable only, and sometimes even seductive, when they are over-spiced and begin to smell dangerously, especially of 'the other world'. That is all of little value when estimated intellectually, and is far from being 'science', much less 'wisdom'; but, repeated once more, and three times repeated, it is expediency, expediency, expediency, mixed with stupidity, stupidity, stupidity – whether it be the indifference and statuesque coldness towards the heated folly of the emotions, which the Stoics advised and fostered; or the no-more-laughing and no-more-weeping of Spinoza, the destruction of the emotions by their analysis and vivisection, which he recommended so naïvely; or the lowering of the emotions to an innocent mean at which they may be satisfied, the Aristotelianism of morals; or even morality as the enjoyment of the emotions in a voluntary attenuation and spiritualisation by the symbolism of art, perhaps as music, or as love of God, and of mankind for God's sake – for in religion the passions are once more enfranchised, provided that . . . ; or, finally, even the complaisant and wanton surrender to the emotions, as has been taught by Hafis and Goethe, the bold letting-go of the reins, the spiritual and corporeal *licentia morum* in the exceptional cases of wise old codgers and drunkards, with whom it 'no longer has much danger'. – This also for the chapter: 'Morals as Timidity'.

199

Inasmuch as in all ages, as long as mankind has existed, there have also been human herds (family alliances, communities, tribes, peoples, states, churches), and always a great number who obey in proportion to the small number who command – in view, therefore, of the fact that obedience has been most practised and fostered among mankind hitherto, one may reasonably suppose that, generally speaking, the need there of is now innate in every one, as a kind of *formal conscience* which gives the command: 'Thou shalt unconditionally do something, unconditionally refrain from something'; in short, 'Thou shalt'. This need tries to satisfy itself and to fill its form with a content; according to its strength, impatience, and eagerness, it at once seizes as an omnivorous appetite with little selection, and accepts whatever is shouted into its ear by all sorts of commanders – parents, teachers, laws, class prejudices, or public opinion. The extraordinary limitation of human development, the hesitation, protractedness, frequent retrogression, and turning thereof, is attributable to the fact that the herd-instinct of obedience is transmitted best, and at the cost of the art of command. If one imagine this instinct increasing to its greatest extent, commanders and independent individuals will finally be lacking altogether; or they will suffer inwardly from a bad conscience, and will have to impose a deception on themselves in the first place in order to be able to command: just as if they also were only obeying. This condition of things actually exists in Europe at present – I call it the moral hypocrisy of the commanding class. They know no other way of protecting themselves from their bad conscience than by playing the rôle of executors of older and higher orders (of predecessors, of the constitution, of justice, of the law, or of God himself), or they even justify themselves by maxims from the current opinions of the herd, as 'first servants of their people', or 'instruments of the public weal'. On the other hand, the gregarious European man nowadays assumes an air as if he were the only kind of man that is allowable; he glorifies his qualities, such as public spirit, kindness, deference, industry, temperance, modesty, indulgence, sympathy, by virtue of which he is gentle, endurable, and useful to the herd, as the peculiarly human virtues. In cases, however, where it is believed that the leader and bell-wether cannot be dispensed with, attempt after attempt is made nowadays to replace commanders by the summing together of clever gregarious men: all representative constitutions, for example, are of this origin. In spite of all, what a blessing, what a deliverance from a weight becoming unendurable, is the appearance of an absolute ruler for these gregarious Europeans – of this fact the effect of the appearance of Napoleon was the last great proof: the history of the influence of Napoleon is almost the history of the higher happiness to which the entire century has attained in its worthiest individuals and periods.

200

The man of an age of dissolution which mixes the races with one another, who has the inheritance of a diversified descent in his body – that is to say, contrary, and often not only contrary, instincts and standards of value, which struggle with one another and are seldom at peace – such a man of late culture and broken lights, will, on an average, be a weak man. His fundamental desire is that the war which is *in him* should come to an end; happiness appears to him in the character of a soothing medicine and mode of thought (for instance, Epicurean or Christian); it is above all things the happiness of repose, of undisturbedness, of repletion, of final unity – it is the 'Sabbath of Sabbaths', to use the expression of the holy rhetorician, St Augustine, who was himself such a man. Should, however, the contrariety and conflict in such natures operate as an *additional* incentive and stimulus to life – and if, on the other hand, in addition to their powerful and irreconcilable instincts, they have also inherited and indoctrinated into them a proper mastery and subtlety for carrying on the conflict with themselves (that is to say, the faculty of self-control and self-deception), there then arise those marvellously incomprehensible and inexplicable beings, those enigmatical men, predestined for conquering and circumventing others, the finest examples of which are Alcibiades and Caesar (with whom I should like to associate the *first* of Europeans according to my taste, the Hohenstaufen, Frederick II), and amongst artists, perhaps Leonardo da Vinci. They appear precisely in the same periods when that weaker type, with its longing for repose, comes to the front; the two types are complementary to each other, and spring from the same causes.

201

As long as the utility which determines moral estimates is only gregarious utility, as long as the preservation of the community is only kept in view, and the immoral is sought precisely and exclusively in what seems dangerous to the maintenance of the community, there can be no 'morality of love to one's neighbour'. Granted even that there is already a little constant exercise of consideration, sympathy, fairness, gentleness, and mutual assistance, granted that even in this condition of society all those instincts are already active which are latterly distinguished by honourable names as 'virtues', and eventually almost coincide with the conception 'morality': in that period they do not as yet belong to the domain of moral valuations – they are still *ultra-moral*. A sympathetic action, for instance, is neither called good nor bad, moral nor immoral, in the best period of the Romans; and should it be praised, a sort of resentful disdain is compatible with this praise, even at the best, directly the sympathetic action is compared with one which contributes to the welfare of the whole, to the *res publica*. After all, 'love to our neighbour' is always a secondary matter, partly conventional and arbitrarily manifested in relation to our *fear of our neighbour*. After the fabric of society seems on the whole established and secured against external dangers, it is this fear of our neighbour which again creates new perspectives of moral valuation. Certain strong and dangerous instincts, such as the love of enterprise, foolhardiness, revengefulness, astuteness, rapacity, and love of power, which up till then had not only to be honoured from the point of view of general utility – under other names, of course, than those here given – but had to be fostered and cultivated (because they were perpetually required in the common danger against the common enemies), are now felt in their dangerousness to be doubly strong – when the outlets for them are lacking – and are gradually branded as immoral and given over to calumny. The contrary instincts and inclinations now attain to moral honour; the gregarious instinct gradually draws its conclusions. How much or how little dangerousness to the community or to equality is contained in an opinion, a condition, an emotion, a disposition, or an endowment – that is now the moral perspective; here again fear is the mother of morals. It is by the loftiest and strongest instincts, when they break out passionately and carry the individual far above and beyond the average, and the low level of the gregarious conscience, that the self-reliance of the community is destroyed; its belief in itself, its backbone, as it were, breaks; consequently these very instincts will be most branded and defamed. The lofty independent spirituality, the will to stand alone, and even the cogent reason, are felt to be dangers; everything that elevates the individual above the herd, and is a source of fear to the neighbour, is henceforth called *evil*; the tolerant, unassuming, self-adapting, self-equalising disposition, the *mediocrity* of desires, attains to moral distinction and honour. Finally, under very peaceful circumstances, there is always less opportunity and necessity for training the feelings to severity and rigour; and now every form of severity, even in justice, begins to disturb the conscience; a lofty and rigorous nobleness and self-responsibility almost offends, and awakens distrust; 'the lamb', and still more 'the sheep', wins respect. There is a point of diseased mellowness and effeminacy in the history of society, at which society itself takes the part of him who injures it, the part of the *criminal*, and does so, in fact, seriously and honestly. To punish, appears to it to be somehow unfair – it is certain that the idea of 'punishment' and 'the obligation to punish' are then painful and alarming to people. 'Is it not sufficient if the criminal be rendered *harmless*? Why should we still punish? Punishment itself is terrible!' – with these questions gregarious morality, the morality of fear, draws its ultimate conclusion. If one could at all do away with danger, the cause of fear, one would have done away with this morality at the same time, it would no longer be necessary, it *would not consider itself* any longer necessary! Whoever examines the conscience of the present-day European, will always elicit the same imperative from its thousand moral folds and hidden recesses, the imperative of the timidity of the herd: 'we wish that some time or other there may be *nothing more to fear*!' Some time or other – the will and the way *thereto* is nowadays called 'progress' all over Europe.

202

Let us at once say again what we have already said

a hundred times, for people's ears nowadays are unwilling to hear such truths – *our* truths. We know well enough how offensively it sounds when any one plainly, and without metaphor, counts man amongst the animals; but it will be accounted to us almost a *crime*, that it is precisely in respect to men of 'modern ideas' that we have constantly applied the terms 'herd', 'herd-instincts', and such like expressions. What avail is it? We cannot do otherwise, for it is precisely here that our new insight is. We have found that in all the principal moral judgments Europe has become unanimous, including likewise the countries where European influence prevails: in Europe people evidently *know* what Socrates thought he did not know, and what the famous serpent of old once promised to teach – they 'know' today what is good and evil. It must then sound hard and be distasteful to the ear, when we always insist that that which here thinks it knows, that which here glorifies itself with praise and blame, and calls itself good, is the instinct of the herding human animal: the instinct which has come and is ever coming more and more to the front, to preponderance and supremacy over other instincts, according to the increasing physiological approxim- ation and resemblance of which it is the symptom. *Morality in Europe at present is herding-animal morality*; and therefore, as we understand the matter, only one kind of human morality, beside which, before which, and after which many other moralities, and above all *higher* moralities, are or should be possible. Against such a 'possibility', against such a 'should be', however, this morality defends itself with all its strength; it says obstinately and inexorably: 'I am morality itself and

nothing else is morality!' Indeed, with the help of a
religion which has humoured and flattered the
sublimest desires of the herding-animal, things have
reached such a point that we always find a more
visible expression of this morality even in political and
social arrangements: the *democratic* movement is the
inheritance of the Christian movement. That its
tempo, however, is much too slow and sleepy for the
more impatient ones, for those who are sick and
distracted by the herding-instinct, is indicated by
the increasingly furious howling, and always less disguised teeth-gnashing of the anarchist dogs, who
are now roving through the highways of European
culture. Apparently in opposition to the peacefully
industrious democrats and Revolution-ideologues,
and still more so to the awkward philosophasters and
fraternity-visionaries who call themselves Socialists
and want a 'free society', those are really at one with
them all in their thorough and instinctive hostility to
every form of society other than that of the *autonomous*
herd (to the extent even of repudiating the notions
'master' and 'servant' – *ni dieu ni maître*, says a
socialist formula); at one in their tenacious opposition
to every special claim, every special right and privilege
(this means ultimately opposition to *every* right, for
when all are equal, no one needs 'rights' any longer);
at one in their distrust of punitive justice (as though it
were a violation of the weak, unfair to the *necessary*
consequences of all former society); but equally at one
in their religion of sympathy, in their compassion for
all that feels, lives, and suffers (down to the very
animals, up even to 'God' – the extravagance of
'sympathy for God' belongs to a democratic age);
altogether at one in the cry and impatience of their

sympathy, in their deadly hatred of suffering generally, in their almost feminine incapacity for witnessing it or *allowing* it; at one in their involuntary beglooming and heart-softening, under the spell of which Europe seems to be threatened with a new Buddhism; at one in their belief in the morality of *mutual* sympathy, as though it were morality in itself, the climax, the *attained* climax of mankind, the sole hope of the future, the consolation of the present, the great discharge from all the obligations of the past; altogether at one in their belief in the community as the *deliverer*, in the herd, and therefore in 'themselves'.

203

We, who hold a different belief – we, who regard the democratic movement, not only as a degenerating form of political organisation, but as equivalent to a degenerating, a waning type of man, as involving his mediocrising, and depreciation: where have *we* to fix our hopes? In *new philosophers* – there is no other alternative: in minds strong and original enough to initiate opposite estimates of value, to transvalue and invert 'eternal valuations'; in forerunners, in men of the future, who in the present shall fix the constraints and fasten the knots which will compel millenniums to take *new* paths. To teach man the future of humanity as his *will*, as depending on human will, and to make preparation for vast hazardous enterprises and collective attempts in rearing and educating, in order thereby to put an end to the frightful rule of folly and chance which has hitherto gone by the name of 'history' (the folly of the 'greatest number' is only its last form) – for that purpose a new type of philosophers and commanders will some time or other be needed, at the very idea of which everything that has existed in the way of occult, terrible, and benevolent beings might look pale and dwarfed. The image of such leaders hovers before *our* eyes – is it lawful for me to say it aloud, ye free spirits? The conditions which one would partly have to create and partly utilise for their genesis; the presumptive methods and tests by virtue of which a soul should grow up to such an elevation and power as to feel a *constraint* to these tasks; a transvaluation of values, under the new pressure and hammer of which a conscience should be steeled and a heart transformed into brass, so as to bear the weight of such responsibility; and on the other hand the necessity for such leaders, the dreadful danger that they might be lacking, or miscarry and degenerate – these are *our* real anxieties and glooms, ye know it well, ye free spirits! These are the heavy distant thoughts and storms which sweep across the heaven of *our* life. There are few pains so grievous as to have seen, divined, or experienced how an exceptional man has missed his way and deteriorated; but he who has the rare eye for the universal danger of 'man' himself *deteriorating*, he who like us has recognised the extraordinary fortuitousness which has hitherto played its game in respect to the future of mankind – a game in which neither the hand, nor even a 'finger of God' has participated! – he who divines the fate that is hidden under the idiotic unwariness and blind confidence of 'modern ideas', and still more under the whole of Christo-European morality – suffers from an anguish with which no other is to be compared. He sees at a glance all that could still *be made out of man* through a favourable accumulation and augmentation of human powers and arrangements; he knows with all the knowledge of his conviction how unexhausted man still is for the greatest possibilities, and how often in the past the type man has stood in presence of mysterious decisions and new paths: – he knows still better from his painfulest recollections on what wretched obstacles promising developments of the highest rank have hitherto usually gone to pieces, broken down, sunk, and become contemptible. The *universal degeneracy of mankind* to the level of the 'man of the future' – as idealised by the socialistic fools and shallow-pates – this degeneracy and dwarfing of man to an absolutely gregarious animal (or as they call it, to a man of 'free society'), this brutalising of man into a pigmy with equal rights and claims, is undoubtedly *possible*! He who has thought out this possibility to its ultimate conclusion knows *another* loathing unknown to the rest of mankind – and perhaps also a new *mission*!

SEVENTH CHAPTER

Our Virtues

228

I hope to be forgiven for discovering that all moral philosophy hitherto has been tedious and has belonged to the soporific appliances – and that 'virtue', in my opinion, has been *more* injured by the *tediousness* of its advocates than by anything else; at the same time, however, I would not wish to overlook their general usefulness. It is desirable that as few people as possible should reflect upon morals, and consequently it is *very* desirable that morals should not some day become interesting! But let us not be afraid! Things still remain today as they have always been: I see no one in Europe who has (or *discloses*) an idea of the fact that philosophising concerning morals might be conducted in a dangerous, captious, and ensnaring manner – that *calamity* might be involved therein. Observe, for example, the indefatigable, inevitable English utilitarians: how ponderously and respectably they stalk on, stalk along (a Homeric metaphor expresses it better) in the footsteps of Bentham, just as he had already stalked in the footsteps of the respectable Helvétius! (no, he was not a dangerous man, Helvétius, *ce sénateur Pococurante*, to use an expression of Galiani). No new thought, nothing of the nature of a finer turning or better expression of an old thought, not even a proper history of what has been previously thought on the subject: an *impossible* literature, taking it all in all, unless one knows how to leaven it with some mischief. In effect, the old English vice called *cant*, which is *moral Tartuffism*, has insinuated itself also into these moralists (whom one must certainly read with an eye to their motives if one *must* read them), concealed this time under the new form of the scientific spirit; moreover, there is not absent from them a secret struggle with the pangs of conscience, from which a race of former Puritans must naturally suffer, in all their scientific tinkering with morals. (Is not a moralist the opposite of a Puritan? That is to say, as a thinker who regards morality as questionable, as worthy of interrogation, in short, as a problem? Is moralising not – immoral?) In the end, they all want *English* morality to be recognised as authoritative, inasmuch as mankind, or the 'general utility', or 'the happiness of the greatest number' – no! the happiness of *England*, will be best served thereby. They would like, by all means, to convince themselves that the striving after *English* happiness, I mean after *comfort* and *fashion* (and in the highest instance, a seat in Parliament), is at the same time the true path of virtue; in fact, that in so far as there has been virtue in the world hitherto, it has just consisted in such striving. Not one of those ponderous, conscience-stricken herding-animals (who undertake to advocate the cause of egoism as conducive to the general welfare) wants to have any knowledge or inkling of the facts that the 'general welfare' is no ideal, no goal, no notion that can be at all grasped, but is only a nostrum – that what is fair to one *may not* at all be fair to another, that the require-ment of one morality for all is really a detriment to higher men, in short, that there is a *distinction of rank* between man and man, and consequently between morality and morality. They are an unassuming and fundamentally mediocre species of men, these utilitarian Englishmen, and, as already remarked, in so far as they are tedious, one cannot think highly enough of their utility. One ought even to *encourage* them, as has been partially attempted in the following rhymes:

> Hail, ye worthies, barrow-wheeling,
> 'Longer – better', aye revealing,
> Stiffer aye in head and knee;
> Unenraptured, never jesting,
> Mediocre everlasting,
> *Sans genie et sans esprit!*

229

In these later ages, which may be proud of their humanity, there still remains so much *superstition* of the fear, of the 'cruel wild beast', the mastering of which constitutes the very pride of these humaner ages – that even obvious truths, as if by the agreement of centuries, have long remained unuttered, because they have the appearance of helping the finally slain wild beast back to life again. I perhaps risk something when I allow such a truth to escape; let others capture it again and give it so much 'milk of pious sentiment' to drink, that it will lie down quiet and forgotten, in its old corner. One ought to learn anew about cruelty, and open one's eyes; one ought at last to learn impatience, in order that such immodest gross errors – as, for instance, have been fostered by ancient and modern philosophers with regard to tragedy – may no longer wander about virtuously and boldly. Almost everything that we call 'higher culture' is based upon the spiritualising and intensifying of *cruelty* – this is my thesis; the 'wild beast' has not been slain at all, it lives, it flourishes, it has only been – transfigured. That which constitutes the painful delight of tragedy is cruelty; that which operates agreeably in so-called tragic sympathy, and at the basis even of everything sublime, up to the highest and most delicate thrills of metaphysics, obtains its sweetness solely from the intermingled ingredient of cruelty. What the Roman enjoys in the arena, the Christian in the ecstasies of the cross, the Spaniard at the sight of the faggot and stake, or of the bull-fight, the present-day Japanese who presses his way to the tragedy, the workman of the Parisian suburbs who has a homesickness for bloody revolutions, the Wagnerienne who, with unhinged will, 'undergoes' the performance of 'Tristan and Isolde' – what all these enjoy, and strive with mysterious ardour to drink in, is the philtre of the great Circe 'cruelty'. Here, to be sure, we must put aside entirely the blundering psychology of former times, which could only teach with regard to cruelty that it originated at the sight of the suffering of *others*: there is an abundant, superabundant enjoyment even in one's own suffering, in causing one's own suffering – and wherever man has allowed himself to be persuaded to self-denial in the *religious* sense, or to self-mutilation, as among the Phoenicians and ascetics, or in general, to desensualisation, decarnalisation, and contrition, to Puritanical repentance-spasms, to vivisection of conscience and to Pascal-like *sacrifizio dell' intelletto*, he is secretly allured and impelled forwards by his cruelty, by the dangerous thrill of cruelty *towards himself*. Finally, let us consider that even the seeker of knowledge operates as an artist and glorifier of cruelty, in that he compels his spirit to perceive *against* its own inclination, and often enough against the wishes of his heart – he forces it to say Nay, where he would like to affirm, love, and adore; indeed, every instance of taking a thing profoundly and funda-mentally, is a violation, an intentional injuring of the fundamental will of the spirit, which instinctively aims at appearance and superficiality – even in every desire for knowledge there is a drop of cruelty.

239

The weaker sex has in no previous age been treated with so much respect by men as at present – this belongs to the tendency and fundamental taste of democracy, in the same way as disrespectfulness to old age – what wonder is it that abuse should be immediately made of this respect? They want more, they learn to make claims, the tribute of respect is at last felt to be well-nigh galling; rivalry for rights, indeed actual strife itself, would be preferred: in a word, woman is losing modesty. And let us immediately add that she is also losing taste. She is unlearning to *fear* man: but the woman who 'unlearns to fear' sacrifices her most womanly instincts. That woman should venture forward when the fear-inspiring quality in man – or more definitely, the *man* in man – is no longer either desired or fully developed, is reasonable enough and also intelligible enough; what is more difficult to understand is that precisely thereby – woman deterior-ates. This is what is happening nowadays: let us not deceive ourselves about it! Wherever the industrial spirit has triumphed over the military and aristocratic spirit, woman strives for the economic and legal independence of a clerk: 'woman as clerkess' is inscribed on the portal of the modern society which is in course of formation. While she thus appropriates new rights, aspires to be 'master', and inscribes 'progress' of woman on her flags and banners, the very opposite realises itself with terrible obviousness: *woman retrogrades.* Since the French Revolution the influence of woman in Europe has *declined* in proportion as she has increased her rights and claims; and the 'emancipation of woman', in so far as it is desired and demanded by women themselves (and not only by masculine shallow-pates), thus proves to be a remarkable symptom of the increased weakening and deadening of the most womanly instincts. There is *stupidity* in this movement, an almost masculine stupidity, of which a well-reared woman – who is always a sensible woman – might be heartily ashamed. To lose the intuition as to the ground upon which she can most surely achieve victory; to neglect exercise in the use of her proper weapons; to let-herself-go before man, perhaps even 'to the book', where formerly she kept herself in control and in refined, artful humility; to neutralise with her virtuous audacity man's faith in a *veiled*, fundamentally different ideal in woman, something eternally, necessarily feminine; to emphatically and loquaciously dissuade man from the idea that woman must be preserved, cared for, protected, and indulged, like some delicate, strangely wild, and often pleasant domestic animal; the clumsy and indignant collection of everything of the nature of servitude and bondage which the position of woman in the hitherto existing order of society has entailed and still entails (as though slavery were a counter-argument, and not rather a condition of every higher culture, of every elevation of culture) – what does all this betoken, if not a disintegration of womanly instincts, a de-feminising? Certainly, there are enough of idiotic friends and corrupters of woman amongst the learned asses of the masculine sex, who advise woman to de-feminise herself in this manner, and to imitate all the stupidities from which 'man' in Europe, European 'manliness', suffers – who would like to lower woman to 'general culture', indeed even to newspaper reading and meddling with politics. Here and there they wish even to make women into free spirits and literary workers: as though a woman without piety would not be something perfectly obnoxious or ludicrous to a profound and godless man; almost everywhere her nerves are being ruined by the most morbid and dangerous kind of music (our latest German music), and she is daily being made more hysterical and more incapable of fulfilling her first and last function, that of bearing robust children. They wish to 'cultivate' her in general still more, and intend, as they say, to make the 'weaker sex' *strong* by culture: as if history did not teach in the most emphatic manner that the 'cultivating' of mankind and his weakening – that is to say, the weakening, dissipating, and languishing of his *force of will* – have always kept pace with one another, and that the most powerful and influential women in the world (and lastly, the mother of Napoleon) had just to thank their force of will – and not their schoolmasters! – for their power and ascendency over men. That which inspires respect in woman, and often enough fear also, is her *nature*, which is more 'natural' than that of man, her genuine, carnivora-like, cunning flexibility, her tiger-claws beneath the glove, her *naïveté* in egoism, her untrainableness and innate wildness, the incomprehensibleness, extent, and deviation of her desires and virtues . . . That which, in spite of fear, excites one's sympathy for the dangerous and beautiful cat, 'woman', is that she seems more afflicted, more vulnerable, more necessitous of love and more condemned to disillusionment than any other creature. Fear and sympathy: it is with these feelings that man has hitherto stood in presence of woman, always with one foot already in tragedy, which rends while it delights. What? And all that is now to be at an end? And the *disenchantment* of woman is in progress? The tediousness of woman is slowly evolving? Oh Europe! Europe! We know the horned animal which was always most attractive to thee, from which danger is ever again threatening thee! Thy old fable might once more become 'history' – an immense stupidity might once again overmaster thee and carry thee away! And no God concealed beneath it – no! only an 'idea', a 'modern idea' . . .

What is Noble?

257

Every elevation of the type 'man', has hitherto been the work of an aristocratic society – and so will it always be – a society believing in a long scale of gradations of rank and differences of worth among human beings, and requiring slavery in some form or other. Without the *pathos of distance*, such as grows out of the incarnated difference of classes, out of the constant outlooking and downlooking of the ruling caste on subordinates and instruments, and out of their equally constant practice of obeying and commanding, of keeping down and keeping at a distance – that other more mysterious pathos could never have arisen, the longing for an ever new widening of distance within the soul itself, the formation of ever higher, rarer, further, more extended, more comprehensive states, in short, just the elevation of the type 'man', the continued 'self-surmounting of man', to use a moral formula in a supermoral sense. To be sure, one must not resign oneself to any humanitarian illusions about the history of the origin of an aristocratic society (that is to say, of the preliminary condition for the elevation of the type 'man'): the truth is hard. Let us acknowledge unprejudicedly how every higher civilisation hitherto has *originated*! Men with a still natural nature, barbarians in every terrible sense of the word, men of prey, still in possession of unbroken strength of will and desire for power, threw themselves upon weaker, more moral, more peaceful races (perhaps trading or cattle-rearing communities), or upon old mellow civilisations in which the final vital force was flickering out in brilliant fireworks of wit and depravity. At the commencement, the noble caste was always the barbarian caste: their superiority did not consist first of all in their physical, but in their psychical power – they were more *complete* men (which at every point also implies the same as 'more complete beasts').

258

Corruption – as the indication that anarchy threatens to break out among the instincts, and that the foundation of the emotions, called 'life', is convulsed – is something radically different according to the organisation in which it manifests itself. When, for instance, an aristocracy like that of France at the beginning of the Revolution, flung away its privileges with sublime disgust and sacrificed itself to an excess of its moral sentiments, it was corruption – it was really only the closing act of the corruption which had existed for centuries, by virtue of which that aristocracy had abdicated step by step its lordly prerogatives and lowered itself to a *function* of royalty (in the end even to its decoration and parade-dress). The essential thing, however, in a good and healthy aristocracy is that it should *not* regard itself as a function either of the kingship or the commonwealth, but as the *significance* and highest justification thereof – that it should therefore accept with a good conscience the sacrifice of a legion of individuals, who, *for its sake*, must be suppressed and reduced to imperfect men, to slaves and instruments. Its fundamental belief must be precisely that society is *not* allowed to exist for its own sake, but only as a foundation and scaffolding, by means of which a select class of beings may be able to elevate themselves to their higher duties, and in general to a higher *existence*: like those sun-seeking climbing plants in Java – they are called *Sipo Matador* – which encircle an oak so long and so often with their arms, until at last, high above it, but supported by it, they can unfold their tops in the open light, and exhibit their happiness.

259

To refrain mutually from injury, from violence, from exploitation, and put one's will on a par with that of others: this may result in a certain rough sense in good conduct among individuals when the necessary conditions are given (namely, the actual similarity of the individuals in amount of force and degree of worth, and their co-relation within one organisation). As soon, however, as one wished to take this principle more generally, and if possible even as *the fundamental principle of society*, it would immediately disclose what it really is – namely, a Will to the *denial* of life, a principle of dissolution and decay. Here one must think profoundly to the very basis and resist all sentimental weakness: life itself is *essentially* appropriation, injury, conquest of the strange and weak, suppression, severity, obtrusion of peculiar forms, incorporation, and at the least, putting it mildest, exploitation – but why should one for ever use precisely these words on which for ages a disparaging purpose has been stamped? Even the organisation within which, as was previously supposed, the individuals treat each other as equal – it takes place in every healthy aristocracy –

must itself, if it be a living and not a dying organisation, do all that towards other bodies, which the individuals within it refrain from doing to each other: it will have to be the incarnated Will to Power, it will endeavour to grow, to gain ground, attract to itself and acquire ascendency – not owing to any morality or immorality, but because it *lives*, and because life *is* precisely Will to Power. On no point, however, is the ordinary consciousness of Europeans more unwilling to be corrected than on this matter; people now rave everywhere, even under the guise of science, about coming conditions of society in which 'the exploiting character' is to be absent – that sounds to my ears as if they promised to invent a mode of life which should refrain from all organic functions. 'Exploitation' does not belong to a depraved, or imperfect and primitive society: it belongs to the *nature* of the living being as a primary organic function; it is a consequence of the intrinsic Will to Power, which is precisely the Will to Life. Granting that as a theory this is a novelty – as a reality it is the *fundamental fact* of all history: let us be so far honest towards ourselves!

260

In a tour through the many finer and coarser moralities which have hitherto prevailed or still prevail on the earth, I found certain traits recurring regularly together, and connected with one another, until finally two primary types revealed themselves to me, and a radical distinction was brought to light. There is *master-morality* and *slave-morality* – I would at once add, however, that in all higher and mixed civilisations, there are also attempts at the reconciliation of the two moralities; but one finds still oftener the confusion and mutual misunderstanding of them, indeed, sometimes their close juxtaposition – even in the same man, within one soul. The distinctions of moral values have either originated in a ruling caste, pleasantly conscious of being different from the ruled – or among the ruled class, the slaves and dependents of all sorts. In the first case, when it is the rulers who determine the conception 'good', it is the exalted, proud disposition which is regarded as the distinguishing feature, and that which determines the order of rank. The noble type of man separates from himself the beings in whom the opposite of this exalted, proud disposition displays itself: he despises them. Let it at once be noted that in this first kind of morality the antithesis 'good' and 'bad' means practically the same as 'noble' and 'despicable'; – the antithesis 'good' and '*evil*' is of a different origin. The cowardly, the timid, the insignificant, and those thinking merely of narrow utility are despised; moreover, also, the distrustful, with their constrained glances, the self-abasing, the doglike kind of men who let themselves be abused, the mendicant flatterers, and above all the liars – it is a fundamental belief of all aristocrats that the common people are untruthful. 'We truthful ones' – the nobility in ancient Greece called themselves. It is obvious that everywhere the designations of moral value were at first applied to *men*, and were only derivatively and at a later period applied to *actions*; it is a gross mistake, therefore, when historians of morals start with questions like, 'Why have sympathetic actions been praised?' The noble type of man regards *himself* as a determiner of values; he does not require to be approved of; he passes the judgment: 'What is injurious to me is injurious in itself'; he knows that it is he himself only who confers honour on things; he is a *creator of values*. He honours whatever he recognises in himself: such morality is self-glorification. In the foreground there is the feeling of plenitude, of power, which seeks to overflow, the happiness of high tension, the consciousness of a wealth which would fain give and bestow: the noble man also helps the unfortunate, but not – or scarcely – out of pity, but rather from an impulse generated by the super-abundance of power. The noble man honours in himself the powerful one, him also who has power over himself, who knows how to speak and how to keep silence, who takes pleasure in subjecting himself to severity and hardness, and has reverence for all that is severe and hard. 'Wotan placed a hard heart in my breast', says an old Scandinavian Saga: it is thus rightly expressed from the soul of a proud Viking. Such a type of man is even proud of *not* being made for sympathy; the hero of the Saga therefore adds warningly: 'He who has not a hard heart when young, will never have one.' The noble and brave who think thus are the furthest removed from the morality which sees precisely in sympathy, or in acting for the good of others, or in *désintéressement*, the characteristic of the moral; faith in oneself, pride in oneself, a radical enmity and irony towards 'selflessness', belong as definitely to noble morality, as do a careless scorn and precaution in presence of sympathy and the 'warm heart'. It is the powerful who *know* how to honour, it is their art, their domain for invention. The profound reverence for age and for tradition – all law rests on this double reverence – the belief and prejudice in favour of ancestors and unfavourable to newcomers, is typical in the morality of the powerful; and if, reversely, men of 'modern ideas' believe almost instinctively in 'progress' and 'the future', and are more and more lacking in respect for old age, the ignoble origin of these 'ideas' has complacently betrayed itself thereby. A morality of the ruling class, however, is more especially foreign and irritating to present-day taste in the sternness of its principle that one has duties only to one's equals; that one may act towards beings of a lower rank, towards all that is foreign, just as seems good to one, or 'as the heart desires', and in any case 'beyond good and evil': it is here that sympathy and similar sentiments can have a place. The ability and obligation to exercise prolonged gratitude and prolonged revenge – both only within the circle of equals – artfulness in retaliation, *raffinement* of the idea in friendship, a certain necessity to have enemies (as outlets for the emotions of envy, quarrel-someness, arrogance – in fact, in order to be a good *friend*): all these are typical characteristics of the noble morality, which, as has been pointed out, is not the morality of 'modern ideas', and is therefore at present difficult to realise, and also to unearth and disclose. It is otherwise with the second type of morality, *slave-morality*. Supposing that the abused, the oppressed, the suffering, the unemancipated, the weary, and those uncertain of themselves, should moralise, what will be the common element in their moral estimates? Probably a pessimistic suspicion with regard to the entire situation of man will find expression, perhaps a condemnation of man, together with his situation. The slave has an unfavourable eye for the virtues of the powerful; he has a scepticism and distrust, a *refinement* of distrust of everything 'good' that is there honoured – he would fain persuade himself that the very happiness there is not genuine. On the other hand, *those* qualities which serve to alleviate the existence of sufferers are brought into prominence and flooded with light; it is here that sympathy, the kind, helping hand, the warm heart, patience, diligence, humility, and friendliness attain to honour; for here these are the most useful qualities, and almost the only means of supporting the burden of existence. Slave-morality is essentially the morality of utility. Here is the seat of the origin of the famous antithesis 'good' and 'evil': power and dangerousness are assumed to reside in the evil, a certain dreadfulness, subtlety, and strength, which do not admit of being despised. According to slave-morality, therefore, the 'evil' man arouses fear; according to master-morality, it is precisely the 'good' man who arouses fear and seeks to arouse it, while the bad man is regarded as the despicable being. The contrast attains its maximum when, in accordance with the logical consequences of slave-morality, a shade of depreciation – it may be slight and well-intentioned – at last attaches itself even to the 'good' man of this morality; because, according to the servile mode of thought, the good man must in any case be the *safe* man: he is good-natured, easily deceived, perhaps a little stupid, *unbonhomme*. Everywhere that slave-morality gains the ascendency, language shows a tendency to approximate the significations of the words 'good' and 'stupid'. – A last fundamental difference: the desire for *freedom*, the instinct for happiness and the refinements of the feeling of liberty belong as necessarily to slave-morals and morality, as artifice and enthusiasm in reverence and devotion are the regular symptoms of an aristocratic mode of thinking and estimating. – Hence we can understand without further detail why love *as a passion* – it is our European speciality – must absolutely be of noble origin; as is well known, its invention is due to the Provençal poet-cavaliers, those brilliant ingenious men of the '*gai saber*', to whom Europe owes so much, and almost owes itself.

261

Vanity is one of the things which are perhaps most difficult for a noble man to understand: he will be tempted to deny it, where another kind of man thinks he sees it self-evidently. The problem for him is to represent to his mind beings who seek to arouse a good opinion of themselves which they themselves do not possess – and consequently also do not 'deserve' – and who yet *believe* in this good opinion afterwards. This seems to him on the one hand such bad taste and so self-disrespectful, and on the other hand so grotesquely unreasonable, that he would like to consider vanity an exception, and is doubtful about it in most cases when it is spoken of. He will say, for instance: 'I may be mistaken about my value, and on the other hand may nevertheless demand that my value should be acknowledged by others precisely as I rate it' – that, however, is not vanity (but self-conceit, or, in most cases, that which is called 'humility', and also 'modesty'). Or he will even say: 'For many reasons I can delight in the good opinion of others, perhaps because I love and honour them, and rejoice in all their joys, perhaps also because their good opinion endorses and strengthens my belief in my own good opinion, perhaps because the good opinion of others, even in cases where I do not share it, is useful to me, or gives promise of usefulness: – all this, however, is not vanity.' The man of noble character must first bring it home forcibly to his mind, especially with the aid of history, that, from time immemorial, in all social strata in any way dependent, the ordinary man *was* only that which he *passed for* – not being at all accustomed to fix values, he did not assign even to himself any other value than that which his master assigned to him (it is the peculiar *right of masters* to create values). It may be looked upon as the result of an extraordinary atavism, that the ordinary man, even at present, is still always *waiting* for an opinion about himself, and then instinctively submitting himself to it; yet by no means only to a 'good' opinion, but also to a bad and unjust one (think, for instance, of the greater part of the self-appreciations and self-depreciations which believing women learn from their confessors, and which in general the believing Christian learns from his Church). In fact, conformably to the slow rise of the democratic social order (and its cause, the blending of the blood of masters and slaves), the originally noble and rare impulse of the masters to assign a value to themselves and to 'think well' of themselves, will now be more and more encouraged and extended; but it has at all times an older, ampler, and more radically ingrained propensity opposed to it – and in the phenomenon of 'vanity' this older propensity over-masters the younger. The vain person rejoices over *every* good opinion which he hears about himself (quite apart from the point of view of its usefulness, and equally regardless of its truth or falsehood), just as he suffers from every bad opinion: for he subjects himself to both, he *feels* himself subjected to both, by that oldest instinct of subjection which breaks forth in him. It is 'the slave' in the vain man's blood, the remains of the slave's craftiness – and how much of the 'slave' is still left in woman, for instance! – which seeks to *seduce* to good opinions of itself; it is the slave, too, who immediately afterwards falls prostrate himself before these opinions, as though he had not called them forth. And to repeat it again: vanity is an atavism.

262

A *species* originates, and a type becomes established and strong in the long struggle with essentially constant *unfavourable* conditions. On the other hand, it is known by the experience of breeders that species which receive superabundant nourishment, and in general a surplus of protection and care, immediately tend in the most marked way to develop variations, and are fertile in prodigies and monstrosities (also in monstrous vices). Now look at an aristocratic common-wealth, say an ancient Greek *polis*, or Venice, as a voluntary or involuntary contrivance for the purpose of *rearing* human beings; there are there men beside one another, thrown upon their own resources, who want to make their species prevail, chiefly because they *must* prevail, or else run the terrible danger of being exterminated. The favour, the superabundance, the protection are there lacking under which variations are fostered; the species needs itself as species, as something which, precisely by virtue of its hardness, its uniformity, and simplicity of structure, can in general prevail and make itself permanent in constant struggle with its neighbours, or with rebellious or rebellion-threatening vassals. The most varied experience teaches it what are the qualities to which it principally owes the fact that it still exists, in spite of all gods and men, and has hitherto been victorious: these qualities it calls virtues, and these virtues alone it develops to maturity. It does so with severity, indeed it desires severity; every aristocratic morality is intolerant in the education of youth, in the control of women, in the marriage customs, in the relations of old and young, in the penal laws (which have an eye only for the degenerating): it counts intolerance itself among the virtues, under the name of 'justice'. A type with few, but very marked features, a species of severe, warlike, wisely silent, reserved and reticent men (and as such, with the most delicate sensibility for the charm and *nuances* of society) is thus established, unaffected by the vicissitudes of generations; the constant struggle with uniform *unfavourable* conditions is, as already remarked, the cause of a type becoming stable and hard. Finally, however, a happy state of things results, the enormous tension is relaxed; there are perhaps no more enemies among the neighbouring peoples, and the means of life, even of the enjoyment of life, are present in superabundance. With one stroke the bond and constraint of the old discipline severs: it is no longer regarded as necessary, as a condition of existence – if it would continue, it can only do so as a form of *luxury*, as an archaïsing *taste*. Variations, whether they be deviations (into the higher, finer, and rarer), or deteriorations and monstrosities, appear suddenly on the scene in the greatest exuberance and splendour; the individual dares to be individual and detach himself. At this turning point of history there manifest themselves, side by side, and often mixed and entangled together, a magnificent, manifold, virgin-forest-like up-growth and up-striving, a kind of *tropical tempo* in the rivalry of growth, and an extraordinary decay and self-destruction, owing to the savagely opposing and seemingly exploding egoisms, which strive with one another 'for sun and light', and can no longer assign any limit, restraint, or forbearance for themselves by means of the hitherto existing morality. It was this morality itself which piled up the strength so enormously, which bent the bow in so threatening a manner – it is now 'out of date', it is getting 'out of date'. The dangerous and disquieting point has been reached when the greater, more manifold, more comprehensive life *is lived beyond* the old morality; the 'individual' stands out, and is obliged to have recourse to his own law-giving, his own arts and artifices for self-preservation, self-elevation, and self-deliverance. Nothing but new 'Whys', nothing but new 'Hows', no common formulas any longer, misunderstanding and disregard in league with each other, decay, deterioration, and the loftiest desires frightfully entangled, the genius of the race over-flowing from all the cornucopias of good and bad, a portentous simultaneousness of Spring and Autumn, full of new charms and mysteries peculiar to the fresh, still inexhausted, still unwearied corruption. Danger is again present, the mother of morality, great danger; this time shifted into the individual, into the neighbour and friend, into the street, into their own child, into their own heart, into all the most personal and secret recesses of their desires and volitions. What will the moral philosophers who appear at this time have to preach? They discover, these sharp onlookers and loafers, that the end is quickly approaching, that everything around them decays and produces decay, that nothing will endure until the day after tomorrow, except one species of man, the incurably *mediocre*.

The mediocre alone have a prospect of continuing and propagating themselves – they will be the men of the future, the sole survivors; 'be like them! become mediocre!' is now the only morality which has still a significance, which still obtains a hearing. – But it is difficult to preach this morality of mediocrity! It can never avow what it is and what it desires! It has to talk of moderation and dignity and duty and brotherly love – it will have difficulty *in concealing its irony*!

263

There is an *instinct for rank*, which more than anything else is already the sign of a *high* rank; there is a *delight* in the *nuances* of reverence which leads one to infer noble origin and habits. The refinement, goodness, and loftiness of a soul are put to a perilous test when something passes by that is of the highest rank, but is not yet protected by the awe of authority from obtrusive touches and incivilities: something that goes its way like a living touchstone, undistinguished, undiscovered, and tentative, perhaps voluntarily veiled and disguised. He whose task and practice it is to investigate souls, will avail himself of many varieties of this very art to determine the ultimate value of a soul, the unalterable, innate order of rank to which it belongs: he will test it by its *instinct for reverence*. *Différence engendre haine*: the vulgarity of many a nature spurts up suddenly like dirty water, when any holy vessel, any jewel from closed shrines, any book bearing the marks of great destiny, is brought before it; while on the other hand, there is an involuntary silence, a hesitation of the eye, a cessation of all gestures, by which it is indicated that a soul *feels* the nearness of what is worthiest of respect. The way in which, on the whole, the reverence for the *Bible* has hitherto been maintained in Europe, is perhaps the best example of discipline and refinement of manners which Europe owes to Christianity: books of such profoundness and supreme significance require for their protection an external tyranny of authority, in order to acquire the *period* of thousands of years which is necessary to exhaust and unriddle them. Much has been achieved when the sentiment has been at last instilled into the masses (the shallow-pates and the boobies of every kind) that they are not allowed to touch everything, that there are holy experiences before which they must take off their shoes and keep away the unclean hand – it is almost their highest advance towards humanity. On the contrary, in the so-called cultured classes, the believers in 'modern ideas', nothing is perhaps so repulsive as their lack of shame, the easy insolence of eye and hand with which they touch, taste, and finger everything; and it is possible that even yet there is more *relative* nobility of taste, and more tact for reverence among the people, among the lower classes of the people, especially among peasants, than among the newspaper-reading *demimonde* of intellect, the cultured class.

264

It cannot be effaced from a man's soul what his ancestors have preferably and most constantly done: whether they were perhaps diligent economisers attached to a desk and a cashbox, modest and citizen-like in their desires, modest also in their virtues; or whether they were accustomed to commanding from morning till night, fond of rude pleasures and probably of still ruder duties and responsibilities; or whether, finally, at one time or another, they have sacrificed old privileges of birth and possession, in order to live wholly for their faith – for their 'God' – as men of an inexorable and sensitive conscience, which blushes at every compromise. It is quite impossible for a man *not* to have the qualities and predilections of his parents and ancestors in his constitution, whatever appearances may suggest to the contrary. This is the problem of race. Granted that one knows something of the parents, it is admissible to draw a conclusion about the child: any kind of offensive incontinence, any kind of sordid envy, or of clumsy self-vaunting – the three things which together have constituted the genuine plebeian type in all times – such must pass over to the child, as surely as bad blood; and with the help of the best education and culture one will only succeed in *deceiving* with regard to such heredity. And what else does education and culture try to do nowadays! In our very democratic, or rather, very plebeian age, 'education' and 'culture' *must* be essentially the art of deceiving – deceiving with regard to origin, with regard to the inherited plebeianism in body and soul. An educator who nowadays preached truthfulness above everything else, and called out constantly to his pupils: 'Be true! Be natural! Show yourselves as you are!' – even such a virtuous and sincere ass would learn in a short time to have recourse to the *furca* of Horace, *naturam expellere*: with what results? 'Plebeianism' *usque recurret*.

265

At the risk of displeasing innocent ears, I submit that egoism belongs to the essence of a noble soul, I mean the unalterable belief that to a being such as 'we', other beings must naturally be in subjection, and have to sacrifice themselves. The noble soul accepts the fact of his egoism without question, and also without consciousness of harshness, constraint, or arbitrariness therein, but rather as something that may have its basis in the primary law of things: if he sought a designation for it he would say: 'It is justice itself.' He acknowledges under certain circumstances, which made him hesitate at first, that there are other equally privileged ones; as soon as he has settled this question of rank, he moves among those equals and equally privileged ones with the same assurance, as regards modesty and delicate respect, which he enjoys in intercourse with himself – in accordance with an innate heavenly mechanism which all the stars understand. It is an *additional* instance of his egoism, this artfulness and self-limitation in intercourse with his equals – every star is a similar egoist; he honours *himself* in them, and in the rights which he concedes to them, he has no doubt that the exchange of honours and rights, as the *essence* of all intercourse, belongs also to the natural condition of things. The noble soul gives as he takes, prompted by the passionate and sensitive instinct of requital, which is at the root of his nature. The notion of 'favour' has, *inter pares*, neither significance nor good repute; there may be a sublime way of letting gifts as it were light upon one from above, and of drinking them thirstily like dewdrops; but for those arts and displays the noble soul has no aptitude. His egoism hinders him here: in general, he looks 'aloft' unwillingly – he looks either *forward*, horizontally and deliberately, or downwards – *he knows that he is on a height*.

332

266

'One can only truly esteem him who does not *look out for* himself.' – Goethe to Rath Schlosser.

267

The Chinese have a proverb which mothers even teach their children: '*Siao-sin*' ('make thy heart *small*'). This is the essentially fundamental tendency in latter-day civilisations. I have no doubt that an ancient Greek, also, would first of all remark the self-dwarfing in us Europeans of today – in this respect alone we should immediately be 'distasteful' to him.

268

What, after all, is ignobleness? Words are vocal symbols for ideas; ideas, however, are more or less definite mental symbols for frequently returning and concurring sensations, for groups of sensations. It is not sufficient to use the same words in order to understand one another: we must also employ the same words for the same kind of internal experiences, we must in the end have experiences *in common*. On this account the people of one nation understand one another better than those belonging to different nations, even when they use the same language; or rather, when people have lived long together under similar conditions (of climate, soil, danger, require-ment, toil) there *originates* therefrom an entity that 'understands itself' – namely, a nation. In all souls a like number of frequently recurring experiences have gained the upper hand over those occurring more rarely: about these matters people understand one another rapidly and always more rapidly – the history of language is the history of a process of abbreviation; on the basis of this quick comprehension people always unite closer and closer. The greater the danger, the greater is the need of agreeing quickly and readily about what is necessary; not to misunderstand one another in danger – that is what cannot at all be dispensed with in intercourse. Also in all loves and friendships one has the experience that nothing of the kind continues when the discovery has been made that in using the same words, one of the two parties has feelings, thoughts, intuitions, wishes, or fears different from those of the other. (The fear of the 'eternal misunderstanding': that is the good genius which so often keeps persons of different sexes from too hasty attachments, to which sense and heart prompt them – and *not* some Schopenhauerian 'genius of the species'!). Whichever groups of sensations within a soul awaken most readily, begin to speak, and give the word of command – these decide as to the general order of rank of its values, and determine ultimately its list of desirable things. A man's estimates of value betray something of the *structure* of his soul, and wherein it sees its conditions of life, its intrinsic needs. Supposing now that necessity has from all time drawn together only such men as could express similar requirements and similar experiences by similar symbols, it results on the whole that the easy *communicability* of need, which implies ultimately the undergoing only of average and *common* experiences, must have been the most potent of all the forces which have hitherto operated upon mankind. The more similar, the more ordinary people, have always had and are still having the advantage; the more select, more refined, more unique, and difficultly comprehensible, are liable to stand alone; they succumb to accidents in their isolation, and seldom propagate themselves. One must appeal to immense opposing forces, in order to thwart this natural, all-too-natural *progressus in simile*, the evolution of man to the similar, the ordinary, the average, the gregarious – to the *ignoble*!

290

Every deep thinker is more afraid of being understood than of being misunderstood. The latter perhaps wounds his vanity; but the former wounds his heart, his sympathy, which always says: 'Ah, why would *you* also have as hard a time of it as I have?'

291

Man, a *complex*, mendacious, artful, and inscrutable animal, uncanny to the other animals by his artifice and sagacity, rather than by his strength, has invented the good conscience in order finally to enjoy his soul as something *simple*; and the whole of morality is a long, audacious falsification, by virtue of which generally enjoyment at the sight of the soul becomes possible. From this point of view there is perhaps much more in the conception of 'art' than is generally believed.

292

A philosopher: that is a man who constantly experiences, sees, hears, suspects, hopes, and dreams extraordinary things; who is struck by his own thoughts as if they came from the outside, from above and below, as a species of events and lightning-flashes *peculiar to him*; who is perhaps himself a storm pregnant with new lightnings; a portentous man, around whom there is always rumbling and mumbling

335

and gaping and something uncanny going on. A philosopher: alas, a being who often runs away from himself, is often afraid of himself – but whose curiosity always makes him 'come to himself' again.

293

A man who says: 'I like that, I take it for my own, and mean to guard and protect it from every one'; a man who can conduct a case, carry out a resolution, remain true to an opinion, keep hold of a woman, punish and overthrow insolence; a man who has his indignation and his sword, and to whom the weak, the suffering, the oppressed, and even the animals willingly submit and naturally belong; in short, a man who is a *master* by nature – when such a man has sympathy, well! *that* sympathy has value! But of what account is the sympathy of those who suffer! Or of those even who preach sympathy! There is nowadays, throughout almost the whole of Europe, a sickly irritability and sensitiveness towards pain, and also a repulsive irrestrainableness in complaining, an effeminising, which, with the aid of religion and philosophical nonsense, seeks to deck itself out as something superior – there is a regular cult of suffering. The *unmanliness* of that which is called 'sympathy' by such groups of visionaries, is always, I believe, the first thing that strikes the eye. One must resolutely and radically taboo this latest form of bad taste; and finally I wish people to put the good amulet, '*gai saber*' ('gay science', in ordinary language), on heart and neck, as a protection against it.

294

The Olympian Vice – Despite the philosopher who, as a genuine Englishman, tried to bring laughter into bad repute in all thinking minds – 'Laughing is a bad infirmity of human nature, which every thinking mind will strive to overcome' (Hobbes) – I would even allow myself to rank philosophers according to the quality of their laughing – up to those who are capable of *golden* laughter. And supposing that gods also philosophise, which I am strongly inclined to believe, owing to many reasons – I have no doubt that they also know how to laugh thereby in an over-manlike and new fashion – and at the expense of all serious things! Gods are fond of ridicule: it seems that they cannot refrain from laughter even in holy matters.

295

The genius of the heart, as that great mysterious one possesses it, the tempter-god and born rat-catcher of consciences, whose voice can descend into the nether-world of every soul, who neither speaks a word nor casts a glance in which there may not be some motive or touch of allurement, to whose perfection it pertains that he knows how to appear – not as he is, but in a guise which acts as an *additional* constraint on his followers to press ever closer to him, to follow him more cordially and thoroughly – the genius of the heart, which imposes silence and attention on everything loud and self-conceited, which smooths rough souls and makes them taste a new longing – to lie placid as a mirror, that the deep heavens may be reflected in them – the genius of the heart, which teaches the clumsy and too hasty hand to hesitate, and to grasp more delicately; which scents the hidden and forgotten treasure, the drop of goodness and sweet spirituality under thick dark ice, and is a divining rod for every grain of gold, long buried and imprisoned in mud and sand; the genius of the heart, from contact with which every one goes away richer, not favoured or surprised, not as though gratified and oppressed by the good things of others; but richer in himself, newer than before, broken up, blown upon, and sounded by a thawing wind; more uncertain perhaps, more delicate, more fragile, more bruised, but full of hopes which as yet lack names, full of a new will and current, full of a new ill-will and counter-current . . . but what am I doing, my friends? Of whom am I talking to you? Have I forgotten myself so far that I have not even told you his name? Unless it be that you have already divined of your own accord who this questionable god and spirit is, that wishes to be *praised* in such a manner? For, as it happens to every one who from childhood onward has always been on his legs, and in foreign lands, I have also encountered on my path many strange and dangerous spirits; above all, however, and again and again, the one of whom I have just spoken: in fact, no less a personage than the god *Dionysus*, the great equivocator and tempter, to whom, as you know, I once offered in all secrecy and reverence my first-fruits – the last, as it seems to me, who has offered a *sacrifice* to him, for I have found no one who could understand what I was then doing. In the meantime, however, I have learned much, far too much, about the philosophy of this god, and, as I said, from mouth to mouth – I, the last disciple and initiate of the god Dionysus: and perhaps I might at last begin to give you, my friends, as far as I am allowed, a little taste of this philosophy? In a hushed voice, as is but seemly: for it has to do with much that is secret, new, strange, wonderful, and uncanny. The very fact that Dionysus is a philosopher, and that therefore gods also philosophise, seems to me a novelty which is not unensnaring, and might perhaps arouse suspicion precisely amongst philosophers – amongst you, my friends, there is less to be said against it, except that it comes too late and not at the right time; for, as it has been disclosed to me, you are loth nowadays to believe in god and gods. It may happen, too, that in the frankness of my story I must go further than is agreeable to the strict usages of your ears? Certainly the god in question went further, very much further, in such dialogues, and was always many paces ahead of me . . . Indeed, if it were allowed, I should have to give him, according to human usage, fine ceremonious titles of lustre and merit, I should have to extol his courage as investigator and discoverer, his fearless honesty, truthfulness, and love of wisdom. But such a god does not know what to do with all that respectable trumpery and pomp. 'Keep that,' he would say, 'for thyself and those like thee, and whoever else require it! I – have no reason to cover my nakedness!' One suspects that this kind of divinity and philosopher perhaps lacks shame? He once said: 'Under certain circumstances I love mankind' – and referred thereby to Ariadne, who was present; 'in my opinion man is an agreeable, brave, inventive animal, that has not his equal upon earth, he makes his way even through all labyrinths. I like man, and often think how I can still further advance him, and make him stronger, more evil, and more profound.' 'Stronger, more evil, and more profound?' I asked in horror. 'Yes,' he said again, 'stronger, more evil, and more profound; also more beautiful' – and thereby the tempter-god smiled with his halcyon smile, as though he had just paid some charming compliment. One here sees at once that it is not only shame that this divinity lacks – and in general there are good grounds for supposing that in some things the gods could all of them come to us men for instruction. We men are – more human.

TWILIGHT OF THE IDOLS

'Reason' in Philosophy

You ask me what all idiosyncrasy is in philosophers? . . . For instance their lack of the historical
sense, their hatred even of the idea of Becoming, their
Egyptianism. They imagine that they do honour to a
thing by divorcing it from history *sub specie aeterni* –
when they make a mummy of it. All the ideas that
philosophers have treated for thousands of years, have
been mummied concepts; nothing real has ever come
out of their hands alive. These idolaters of concepts
merely kill and stuff things when they worship – they
threaten the life of everything they adore. Death,
change, age, as well as procreation and growth, are in
their opinion objections – even refutations. That which
is cannot evolve; that which evolves *is* not. Now all of
them believe, and even with desperation, in Being.
But, as they cannot lay hold of it, they try to discover
reasons why this privilege is withheld from them.
'Some merely apparent quality, some deception must
be the cause of our not being able to ascertain the
nature of Being: where is the deceiver?' 'We have him,'
they cry rejoicing, 'it is sensuality!' These senses, *which
in other things are so immoral*, cheat us concerning the
true world. Moral: we must get rid of the deception of
the senses, of Becoming, of history, of falsehood.
History is nothing more than the belief in the senses,
the belief in falsehood. Moral: we must say 'no' to
everything in which the senses believe: to all the rest

of mankind: all that belongs to the 'people'. Let us be philosophers, mummies, monotono-theists, gravediggers! – And above all, away with the *body*, this wretched *idée fixe* of the senses, infected with all the faults of logic that exist, refuted, even impossible, although it be impudent enough to pose as if it were real!

2

With a feeling of great reverence I except the name of *Heraclitus*. If the rest of the philosophic gang rejected the evidences of the senses, because the latter revealed a state of multifariousness and change, he rejected the same evidence because it revealed things as if they possessed permanence and unity. Even Heraclitus did an injustice to the senses. The latter lie neither as the Eleatics believed them to lie, nor as he believed them to lie – they do not lie at all. The interpretations we give to their evidence is what first introduces falsehood into it; for instance the lie of unity, the lie of matter, of substance and of permanence. Reason is the cause of our falsifying the evidence of the senses. In so far as the senses show us a state of Becoming, of transiency, and of change, they do not lie. But in declaring that Being was an empty illusion, Heraclitus will remain eternally right. The 'apparent' world is the only world: the 'true world' is no more than a false adjunct thereto.

3

And what delicate instruments of observation we have in our senses! This human nose, for instance, of which no philosopher has yet spoken with reverence and gratitude, is, for the present, the most finely adjusted instrument at our disposal: it is able to register even such slight changes of movement as the spectroscope would be unable to record. Our scientific triumphs at the present day extend precisely so far as we have accepted the evidence of our senses – as we have sharpened and armed them, and learned to follow them up to the end. What remains is abortive and not yet science – that is to say, metaphysics, theology, psychology, epistemology, or formal science, or a doctrine of symbols, like logic and its applied form mathematics. In all these things reality does not come into consideration at all, even as a problem; just as little as does the question concerning the general value of such a convention of symbols as logic.

4

The other idiosyncrasy of philosophers is no less dangerous; it consists in confusing the last and the first things. They place that which makes its appearance last – unfortunately! for it ought not to appear at all! – the 'highest concept', that is to say, the most general, the emptiest, the last cloudy streak of evaporating reality, at the beginning as the beginning. This again is only their manner of expressing their veneration: the highest thing must not have grown out of the lowest, it must not have grown at all . . . Moral: everything of the first rank must be *causa sui*. To have been derived from something else, is as good as an objection, it sets the value of a thing in question. All superior values are of the first rank, all the highest concepts – that of Being, of the Absolute, of Goodness, of Truth, and of Perfection; all these things cannot have been evolved, they must therefore be *causa sui*. All these things cannot however be unlike one another, they cannot be opposed to one another. Thus they attain to their

345

stupendous concept 'God'. The last, most attenuated and emptiest thing is postulated as the first thing, as the absolute cause, as *ens realissimum*. Fancy humanity having to take the brain diseases of morbid cobweb spinners seriously! And it has paid dearly for having done so.

5

Against this let us set the different manner in which we (– you observe that I am courteous enough to say 'we') conceive the problem of the error and deceptiveness of things. Formerly people regarded change and evolution in general as the proof of appearance, as a sign of the fact that something must be there that leads us astray. Today, on the other hand, we realise that precisely as far as the rational bias forces us to postulate unity, identity, permanence, substance, cause, materiality and being, we are in a measure involved in error, driven necessarily to error; however certain we may feel, as the result of a strict examination of the matter, that the error lies here. It is just the same here as with the motion of the sun: in its case it was our eyes that were wrong; in the matter of the concepts above mentioned it is our language itself that pleads most constantly in their favour. In its origin language belongs to an age of the most rudimentary forms of psychology: if we try to conceive of the first conditions of the metaphysics of language, *i.e.*, in plain English, of reason, we immediately find ourselves in the midst of a system of fetishism. For here, the doer and his deed are seen in all circumstances, will is believed in as a cause in general; the ego is taken for granted, the ego as Being, and as substance, and the faith in the ego as substance is projected into all things – in this way, alone, the concept 'thing' is created. Being is thought into and insinuated into everything as cause; from the concept 'ego', alone, can the concept 'Being' proceed. At the beginning stands the tremendously fatal error of supposing the will to be something that actuates – a faculty. Now we know that it is only a word. Very much later, in a world a thousand times more enlightened, the assurance, the subjective certitude, in the handling of the categories of reason came into the minds of philosophers as a surprise. They concluded that these categories could not be derived from experience – on the contrary, the whole of experience rather contradicts them. *Whence do they come therefore?* In India, as in Greece, the same mistake was made: 'we must already once have lived in a higher world (– instead of in a much lower one, which would have been the truth!), we must have been divine, for we possess reason!' . . . Nothing indeed has exercised a more simple power of persuasion hitherto than the error of Being, as it was formulated by the Eleatics for instance: in its favour are every word and every sentence that we utter! Even the opponents of the Eleatics succumbed to the seductive powers of their concept of Being. Among others there was Democritus in his discovery of the atom. 'Reason' in language! – oh what a deceptive old witch it has been! I fear we shall never be rid of God, so long as we still believe in grammar.

6

People will feel grateful to me if I condense a point of view, which is at once so important and so new, into four theses: by this means I shall facilitate comprehension, and shall likewise challenge contradiction.

Proposition One. The reasons upon which the apparent nature of 'this' world have been based, rather tend to prove its reality – any other kind of reality defies demonstration.

Proposition Two. The characteristics with which man has endowed the 'true Being' of things, are the characteristics of non-Being, of *nonentity*. The 'true world' has been erected upon a contradiction of the real world; and it is indeed an apparent world, seeing that it is merely a *moralo-optical* delusion.

Proposition Three. There is no sense in spinning yarns about another world, provided, of course, that we do not possess a mighty instinct which urges us to slander, belittle, and cast suspicion upon this life: in this case we should be avenging ourselves on this life with the phantasmagoria of 'another', of a 'better' life.

Proposition Four. To divide the world into a 'true' and an 'apparent' world, whether after the manner of Christianity or of Kant (after all a Christian in disguise), is only a sign of decadence – a symptom of *degenerating* life. The fact that the artist esteems the appearance of a thing higher than reality, is no objection to this statement. For 'appearance' signifies once more reality here, but in a selected, strengthened and corrected form. The tragic artist is no pessimist – he says *Yea* to everything questionable and terrible, he is Dionysian.

Morality as the Enemy of Nature

I

There is a time when all passions are simply fatal in their action, when they wreck their victims with the weight of their folly – and there is a later period, a very much later period, when they marry with the spirit, when they 'spiritualise' themselves. Formerly, owing to the stupidity inherent in passion, men waged war against passion itself: men pledged themselves to annihilate it – all ancient moral-mongers were unanimous on this point, '*il faut tuer les passions.*' The most famous formula for this stands in the New Testament, in that Sermon on the Mount, where, let it be said incidentally, things are by no means regarded *from a height*. It is said there, for instance, with an application to sexuality: 'if thy eye offend thee, pluck it out': fortunately no Christian acts in obedience to this precept. To annihilate the passions and desires, simply on account of their stupidity, and to obviate the unpleasant consequences of their stupidity, seems to us today merely an aggravated form of stupidity. We no longer admire those dentists who extract teeth simply in order that they may not ache again. On the other hand, it will be admitted with some reason, that on the soil from which Christianity grew, the idea of the 'spiritualisation of passion' could not possibly have been conceived. The early Church, as everyone knows, certainly did wage war against the 'intelligent', in favour of the 'poor in spirit'. In these circumstances how could the passions be combated intelligently? The Church combats passion by means of excision of all kinds: its practice, its 'remedy', is *castration*. It never inquires 'how can a desire be spiritualised, beautified, deified?' In all ages it has laid the weight of discipline in the process of extirpation (the extirpation of sensuality, pride, lust of dominion, lust of property, and revenge). But to attack the passions at their roots, means attacking life itself at its source: the method of the Church is hostile to life.

2

The same means, castration and extirpation, are instinctively chosen for waging war against a passion, by those who are too weak of will, too degenerate, to impose some sort of moderation upon it; by those natures who, to speak in metaphor (– and without metaphor), need *la Trappe*, or some kind of ultimatum of war, a *gulf* set between themselves and a passion. Only degenerates find radical methods indispensable: weakness of will, or more strictly speaking, the inability not to react to a stimulus, is in itself simply another form of degeneracy. Radical and mortal hostility to sensuality, remains a suspicious symptom: it justifies one in being suspicious of the general state of one who goes to such extremes. Moreover, that hostility and hatred reach their height only when such natures no longer possess enough strength of character to adopt the radical remedy, to renounce their inner 'Satan'. Look at the whole history of the priests, the philosophers, and the artists as well: the most poisonous diatribes against the senses have not been said by the impotent, nor by the ascetics, but by those impossible ascetics, by those who found it necessary to be ascetics.

3

The spiritualisation of sensuality is called *love*: it is a great triumph over Christianity. Another triumph is our spiritualisation of hostility. It consists in the fact that we are beginning to realise very profoundly the value of having enemies: in short that with them we are forced to do and to conclude precisely the reverse of what we previously did and concluded. In all ages the Church wished to annihilate its enemies: we, the immoralists and Antichrists, see our advantage in the survival of the Church. Even in political life, hostility has now become more spiritual – much more cautious, much more thoughtful, and much more moderate. Almost every party sees its self-preservative interests in preventing the Opposition from going to pieces; and the same applies to politics on a grand scale. A new creation, more particularly, like the new Empire, has more need of enemies than friends: only as a contrast does it begin to feel necessary, only as a contrast does it *become* necessary. And we behave in precisely the same way to the 'inner enemy': in this quarter too we have spiritualised enmity, in this quarter too we have understood its value. A man is productive only in so far as he is rich in contrasted instincts; he can remain young only on condition that his soul does not begin to take things easy and to yearn for peace. Nothing has grown more alien to us than that old desire – the 'peace of the soul', which is the aim of Christianity. Nothing could make us less envious than the moral cow and the plump happiness of a clean conscience. The man who has renounced war has renounced a grand life. In many cases, of course, 'peace of the soul' is merely a misunderstanding – it is something *very different* which has failed to find a more honest name for itself. Without either circumlocution or prejudice I will suggest a few cases. 'Peace of the soul' may for instance be the sweet effulgence of rich animality in the realm of morality (or religion). Or the first presage of weariness, the first shadow that evening, every kind of evening, is wont to cast. Or a sign that the air is moist, and that winds are blowing up from the south. Or unconscious gratitude for a good digestion (sometimes called 'brotherly love'). Or the serenity of the convalescent, on whose lips all things have a new taste, and who bides his time. Or the condition which follows upon a thorough gratification of our strongest passion, the well-being of unaccustomed satiety. Or the senility of our will, of our desires, and of our vices. Or laziness, coaxed by vanity into togging itself out in a moral garb. Or the ending of a state of long suspense and of agonising uncertainty, by a state of certainty, of even terrible certainty. Or the expression of ripeness and mastery in the midst of a task, of a creative work, of a production, of a thing willed, the calm breathing that denotes that 'freedom of will' has been attained. Who knows? Maybe *The Twilight of the Idols* is only a sort of 'peace of the soul'.

4

I will formulate a principle. All naturalism in morality (that is to say, every sound morality) is ruled by a life instinct – any one of the laws of life is fulfilled by the definite canon 'thou shalt', 'thou shalt not', and any sort of obstacle or hostile element in the road of life is thus cleared away. Conversely, the morality which is antagonistic to nature – that is to say, almost every

morality that has been taught, honoured and preached
hitherto, is directed precisely against the life-instincts
– it is a condemnation, now secret, now blatant and
impudent, of these very instincts. Inasmuch as it says
'God sees into the heart of man,' it says Nay to the
profoundest and most superior desires of life and takes
God as the enemy of life. The saint in whom God is
well pleased, is the ideal eunuch. Life terminates
where the 'Kingdom of God' begins.

5

Admitting that you have understood the villainy of
such a mutiny against life as that which has become
almost sacrosanct in Christian morality, you have
fortunately understood something besides; and that is
the futility, the fictitiousness, the absurdity and the
falseness of such a mutiny. For the condemnation of
life by a living creature is after all but the symptom of
a definite kind of life: the question as to whether the
condemnation is justified or the reverse is not even
raised. In order even to approach the problem of the
value of life, a man would need to be placed outside
life, and moreover know it as well as one, as many, as
all in fact, who have lived it. These are reasons enough
to prove to us that this problem is an inaccessible one
to us. When we speak of values, we speak under the
inspiration, and through the optics of life: life itself
urges us to determine values: life itself values through
us when we determine values. From which it follows
that even that morality which is antagonistic to life,
and which conceives God as the opposite and the
condemnation of life, is only a valuation of life – of
what life? Of what kind of life? But I have already
answered this question: it is the valuation of declining,

of enfeebled, of exhausted and of condemned life. Morality, as it has been understood hitherto – as it was finally formulated by Schopenhauer in the words 'The Denial of the Will to Life,' is the instinct of degeneration itself, which converts itself into an imperative: it says: 'Perish!' It is the death sentence of men who are already doomed.

6

Let us at last consider how exceedingly simple it is on our part to say: 'Man should be thus and thus!' Reality shows us a marvellous wealth of types, and a luxuriant variety of forms and changes: and yet the first wretch of a moral loafer that comes along cries 'No! Man should be different!' He even knows what man should be like, does this sanctimonious prig: he draws his own face on the wall and declares: '*ecce homo!*' But even when the moralist addresses himself only to the individual and says 'thus and thus shouldst thou be!' he still makes an ass of himself. The individual in his past and future is a piece of fate, one law the more, one necessity the more for all that is to come and is to be. To say to him 'change thyself', is tantamount to saying that everything should change, even backwards as well. Truly these have been consistent moralists, they wished man to be different, *i.e.* virtuous; they wished him to be after their own image – that is to say sanctimonious humbugs. And to this end they denied the world! No slight form of insanity! No modest form of immodesty! Morality, in so far it condemns *per se*, and *not* out of any aim, consideration or motive of life, is a specific error, for which no one should feel any mercy, a degenerate idiosyncrasy, that has done an unutterable amount of harm. We others, we immoralists, on the contrary, have opened our hearts wide to all kinds of comprehension, understanding and approbation. We do not deny readily, we glory in saying yea to things. Our eyes have opened ever wider and wider to that economy which still employs and knows how to use to its own advantage all that which the sacred craziness of priests and the morbid reason in priests, rejects; to that economy in the law of life which draws its own advantage even out of the repulsive race of bigots, the priests and the virtuous – what advantage? But we ourselves, we immoralists, are the reply to this question.

The Four Great Errors

I

The error of the confusion of cause and effect – There is no more dangerous error than to confound the effect with the cause: I call this error the intrinsic perversion of reason. Nevertheless this error is one of the most ancient and most recent habits of mankind. In one part of the world it has even been canonised; and it bears the name of 'Religion' and 'Morality'. Every postulate formulated by religion and morality contains it. Priests and the promulgators of moral laws are the promoters of this perversion of reason. Let me give you an example. Everybody knows the book of the famous Cornaro, in which he recommends his slender diet as the recipe for a long, happy and also virtuous life. Few books have been so widely read, and to this day many thousand copies of it are still printed annually in England. I do not doubt that there is scarcely a single book (the Bible of course excepted) that has worked more mischief, shortened more lives, than this well-meant curiosity. The reason of this is the confusion of effect and cause. This worthy Italian saw the cause of his long life in his diet: whereas the prerequisites of long life, which are exceptional slowness of molecular change, and a low rate of expenditure in energy, were the cause of his meagre diet. He was not at liberty to eat a small or a great amount. His frugality was not the result of free choice, he would have been ill had he eaten more. He who does not happen to be a carp, however, is not only wise to eat well, but is also compelled to do so. A scholar of the present day, with his rapid consumption of nervous energy, would soon go to the dogs on Cornaro's diet. *Crede experto.*

2

The most general principle lying at the root of every religion and morality, is this: 'Do this and that and avoid this and that, and thou wilt be happy. Otherwise – ' Every morality and every religion is this Imperative – I call it the great original sin of reason – *immortal unreason*. In my mouth this principle is converted into its opposite – first example of my 'Transvaluation of all Values': a well-constituted man, a man who is one of 'Nature's lucky strokes', *must* perform certain actions and instinctively fear other actions; he introduces the element of order, of which he is the physiological manifestation, into his relations with men and things. In a formula: his virtue is the consequence of his good constitution. Longevity and plentiful offspring are not the reward of virtue, virtue itself is on the contrary that retardation of the metabolic process which, among other things, results in a long life and in plentiful offspring, in short in *Cornarism*. The Church and morality say: 'A race, a people perish through vice and luxury.' My reinstated reason says: when a people are going to the dogs, when they are degenerating physiologically, vice and luxury (that is to say, the need of ever stronger and more frequent stimuli such as all exhausted natures are acquainted with) are bound to result. Such and such a young man grows pale and withered prematurely. His friends say this or that illness is the cause of it. I say: the fact that he became ill, the fact that he did not resist illness, was in itself already the outcome of impoverished life, of hereditary exhaustion. The newspaper reader says: such and such a party by committing such an error will meet its death. My superior politics say: a party that can make such mistakes, is in its last agony – it no longer possesses any certainty of instinct. Every mistake is in every sense the sequel to degeneration of the instincts, to disintegration of the will. This is almost the definition of evil, Everything valuable is instinct – and consequently easy, necessary, free. Exertion is an objection, the god is characteristically different from the hero (in my language: light feet are the first attribute of divinity).

3

The error of false causality – In all ages men have believed that they knew what a cause was: but whence did we derive this knowledge, or more accurately, this faith in the fact that we know? Out of the realm of the famous 'inner facts of consciousness', not one of which has yet proved itself to be a fact. We believed ourselves to be causes even in the action of the will; we thought that in this matter at least we caught causality red-handed. No one doubted that all the *antecedentia* of an action were to be sought in consciousness, and could be discovered there – as 'motive' – if only they were sought. Otherwise we should not be free to perform them, we should not have been responsible for them. Finally who would have questioned that a thought is caused? That the ego causes the thought? Of these three 'facts of inner consciousness' by means of which causality seemed to be guaranteed, the first and most convincing is that of the will as cause; the conception of consciousness ('spirit') as a cause, and subsequently that of the ego (the 'subject') as a cause, were merely born afterwards, once the causality of the will stood established as 'given', as a fact of experience. Meanwhile we have come to our senses. Today we no longer believe a word of all this. The 'inner world' is full of phantoms and will-o'-the-wisps: the will is one of these. The will no longer actuates, consequently it no longer explains anything – all it does is to accompany processes; it may even be absent. The so-called 'motive' is another error. It is merely a ripple on the surface of consciousness, a side issue of the action, which is much more likely to conceal than to reveal the *antecedentia* of the latter. And as for the ego! It has become legendary, fictional, a play upon words: it has ceased utterly and completely from thinking, feeling, and willing! What is the result of it all? There are no such things as spiritual causes. The whole of popular experience on this subject went to the devil! That is the result of it all. For we had blissfully abused that experience, we had built the world upon it as a world of causes, as a world of will, as a world of spirit. The most antiquated and most traditional psychology has been at work here, it has done nothing else: all phenomena were deeds in the light of this psychology, and all deeds were the result of will; according to it the world was a complex mechanism of agents, an agent (a 'subject') lay at the root of all things. Man projected his three 'inner facts of consciousness', the will, the spirit, and the ego in which he believed most firmly, outside himself. He first deduced the concept Being out of the concept Ego, he supposed 'things' to exist as he did himself, according to his notion of the ego as cause. Was it to be wondered at that later on he always found in things only that which he had laid in them? The thing itself, I repeat, the concept 'thing' was merely a reflex of the belief in the ego as cause. And even your atom, my dear good Mechanists and Physicists, what an amount of error, of rudimentary psychology still adheres to it! Not to speak of the 'thing-in-itself', of the *horrendum pudendum* of the metaphysicians! The error of spirit regarded as a cause, confounded with reality! And made the measure of reality! And called *God*!

4

The error of imaginary causes – Starting out from dreamland, we find that to any definite sensation, like that produced by a distant cannon shot for instance, we are wont to ascribe a cause after the fact (very often quite a little romance in which the dreamer himself is, of course, the hero). Meanwhile the sensation becomes protracted like a sort of continuous echo, until, as it were, the instinct of causality allows it to come to the front rank, no longer however as a chance occurrence, but as a thing which has some meaning. The cannon shot presents itself in a *causal* manner, by means of an apparent reversal in the order of time. That which occurs last, the motivation, is experienced first, often with a hundred details which flash past like lightning, and the shot is the *result*. What has happened? The ideas suggested by a particular state of our senses, are misinterpreted as the cause of that state. As a matter of fact we proceed in precisely the same manner when we are awake. The greater number of our general sensations – every kind of obstacle, pressure, tension, explosion in the interplay of the organs, and more particularly the condition of the *nervus sympathicus* – stimulate our instinct of causality: we will have a reason which will account for our feeling thus or thus – for feeling ill or well. We are never satisfied by merely ascertaining the fact that we feel thus or thus: we admit this fact – we become conscious of it – only when we have attributed it to some kind of motivation. Memory, which, in such circumstances unconsciously becomes active, adduces former conditions of a like kind, together with the causal interpretations with which they are associated – but not their real cause. The belief that the ideas, the accompanying processes of consciousness, have been the causes, is certainly produced by the agency of memory. And in this way we become *accustomed* to a particular interpretation of causes which, truth to tell, actually hinders and even utterly prevents the investigation of the proper cause.

5

The psychological explanation of the above fact – To trace something unfamiliar back to something familiar, is at once a relief, a comfort and a satisfaction, while it also produces a feeling of power. The unfamiliar involves danger, anxiety and care – the fundamental instinct is to get rid of these painful circumstances. First principle: any explanation is better than none at all. Since, at bottom, it is only a question of shaking one's self free from certain oppressive ideas, the means employed to this end are not selected with overmuch punctiliousness: the first idea by means of which the unfamiliar is revealed as familiar, produces a feeling of such comfort that it is 'held to be true'. The proof of happiness ('of power') as the criterion of truth. The instinct of causality is therefore conditioned and stimulated by the feeling of fear. Whenever possible, the question 'why?' should not only educe the cause as cause, but rather a certain kind of cause – a comforting, liberating and reassuring cause. The first result of this need is that something known or already experienced, and recorded in the memory, is posited as the cause. The new factor, that which has not been experienced and which is unfamiliar, is excluded from the sphere of causes. Not only do we try to find a certain kind of explanation as the cause, but those kinds of explanations are selected and preferred which dissipate most rapidly the sensation of strangeness, novelty and unfamiliarity – in fact the most ordinary explanations. And the result is that a certain manner of postulating causes tends to predominate ever more and more, becomes concentrated into a system, and finally reigns supreme, to the complete exclusion of all other causes and explanations. The banker thinks immediately of business, the Christian of 'sin', and the girl of her love affair.

6

The whole domain of morality and religion may be classified under the Rubric 'Imaginary Causes'. The 'explanation' of general unpleasant sensations. These sensations are dependent upon certain creatures who are hostile to us (evil spirits: the most famous example of this – the mistaking of hysterical women for witches). These sensations are dependent upon actions which are reprehensible (the feeling of 'sin', 'sinfulness' is a manner of accounting for a certain physiological disorder – people always find reasons for being dissatisfied with themselves). These sensations depend upon punishment, upon compensation for something which we ought not to have done, which we ought not to have been (this idea was generalised in a more impudent form by Schopenhauer, into that principle in which morality appears in its real colours – that is to say, as a veritable poisoner and slanderer of life: 'all great suffering, whether mental or physical, reveals what we deserve: for it could not visit us if we did not deserve it' – *The World as Will and Idea*, vol. 2, p. 666). These sensations are the outcome of ill-considered actions, having evil consequences (– the passions, the senses, postulated as causes, as guilty. By means of other calamities distressing physiological conditions are interpreted as 'merited'). The 'explanation' of pleasant sensations. These sensations are dependent upon a trust in God. They may depend upon our consciousness of having done one or two good actions (a so-called 'good conscience' is a physiological condition, which may be the outcome of good digestion). They may depend upon the happy issue of certain undertakings (an ingenuous mistake: the happy issue of an undertaking certainly does not give a hypochondriac or a Pascal any general sensation of pleasure). They may depend upon faith, love and hope – the Christian virtues. As a matter of fact all these pretended explanations are but the results of certain states, and as it were translations of feelings of pleasure and pain into a false dialect: a man is in a condition of hopefulness because the dominant physiological sensation of his being is again one of strength and wealth; he trusts in God because the feeling of abundance and power gives him a peaceful state of mind. Morality and religion are completely and utterly parts of the psychology of error: in every particular case cause and effect are confounded; as truth is confounded with the effect of that which is believed to be true; or a certain state of consciousness is confounded with the chain of causes which brought it about.

7

The error of free-will – At present we no longer have any mercy upon the concept 'free-will': we know only too well what it is – the most egregious theological trick that has ever existed for the purpose of making mankind 'responsible' in a theological manner – that is to say, to make mankind dependent upon theologians. I will now explain to you only the psychology of the whole process of inculcating the sense of responsibility. Wherever men try to trace responsibility home to anyone, it is the instinct of punishment and of the desire to judge which is active. Becoming is robbed of its innocence when any particular condition of things is traced to a will, to intentions and to responsible actions. The doctrine of the will was invented principally for the purpose of punishment – that is to say, with the intention of tracing guilt. The whole of ancient psychology, or the psychology of the will, is the outcome of the fact that its originators, who were the priests at the head of ancient communities, wanted to create for themselves a right to administer punishments – or the right for God to do so. Men were thought of as 'free' in order that they might be judged and punished – in order that they might be held guilty: consequently every action had to be regarded as voluntary, and the origin of every action had to be imagined as lying in consciousness (– in this way the most fundamentally

THE FOUR GREAT ERRORS

fraudulent character of psychology was established as
the very principle of psychology itself). Now that we
have entered upon the opposite movement, now that
we immoralists are trying with all our power to
eliminate the concepts of guilt and punishment from
the world once more, and to cleanse psychology,
history, nature and all social institutions and customs
of all signs of those two concepts, we recognise no
more radical opponents than the theologians, who
with their notion of 'a moral order of things', still
continue to pollute the innocence of Becoming with
punishment and guilt. Christianity is the metaphysics
of the hangman.

8

What then, alone, can our teaching be? That no one
gives man his qualities, neither God, society, his
parents, his ancestors, nor himself (– this nonsensical
idea which is at last refuted here, was taught as
'intelligible freedom' by Kant, and perhaps even as
early as Plato himself). No one is responsible for the
fact that he exists at all, that he is constituted as he is,
and that he happens to be in certain circumstances
and in a particular environment. The fatality of his
being cannot be divorced from the fatality of all that
which has been and will be. This is not the result of an
individual intention, of a will, of an aim, there is no
attempt at attaining to any 'ideal man', or 'ideal
happiness' or 'ideal morality' with him – it is absurd to
wish him to be careering towards some sort of
purpose. *We* invented the concept 'purpose'; in reality
purpose is altogether lacking. One is necessary, one
is a piece of fate, one belongs to the whole, one is in the
whole – there is nothing that could judge, measure,

365

compare, and condemn our existence, for that would mean judging, measuring, comparing and condemning the whole. *But there is nothing outside the whole!* The fact that no one shall any longer be made responsible, that the nature of existence may not be traced to a *causa prima*, that the world is an entity neither as a sensorium nor as a spirit – *this alone is the great deliverance* – thus alone is the innocence of Becoming restored . . . The concept 'God' has been the greatest objection to existence hitherto . . . We deny God, we deny responsibility in God: thus alone do we save the world.

The 'Improvers' of Mankind

You are aware of my demand upon philosophers, that they should take up a stand Beyond Good and Evil – that they should have the illusion of the moral judgment beneath them. This demand is the result of a point of view which I was the first to formulate: *that there are no such things as moral facts.* Moral judgment has this in common with the religious one, that it believes in realities which are not real. Morality is only an interpretation of certain phenomena: or, more strictly speaking, a misinterpretation of them. Moral judgment, like the religious one, belongs to a stage of ignorance in which even the concept of reality, the distinction between real and imagined things, is still lacking: so that truth, at such a stage, is applied to a host of things which today we call 'imaginary'. That is why the moral judgment must never be taken quite literally: as such it is sheer nonsense. As a sign code, however, it is invaluable: to him at least who knows, it reveals the most valuable facts concerning cultures and inner conditions, which did not know enough to 'understand' themselves. Morality is merely a sign-language, simply symptomatology: one must already know what it is all about in order to turn it to any use.

2

Let me give you one example, quite provisionally. In all ages there have been people who wished to 'improve' mankind: this above all is what was called morality. But the most different tendencies are concealed beneath the same word. Both the taming of the beast man, and the rearing of a particular type of man, have been called 'improvement': these zoological *termini*, alone, represent real things – real things of which the typical 'improver', the priest, naturally knows nothing, and will know nothing. To call the taming of an animal 'improving' it, sounds to our ears almost like a joke. He who knows what goes on in menageries, doubts very much whether an animal is improved in such places. It is certainly weakened, it is made less dangerous, and by means of the depressing influence of fear, pain, wounds, and hunger, it is converted into a sick animal. And the same holds good of the tamed man whom the priest has 'improved'. In the early years of the Middle Ages, during which the Church was most distinctly and above all a menagerie, the most beautiful examples of the 'blond beast' were hunted down in all directions – the noble Germans, for instance, were 'improved'. But what did this 'improved' German, who had been lured to the monastery look like after the process? He looked like a caricature of man, like an abortion: he had become a 'sinner', he was caged up, he had been imprisoned behind a host of appalling notions. He now lay there, sick, wretched, malevolent even toward himself: full of hate for the instincts of life, full of suspicion in regard to all that is still strong and happy. In short a 'Christian'. In physiological terms: in a fight with an animal, the only way of making it weak may be to make it sick. The Church understood this: it ruined man, it made him weak – but it laid claim to having 'improved' him.

3

Now let us consider the other case which is called morality, the case of the rearing of a particular race and species. The most magnificent example of this is offered by Indian morality, and is sanctioned religiously as the 'Law of Manu'. In this book the task is set of rearing no less than four races at once: a priestly race, a warrior race, a merchant and agricultural race, and finally a race of servants – the Sudras. It is quite obvious that we are no longer in a circus watching tamers of wild animals in this book. To have conceived even the plan of such a breeding scheme, presupposes the existence of a man who is a hundred times milder and more reasonable than the mere lion-tamer. One breathes more freely, after stepping out of the Christian atmosphere of hospitals and prisons, into this more salubrious, loftier and more spacious world. What a wretched thing the New Testament is beside Manu, what an evil odour hangs around it! But even this organisation found it necessary to be terrible – not this time in a struggle with the animal-man, but with his opposite, the non-caste man, the hotchpotch man, the Chandala. And once again it had no other means of making him weak and harmless, than by making him sick – it was the struggle with the greatest 'number'. Nothing perhaps is more offensive to our feelings than these measures of security on the part of Indian morality. The third edict, for instance (Avadana-Sastra I.), which treats 'of impure vegetables', ordains that the only nourishment that the Chandala should be allowed must consist of garlic and onions, as the holy scriptures forbid their being given corn or grain-bearing fruit, water and fire. The same edict declares that the water which they need must be drawn neither out of rivers, wells or ponds, but only out of the ditches leading to swamps and out of the holes left by the footprints of animals. They are likewise forbidden to wash either their linen or themselves, since the water which is graciously granted to them must only be used for quenching their thirst. Finally Sudra women are forbidden to assist Chandala women at their confinements, while Chandala women are also forbidden to assist each other at such times. The results of sanitary regulations of this kind could not fail to make themselves felt; deadly epidemics and the most ghastly venereal diseases soon appeared, and in consequence of these again 'the Law of the Knife' – that is to say circumcision, was prescribed for male children and the removal of the small labia from the females. Manu himself says: 'the Chandala are the fruit of adultery, incest, and crime (this is the necessary consequence of the idea of breeding). Their clothes shall consist only of the rags torn from corpses, their vessels shall be the fragments of broken pottery, their ornaments shall be made of old iron, and their religion shall be the worship of evil spirits; without rest they shall wander from place to place. They are forbidden to write from left to right or to use their right hand in writing: the use of the right hand and writing from left to right are reserved to people of virtue, to people of race.'

4

These regulations are instructive enough: we can see in them the absolutely pure and primeval humanity of the Aryans – we learn that the notion 'pure blood', is the reverse of harmless. On the other hand it becomes clear among which people the hatred, the Chandala hatred of this humanity has been immortalised, among which people it has become religion and genius. From this point of view the gospels are documents of the highest value; and the Book of Enoch is still more so. Christianity as sprung from Jewish roots and comprehensible only as grown upon this soil, represents the counter-movement against that morality of breeding, of race and of privilege – it is essentially an anti-Aryan religion: Christianity is the transvaluation of all Aryan values, the triumph of Chandala values, the proclaimed gospel of the poor and of the low, the general insurrection of all the down-trodden, the wretched, the bungled and the botched, against the 'race' – the immortal revenge of the Chandala as the *religion of love*.

5

The morality of breeding and the morality of taming, in the means which they adopt in order to prevail, are quite worthy of each other: we may lay down as a leading principle that in order to create morality a man must have the absolute will to immorality. This is the great and strange problem with which I have so long been occupied: the psychology of the 'Improvers' of mankind. A small, and at bottom perfectly insignificant fact, known as the '*pia fraus*', first gave me access to this problem: the *pia fraus*, the heirloom of all philosophers and priests who 'improve' mankind. Neither Manu, nor Plato, nor Confucius, nor the teachers of Judaism and Christianity, have ever doubted their right to falsehood. They have never doubted their right to quite a number of other things. To express oneself in a formula, one might say: all means which have been used heretofore with the object of making man moral, were through and through immoral.

Things I owe to the Ancients

I

In conclusion I will just say a word concerning that world to which I have sought new means of access, to which I may perhaps have found a new passage – the ancient world. My taste, which is perhaps the reverse of tolerant, is very far from saying yea through and through even to this world: on the whole it is not over eager to say *Yea*, it would prefer to say *Nay*, and better still nothing whatever . . . This is true of whole cultures; it is true of books – it is also true of places and of landscapes. Truth to tell, the number of ancient books that count for something in my life is but small; and the most famous are not of that number. My sense of style, for the epigram as style, was awakened almost spontaneously upon my acquaintance with Sallust. I have not forgotten the astonishment of my respected teacher Corssen, when he was forced to give his worst Latin pupil the highest marks – at one stroke I had learned all there was to learn. Condensed, severe, with as much substance as possible in the background, and with cold but roguish hostility towards all 'beautiful words' and 'beautiful feelings' – in these things I found my own particular bent. In my writings up to my 'Zarathustra', there will be found a very earnest ambition to attain to the *Roman* style, to the '*aere perennius*' in style. – The same thing happened on my first acquaintance with Horace. Up to the present no poet has given me the same artistic raptures as those which from the first I received from an Horatian ode. In certain languages it would be absurd even to aspire to what is accomplished by this poet. This mosaic of words, in which every unit spreads its power to the left and to the right over the whole, by its sound, by its place in the sentence, and by its meaning, this *minimum* in the compass and number of the signs, and the *maximum* of energy in the signs which is thereby achieved – all this is Roman, and, if you will believe me, noble *par excellence*. By the side of this all the rest of poetry becomes something popular – nothing more than senseless sentimental twaddle.

2

I am not indebted to the Greeks for anything like such strong impressions; and, to speak frankly, they cannot be to us what the Romans are. One cannot *learn* from the Greeks – their style is too strange, it is also too fluid, to be imperative or to have the effect of a classic. Who would ever have learnt writing from a Greek? Who would ever have learned it without the Romans? . . . Do not let anyone suggest Plato to me. In regard to Plato I am a thorough sceptic, and have never been able to agree to the admiration of Plato the *artist*, which is traditional among scholars. And after all, in this matter, the most refined judges of taste in antiquity are on my side. In my opinion Plato bundles all the forms of style pell-mell together, in this respect he is one of the first decadents of style: he has something similar on his conscience to that which the Cynics had who invented the *satura Menippea*. For the Platonic dialogue – this revoltingly self-complacent and childish kind of dialectics – to exercise any charm over you, you must never have read any good French authors – Fontenelle for instance. Plato is boring. In reality my distrust of Plato is fundamental. I find him so very much astray from all the deepest instincts of the Hellenes, so steeped in moral prejudices, so pre-existently Christian – the concept 'good' is already the highest value with him – that rather than use any other expression I would prefer to designate the whole phenomenon Plato with the hard word 'superior bunkum', or, if you would like it better, 'idealism'. Humanity has had to pay dearly for this Athenian having gone to school among the Egyptians (or among the Jews in Egypt?). In the great fatality of Christianity, Plato is that double-faced fascination called the 'ideal', which made it possible for the more noble natures of antiquity to misunderstand themselves and to tread the *bridge* which led to the 'cross'. And what an amount of Plato is still to be found in the concept 'church', and in the construction, the system and the practice of the church! My recreation, my predilection, my cure, after all Platonism, has always been Thucydides. Thucyd-ides and perhaps Machiavelli's *principe* are most closely related to me owing to the absolute determination which they show of refusing to deceive themselves and of seeing reason in *reality* – not in 'rationality', and still less in 'morality'. There is no more radical cure than Thucydides for the lamentably rose-coloured idealis-ation of the Greeks which the 'classically-cultured' stripling bears with him into life, as a reward for his public school training. His writings must be carefully studied line by line, and his unuttered thoughts must be read as distinctly as what he actually says. There are few thinkers so rich in unuttered thoughts. In him the culture 'of the Sophists' – that is to say, the culture of

realism, receives its most perfect expression: this in-
estimable movement in the midst of the moral and
idealistic knavery of the Socratic schools which was
then breaking out in all directions. Greek philosophy is
the decadence of the Greek instinct: Thucydides is the
great summing up, the final manifestation of that
strong, severe positivism which lay in the instincts of
the ancient Hellene. After all, it is courage in the face of
reality that distinguishes such natures as Thucydides
from Plato: Plato is a coward in the face of reality –
consequently he takes refuge in the ideal: Thucydides
is master of himself – consequently he is able to master
life.

3

To rout up cases of 'beautiful souls', 'golden means'
and other perfections among the Greeks, to admire,
say, their calm grandeur, their ideal attitude of mind,
their exalted simplicity – from this 'exalted simplicity',
which after all is a piece of *niaiserie allemande*, I was
preserved by the psychologist within me. I saw their
strongest instinct, the Will to Power, I saw them
quivering with the fierce violence of this instinct – I
saw all their institutions grow out of measures of
security calculated to preserve each member of their
society from the inner *explosive material* that lay in his
neighbour's breast. This enormous internal tension
thus discharged itself in terrible and reckless hostility
outside the state: the various states mutually tore each
other to bits, in order that each individual state could
remain at peace with itself. It was then necessary to be
strong; for danger lay close at hand – it lurked in
ambush everywhere. The superb suppleness of their
bodies, the daring realism and immorality which is

peculiar to the Hellenes, was a necessity not an inherent quality. It was a result, it had not been there from the beginning. Even their festivals and their arts were but means in producing a feeling of superiority, and of showing it: they are measures of self-glorification; and in certain circumstances of making one's self terrible . . . Fancy judging the Greeks in the German style, from their philosophers; fancy using the suburban respectability of the Socratic schools as a key to what is fundamentally Hellenic! . . . The philosophers are of course the decadents of Hellas, the counter-movement directed against the old and noble taste (against the agonal instinct, against the *polis*, against the value of the race, against the authority of tradition). Socratic virtues were preached to the Greeks, *because* the Greeks had lost virtue: irritable, cowardly, unsteady, and all turned to play-actors, they had more than sufficient reason to submit to having morality preached to them. Not that it helped them in any way; but great words and attitudes are so becoming to decadents.

4

I was the first who, in order to understand the ancient, still rich and even superabundant Hellenic instinct, took that marvellous phenomenon, which bears the name of Dionysus, seriously: it can be explained only as a manifestation of excessive energy. Whoever had studied the Greeks, as that most profound of modern connoisseurs of their culture, Jakob Burckhardt of Basle, had done, knew at once that something had been achieved by means of this interpretation. And in his '*Cultur der Griechen*', Burckhardt inserted a special chapter on the phenomenon in question. If you would like a glimpse of the other side, you have only to refer to the almost laughable poverty of instinct among German philologists when they approach the Dionysian question. The celebrated Lobeck, especially, who with the venerable assurance of a worm dried up between books, crawled into this world of mysterious states, succeeded in convincing himself that he was scientific, whereas he was simply revoltingly superficial and childish – Lobeck, with all the pomp of profound erudition, gave us to understand that, as a matter of fact, there was nothing at all in all these curiosities. Truth to tell, the priests may well have communicated not a few things of value to the participators in such orgies; for instance, the fact that wine provokes desire, that man in certain circumstances lives on fruit, that plants bloom in the spring and fade in the autumn. As regards the astounding wealth of rites, symbols and myths which take their origin in the orgy, and with which the world of antiquity is literally smothered, Lobeck finds that it prompts him to a feat of even greater ingenuity than the foregoing phenomenon did. 'The Greeks,' he says, (*Aglaophamus*, I, p. 672), 'when they had nothing better to do, laughed, sprang and romped about, or, inasmuch as men also like a change at times, they would sit down, weep and bewail their lot. Others then came up who tried to discover some reason for this strange behaviour; and thus, as an explanation of these habits, there arose an incalculable number of festivals, legends, and myths. On the other hand it was believed that the *farcical performances* which then perchance began to take place on festival days, necessarily formed part of the celebrations, and they were retained as an indispensable part of the ritual.' – This is contemptible nonsense, and no one will take a man like Lobeck seriously for a moment. We are very differently affected when we examine the notion 'Hellenic', as Winckelmann and Goethe conceived it, and find it incompatible with that element out of which Dionysian art springs – I speak of orgiasm. In reality I do not doubt that Goethe would have completely excluded any such thing from the potentialities of the Greek soul. *Consequently Goethe did not understand the Greeks.* For it is only in the Dionysian mysteries, in the psychology of the Dionysian state, that the *fundamental fact* of the Hellenic instinct – its 'will to life' – is expressed. What did the Hellene secure himself with these mysteries? *Eternal* life, the eternal recurrence of life; the future promised and hallowed in the past; the triumphant Yea to life despite death and change; real life conceived as the collective prolongation of life through procreation, through the mysteries of sexuality. To the Greeks, the symbol of sex was the most venerated of symbols, the really deep significance of all the piety of antiquity. All the details of the act of procreation, pregnancy and birth gave rise to the loftiest and most solemn feelings. In the doctrine of mysteries, *pain* was pronounced holy: the 'pains of childbirth' sanctify pain in general – all becoming and all growth, everything that guarantees the future *involves* pain . . . In order that there may be eternal joy in creating, in order that the will to life may say Yea to itself in all eternity, the 'pains of childbirth' must also be eternal. All this is what the word Dionysus signifies: I know of no higher symbolism than this Greek symbolism, this symbolism of the Dionysian phenomenon. In it the profoundest instinct of life, the instinct that guarantees the future of life and life eternal, is understood religiously – the road to life itself, procreation, is pronounced *holy* . . . It was only Christianity which, with its fundamental resentment against life, made something impure out of sexuality: it flung *filth* at the very basis, the very first condition of our life.

5

The psychology of orgiasm conceived as the feeling of a superabundance of vitality and strength, within the scope of which even pain acts as a *stimulus*, gave me the key to the concept *tragic* feeling, which has been misunderstood not only by Aristotle, but also even more by our pessimists. Tragedy is so far from proving anything in regard to the pessimism of the Greeks, as Schopenhauer maintains, that it ought rather to be considered as the categorical repudiation and *condemnation* thereof. The saying of Yea to life, including even its most strange and most terrible problems, the will to life rejoicing over its own inexhaustibleness in the *sacrifice* of its highest types – this is what I called Dionysian, this is what I divined as the bridge leading to the psychology of the *tragic* poet. Not in order to escape from terror and pity, not to purify one's self of a dangerous passion by discharging it with vehemence – this is how Aristotle understood it – but to be far beyond terror and pity and to be the eternal lust of Becoming itself – that lust which also involves the *lust of destruction*. And with this I once more come into touch with the spot from which I once set out – the 'Birth of Tragedy' was my first transvaluation of all values: with this I again take my stand upon the soil from out of which my will and my capacity spring – I, the last disciple of the philosopher Dionysus – I, the prophet of eternal recurrence.

THE ANTICHRIST

An attempted criticism of Christianity

This book belongs to the very few. Maybe not one of them is yet alive; unless he be of those who understand my Zarathustra. How *can* I confound myself with those who today already find a hearing? Only the day after tomorrow belongs to me. Some are born posthumously.

I am only too well aware of the conditions under which a man understands me, and then *necessarily* understands. He must be intellectually upright to the point of hardness, in order even to endure my seriousness and my passion. He must be used to living on mountain-tops – and to feeling the wretched gabble of politics and national egotism *beneath* him. He must have become indifferent; he must never inquire whether truth is profitable or whether it may prove fatal . . . Possessing from strength a predilection for questions for which no one has enough courage nowadays; the courage for the *forbidden*; his predestination must be the labyrinth. The experience of seven solitudes. New ears for new music. New eyes for the most remote things. A new conscience for truths which hitherto have remained dumb. And the will to economy on a large scale: to husband his strength and his enthusiasm . . . He must honour himself, he must love himself; he must be absolutely free with regard to himself . . . Very well then! Such men alone are my readers, my proper readers, my preordained readers: of what account are the rest? The rest are simply –

humanity. – One must be superior to humanity in power, in loftiness of soul – in contempt.

FRIEDRICH NIETZSCHE

Let us look each other in the face. We are hyper-boreans – we know well enough how far outside the crowd we stand. 'Thou wilt find the way to the Hyperboreans neither by land nor by water': Pindar already knew this much about us. Beyond the north, the ice, and death – *our life, our happiness* . . . We discovered happiness; we know the way; we found the way out of thousands of years of labyrinth. Who *else* would have found it? Not the modern man, surely? 'I do not know where I am or what I am to do; I am everything that knows not where it is or what to do' – sighs the modern man. We were made quite ill by *this* modernity – with its indolent peace, its cowardly compromise, and the whole of the virtuous filth of its Yea and Nay. This tolerance and *largeur de coeur* which 'forgives' everything because it 'understands' every-thing, is a Sirocco for us. We prefer to live amid ice than to be breathed upon by modern virtues and other southerly winds . . . We were brave enough; we spared neither ourselves nor others: but we were very far from knowing whither to direct our bravery. We were becoming gloomy; people called us fatalists. *Our* fate – it was the abundance, the tension and the storing up of power. We thirsted for thunderbolts and great deeds; we kept at the most respectful distance from the joy of the weakling, from 'resignation' . . . Thunder was in our air, that part of nature which we are, became overcast – *for we had no direction*. The formula of our happiness: a Yea, a Nay, a straight line, a goal.

2

What is good? All that enhances the feeling of power, the Will to Power, and power itself in man. What is bad? All that proceeds from weakness. What is happiness? The feeling that power is *increasing* – that resistance has been overcome.

Not contentment, but more power; not peace at any price, but war; not virtue, but efficiency (virtue in the Renaissance sense, *virtù*, free from all moralic acid). The weak and the botched shall perish: first principle of our humanity. And they ought even to be helped to perish.

What is more harmful than any vice? Practical sympathy with all the botched and the weak – Christianity.

3

The problem I set in this work is not what will replace mankind in the order of living beings (Man is an *end*); but, what type of man must be *reared*, must be *willed*, as having the highest value, as being the most worthy of life and the surest guarantee of the future.

This more valuable type has appeared often enough already: but as a happy accident, as an exception, never as *willed*. He has rather been precisely the most feared; hitherto he has been almost the terrible in itself – and from out the very fear he provoked there arose the will to rear the type which has now been reared, *attained*: the domestic animal, the gregarious animal, the sick animal man – the Christian.

4

Mankind does *not* represent a development towards a better, stronger or higher type, in the sense in which this is supposed to occur today. 'Progress' is merely a modern idea – that is to say, a false idea. The modern European is still far below the European of the Renaissance in value. The process of evolution does not by any means imply elevation, enhancement and increasing strength.

On the other hand isolated and individual cases are continually succeeding in different places on earth, as the outcome of the most different cultures, and in these a *higher type* certainly manifests itself: something which by the side of mankind in general, represents a kind of superman. Such lucky strokes of great success have always been possible and will perhaps always be possible. And even whole races, tribes and nations may in certain circumstances represent such *lucky strokes*.

5

We must not deck out and adorn Christianity: it has waged a deadly war upon this *higher* type of man, it has set a ban upon all the fundamental instincts of this type, and has distilled evil and the devil himself out of these instincts – the strong man as the typical pariah, the villain. Christianity has sided with everything weak, low, and botched; it has made an ideal out of *antagonism* towards all the self-preservative instincts of strong life: it has corrupted even the reason of the strongest intellects, by teaching that the highest values of intellectuality are sinful, misleading and full of temptations. The most lamentable example of this was the corruption of Pascal, who believed in the perversion of his reason through original sin, whereas it had only been perverted by his Christianity.

6

A painful and ghastly spectacle has just risen before my eyes. I tore down the curtain which concealed mankind's *corruption*. This word in my mouth is at least secure from the suspicion that it contains a moral charge against mankind. It is – I would fain emphasise this again – free from moralic acid: to such an extent is this so, that I am most thoroughly conscious of the corruption in question precisely in those quarters in which hitherto people have aspired with most determination to 'virtue' and to 'godliness'. As you have already surmised, I understand corruption in the sense of *decadence*. What I maintain is this, that all the values upon which mankind builds its highest hopes and desires are *decadent* values.

I call an animal, a species, an individual corrupt, when it loses its instincts, when it selects and *prefers* that which is detrimental to it. A history of the 'higher feelings', of 'human ideals' – and it is not impossible that I shall have to write it – would almost explain why man is so corrupt. Life itself, to my mind, is nothing more nor less than the instinct of growth, of permanence, of accumulating forces, of power: where the will to power is lacking, degeneration sets in. My contention is that all the highest values of mankind *lack* this will – that the values of decline and of *nihilism* are exercising the sovereign power under the cover of the holiest names.

7

Christianity is called the religion of *pity*. Pity is opposed to the tonic passions which enhance the energy of the feeling of life: its action is depressing. A man loses power when he pities. By means of pity the drain on strength which suffering itself already introduces into the world is multiplied a thousandfold. Through pity, suffering itself becomes infectious; in certain circumstances it may lead to a total loss of life and vital energy, which is absurdly out of proportion to the magnitude of the cause (– the case of the death of the Nazarene). This is the first standpoint; but there is a still more important one. Supposing one measures pity according to the value of the reactions it usually stimulates, its danger to life appears in a much more telling light. On the whole, pity thwarts the law of development which is the law of selection. It preserves that which is ripe for death, it fights in favour of the disinherited and the condemned of life; thanks to the multitude of abortions of all kinds which it maintains in life, it lends life itself a sombre and questionable aspect. People have dared to call pity a virtue (– in every *noble* culture it is considered as a weakness –); people went still further, they exalted it to *the* virtue, the root and origin of all virtues – but, of course, what must never be forgotten is the fact that this was done from the standpoint of a philosophy which was nihilistic, and on whose shield the device *The Denial of Life* was inscribed. Schopenhauer was right in this respect: by means of pity, life is denied and made *more worthy of denial* – pity is the *praxis* of Nihilism. I repeat, this depressing and infectious instinct thwarts those instincts which aim at the preservation and enhancement of the value life: by *multiplying* misery quite as much as by preserving all that is miserable, it is the principal agent in promoting decadence – pity exhorts people to nothing, to *nonentity*! But they do not say '*nonentity*', they say 'Beyond', or 'God', or 'the true life'; or Nirvana, or Salvation, or Blessedness, instead. This innocent rhetoric, which belongs to the realm of the religio-moral idiosyncrasy, immediately appears to be *very much less innocent* if one realises what the tendency is which here tries to drape itself in the mantle of sublime expressions – the tendency of hostility to life. Schopenhauer was hostile to life: that is why he elevated pity to a virtue . . . Aristotle, as you know, recognised in pity a morbid and dangerous state, of which it was wise to rid one's self from time to time by a purgative: he regarded tragedy as a purgative. For the sake of the instinct of life, it would certainly seem necessary to find some means of lancing any such morbid and dangerous accumulation of pity, as that which possessed Schopenhauer (and unfortunately the whole of our literary and artistic decadence as well, from St Petersburg to Paris, from Tolstoy to Wagner), if only to make it *burst* . . . Nothing is more unhealthy in the midst of our unhealthy modernity, than Christian pity. To be doctors *here*, to be inexorable *here*, to wield the knife effectively *here* – all this is our business, all this is *our* kind of love to our fellows, this is what makes *us* philosophers, us hyperboreans!

8

It is necessary to state whom we regard as our antithesis: the theologians, and all those who have the blood of theologians in their veins – the whole of our philosophy . . . A man must have had his very nose upon this fatality, or better still he must have experienced it in his own soul; he must almost have perished through it, in order to be unable to treat this matter lightly (the free-spiritedness of our friends the naturalists and physiologists is, in my opinion, a *joke* – what they lack in these questions is passion, what they lack is having suffered from these questions). This poisoning extends much further than people think: I unearthed the 'arrogant' instinct of the theologian, wherever nowadays people feel themselves idealists – wherever, thanks to superior antecedents, they claim the right to rise above reality and to regard it with suspicion . . . Like the priest the idealist has every grandiloquent concept in his hand (and not only in his hand!), he wields them all with kindly contempt against the 'understanding', the 'senses', 'honours', 'decent living', 'science'; he regards such things as *beneath* him, as detrimental and seductive forces, upon the face of which, 'the Spirit' moves in pure absoluteness: – as if humility, chastity, poverty, in a word *holiness*, had not done incalculably more harm to life hitherto, than any sort of horror and vice . . . Pure spirit is pure falsehood . . . As long as the priest, the *professional* denier, calumniator and poisoner of life, is considered as the *highest* kind of man, there can be no answer to the question, what *is* truth? Truth has already been turned topsy-turvy, when the conscious advocate of nonentity and of denial passes as the representative of 'truth'.

9

It is upon this theological instinct that I wage war. I find traces of it everywhere. Whoever has the blood of theologians in his veins, stands from the start in a false and dishonest position to all things. The pathos which grows out of this state, is called *Faith*: that is to say, to shut one's eyes once and for all, in order not to suffer at the sight of incurable falsity. People convert this faulty view of all things into a moral, a virtue, a thing of holiness. They endow their distorted vision with a good conscience – they claim that no *other* point of view is any longer of value, once theirs has been made sacrosanct with the names 'God', 'Salvation', 'Eternity'. I unearthed the instinct of the theologian everywhere: it is the most universal, and actually the most subterranean form of falsity on earth. That which a theologian considers true, *must* of necessity be false: this furnishes almost the criterion of truth. It is his most profound self-preservative instinct which forbids reality ever to attain to honour in any way, or even to raise its voice. Whithersoever the influence of the theologian extends, *valuations* are topsy-turvy, and the concepts 'true' and 'false' have necessarily changed places: that which is most deleterious to life, is here called 'true', that which enhances it, elevates it, says Yea to it, justifies it and renders it triumphant, is called 'false' . . . If it should happen that theologians, *via* the 'conscience' either of princes or of the people, stretch out their hand for power, let us not be in any doubt as to what results there-from each time, namely: the will to the end, the *nihilistic* will to power . . .

10

Among Germans I am immediately understood when I say, that philosophy is ruined by the blood of theologians. The Protestant minister is the grandfather of German philosophy, Protestantism itself is the latter's *peccatum originale*. Definition of Protestantism:

the partial paralysis of Christianity – and of reason . . . One needs only to pronounce the words 'Tübingen Seminary', in order to understand what German philosophy really is at bottom, *i.e.* theology *in disguise* . . . The Swabians are the best liars in Germany, they lie innocently . . . Whence came all the rejoicing with which the appearance of Kant was greeted by the scholastic world of Germany, three-quarters of which consist of clergymen's and school-masters' sons? Whence came the German conviction, which finds an echo even now, that Kant inaugurated a change for the *better*? The theologian's instinct in the German scholar divined what had once again been made possible . . . A back-staircase leading into the old ideal was discovered, the concept 'true world', the concept morality as the *essence* of the world (those two most vicious errors that have ever existed!), were, thanks to a subtle and wily scepticism, once again, if not demonstrable, at least no longer *refutable* . . . Reason, the *prerogative* of reason, does not extend so far . . . Out of reality they had made 'appearance'; and an absolutely false world – that of being – had been declared to be reality. Kant's success is merely a theologian's success. Like Luther, and like Leibniz, Kant was one brake the more upon the already squeaky wheel of German uprightness.

11

One word more against Kant as a *moralist*. A virtue *must* be *our* invention, our most personal defence and need: in every other sense it is merely a danger. That which does not constitute a condition of our life, is merely harmful to it: to possess a virtue merely because one happens to respect the concept 'virtue', as Kant

393

would have us do, is pernicious. 'Virtue', 'Duty', 'Goodness in itself', goodness stamped with the character of impersonality and universal validity – these things are mere mental hallucinations, in which decline the final devitalisation of life and Königsbergian Chinadom find expression. The most fundamental laws of preservation and growth, demand precisely the reverse, namely: that each should discover *his* own virtue, his own Categorical Imperative. A nation goes to the dogs when it confounds its concept of duty with the general concept of duty. Nothing is more profoundly, more thoroughly pernicious, than every impersonal feeling of duty, than every sacrifice to the Moloch of abstraction. Fancy no one's having thought Kant's Categorical Imperative *dangerous to life*!. . . The instinct of the theologist alone took it under its wing! An action stimulated by the instinct of life, is proved to be a proper action by the happiness that accompanies it: and that nihilist with the bowels of a Christian dogmatist regarded happiness as an *objection* . . . What is there that destroys a man more speedily than to work, think, feel, as an automaton of 'duty', without internal promptings, without a profound personal predilection, without joy? This is the recipe *par excellence* of decadence and even of idiocy . . . Kant became an idiot. And he was the contemporary of Goethe! This fatal spider was regarded as *the* German philosopher – is still regarded as such! . . . I refrain from saying what I think of the Germans . . . Did Kant not see in the French Revolution the transition of the State from the inorganic to the *organic* form? Did he not ask himself whether there was a single event on record which could be explained otherwise than as a moral faculty of mankind; so that by means of it, 'mankind's tendency towards good' might be *proved* once and for all? Kant's reply: 'that is the Revolution'. Instinct at fault in anything and everything, hostility to nature as an instinct, German decadence made into philosophy – *that is Kant*!

12

Except for a few sceptics, the respectable type in the history of philosophy, the rest do not know the very first pre-requisite of intellectual uprightness. They all behave like females, do these great enthusiasts and animal prodigies – they regard 'beautiful feelings' themselves as arguments, the 'heaving breast' as the bellows of divinity, and conviction as the *criterion* of truth. In the end, even Kant, with 'Teutonic' innocence, tried to dress this lack of intellectual conscience up in a scientific garb by means of the concept 'practical reason'. He deliberately invented a kind of reason which at times would allow one to dispense with reason, that is to say when 'morality', when the sublime command 'thou shalt', makes itself heard. When one remembers that in almost all nations the philosopher is only a further development of the priestly type, this heirloom of priesthood, this *fraud towards one's self*, no longer surprises one. When a man has a holy life-task, as for instance to improve, save, or deliver mankind, when a man bears God in his breast, and is the mouthpiece of imperatives from another world – with such a mission he stands beyond the pale of all merely reasonable valuations. He is even sanctified by such a taste, and is already the type of a higher order! What does a priest care about science? He stands too high for that! And until now the priest has *ruled*! – He it was who determined the concept 'true and false'.

395

13

Do not let us undervalue the fact that we *ourselves*, we free spirits, are already a 'transvaluation of all values', an incarnate declaration of war against all the old concepts 'true' and 'untrue' and of a triumph over them. The most valuable standpoints are always the last to be found: but the most valuable standpoints are the methods. All the methods and the first principles of our modern scientific procedure, had for years to encounter the profoundest contempt: association with them meant exclusion from the society of decent people – one was regarded as an 'enemy of God', as a scoffer at truth and as 'one possessed'. With one's scientific nature, one belonged to the Chandala. We have had the whole feeling of mankind against us; hitherto their notion of that which ought to be truth, of that which ought to serve the purpose of truth: every 'thou shalt', has been directed against us . . . Our objects, our practices, our calm, cautious distrustful manner – everything about us seemed to them absolutely despicable and beneath contempt. After all, it might be asked with some justice, whether the thing which kept mankind blindfold so long, were not an aesthetic taste: what they demanded of truth was a *picturesque* effect, and from the man of science what they expected was that he should make a forcible appeal to their senses. It was our *modesty* which ran counter to their taste so long . . . And oh! how well they guessed this, did these divine turkey-cocks!

We have altered our standpoint. In every respect we have become more modest. We no longer derive man from the 'spirit', and from the 'godhead'; we have thrust him back among the beasts. We regard him as the strongest animal, because he is the craftiest: one of the results thereof is his intellectuality. On the other hand we guard against the vain pretension, which even here would fain assert itself: that man is the great *arrière pensée* of organic evolution! He is by no means the crown of creation; beside him, every other creature stands at the same stage of perfection . . . And even in asserting this we go a little too far; for, relatively speaking, man is the most botched and diseased of animals, and he has wandered furthest from his instincts. Be all this as it may, he is certainly the most *interesting*! As regards animals, Descartes was the first, with really admirable daring, to venture the thought that the beast was *machina*, and the whole of our physiology is endeavouring to prove this proposition. Moreover, logically we do not set man apart, as Descartes did: the extent to which man is understood today goes only so far as he has been understood mechanistically. Formerly man was given 'free will', as his dowry from a higher sphere; nowadays we have robbed him even of will, in view of the fact that no such faculty is any longer known. The only purpose served by the old word 'will', is to designate a result, a sort of individual reaction which necessarily follows upon a host of partly discordant and partly harmonious stimuli – the will no longer 'effects' or 'moves' anything . . . Formerly people thought that man's consciousness, his 'spirit', was a proof of his lofty origin, of his divinity. With the idea of perfecting man, he was conjured to draw his senses inside himself, after the manner of the tortoise, to cut off all relations with terrestrial things, and to divest himself of his mortal shell. Then the most important thing about him, the 'pure spirit', would remain over. Even concerning these things we have improved our standpoint. Consciousness, 'spirit', now seems to us rather a symptom of relative imperfection in the organism, as an experiment, a groping, a misapprehension, an affliction which absorbs an unnecessary quantity of nervous energy. We deny that anything can be done perfectly so long as it is done consciously. 'Pure spirit' is a piece of 'pure stupidity': if we discount the nervous system, the senses and the 'mortal shell', we have miscalculated – that it is all . . .

15

In Christianity, neither morality nor religion comes in touch at all with reality. Nothing but imaginary *causes* (God, the soul, the ego, spirit, free will – or even non-free will); nothing but imaginary *effects* (sin, salvation, grace, punishment, forgiveness of sins). Imaginary beings are supposed to have intercourse (God, spirits, souls); imaginary Natural History (anthropocentric: total lack of the notion 'natural causes'); an imaginary *psychology* (nothing but misunderstandings of self, interpretations of pleasant or unpleasant general feelings; for instance of the states of the *nervus sympathicus*, with the help of the sign language of a religio-moral idiosyncrasy – repentance, pangs of conscience, the temptation of the devil, the presence of God); an imaginary teleology (the Kingdom of God, the Last Judgment, Everlasting Life). This purely fictitious world distinguishes itself very unfavourably from the world of dreams: the latter *reflects* reality, whereas the former falsifies, depreciates and denies it. Once the concept 'nature' was taken to mean the opposite of the concept God, the word 'natural' had to acquire the meaning of abominable – the whole of that fictitious world takes its root in the hatred of nature (reality!), it is the expression of profound discomfiture in the presence of reality . . . *But this explains everything.* What is the only kind of man who has reasons for wriggling out of reality by lies? The man who suffers from reality. But in order to suffer from reality one must be a bungled portion of it. The preponderance of pain over pleasure is the *cause* of that fictitious morality and religion: but any such preponderance furnishes the formula for decadence.

16

A criticism of the Christian concept of God inevitably leads to the same conclusion: a nation that still believes in itself, also has its own god. In him it honours the conditions which enable it to remain uppermost – that is to say, its virtues. It projects its joy over itself, its feeling of power, into a being, to whom it can be thankful for such things. He who is rich, will give of his riches: a proud people requires a god unto whom it can *sacrifice* things . . . Religion, when restricted to these principles, is a form of gratitude. A man is grateful for his own existence; for this he must have a god. – Such a god must be able to able to benefit and to injure him, he must be able to act the friend and the foe. He must be esteemed for his good as well as for his evil qualities. The monstrous castration of a god by making him a god only of goodness, would lie beyond the pale of the

desires of such a community. The evil god is just as
urgently needed as the good god: for a people in such a
form of society certainly does not owe its existence to
toleration and humaneness . . . What would be the
good of a god who knew nothing of anger, revenge,
envy, scorn, craft, and violence – who had perhaps
never experienced the rapturous *ardeurs* of victory and
of annihilation? No one would understand such a god:
why should one possess him? – Of course, when a
people is on the road to ruin; when it feels its belief in a
future, its hope of freedom vanishing for ever; when it
becomes conscious of submission as the most useful
quality, and of the virtues of the submissive as self-
preservative measures, then its god must also modify
himself. He then becomes a tremulous and unassuming sneak; he counsels 'peace of the soul', the
cessation of all hatred, leniency and 'love' even
towards friend and foe. He is for ever moralising, he
crawls into the heart of every private virtue, becomes
a god for everybody, he retires from active service and
becomes a Cosmopolitan . . . Formerly he represented
a people, the strength of a people, everything aggres-
sive and desirous of power lying concealed in the heart
of a nation: now he is merely the good god . . . In very
truth gods have no other alternative, they are *either* the
Will to Power – in which case they are always the gods
of whole nations – or, on the other hand, the incapacity
for power – in which case they necessarily become
good.

17

Wherever the Will to Power, no matter in what
form, begins to decline, a physiological retrogression, decadence, always supervenes. The godhead of

decadence, shorn of its masculine virtues and passions is perforce converted into the god of the physiologically degraded, of the weak. Of course they do not call themselves the weak, they call themselves 'the good' . . . No hint will be necessary to help you to understand at what moment in history the dualistic fiction of a good and an evil god first became possible. With the same instinct by which the subjugated reduce their god to 'Goodness in itself', they also cancel the good qualities from their conquerer's god; they avenge themselves on their masters by diabolising the latter's god. The *good god* and the devil as well – both the abortions of decadence. How is it possible that we are still so indulgent towards the simplicity of Christian theologians today, as to declare with them that the evolution of the concept God, from the 'God of Israel', the god of a people, to the Christian God, the quintessence of all goodness, marks a *step forward*? But even Renan does this. As if Renan had a right to simplicity! Why, the very contrary stares one in the face. When the pre-requisites of *ascending* life, when everything strong, plucky, masterful and proud has been eliminated from the concept of god, and step by step he has sunk down to the symbol of a staff for the weary, of a last straw for all those who are drowning; when he becomes the pauper's god, the sinner's god, the sick man's god *par excellence*, and the attribute 'Saviour', 'Redeemer', remains *over* as the one essential attribute of divinity: what does such a metamorphosis, such an abasement of the godhead imply? Undoubtedly, 'the kingdom of God' has thus become larger. Formerly all he had was his people, his 'chosen' people. Since then he has gone travelling over foreign lands, just as his people have done; since then he has never rested anywhere: until one day he felt at home everywhere, the Great Cosmopolitan – until he got the 'greatest number', and half the world on his side. But the god of the 'greatest number', the democrat among gods, did not become a proud heathen god notwithstanding: he remained a Jew, he remained the god of the back streets, the god of all dark corners and hovels, of all the unwholesome quarters of the world! . . . His universal empire is now as ever a netherworld empire, an infirmary, a subterranean empire, a ghetto-empire . . . And he himself is so pale, so weak, so decadent . . . Even the palest of the pale were able to master him – our friends the metaphysicians, those albinos of thought. They spun their webs around him so long that ultimately he was hypnotised by their movements and himself became a spider, a metaphysician. Thenceforward he once more began spinning the world out of his inner being – *sub specie Spinozae* – thenceforward he transfigured himself into something ever thinner and ever more anaemic, became 'ideal', became 'pure spirit', became '*absolutum*', and 'thing-in-itself' . . . *The decline and fall of a god*: God became the 'thing-in-itself'.

18

The Christian concept of God – god as the deity of the sick, god as a spider, god as spirit – is one of the most corrupt concepts of god that has ever been attained on earth. Maybe it represents the low-water mark in the evolutionary ebb of the godlike type. God degenerated into the *contradiction of life*, instead of being its transfiguration and eternal Yea! With God war is declared on life, nature, and the will to life! God is the formula for every calumny of this world and for every lie concerning a beyond! In God, nonentity is deified, and the will to nonentity is declared holy!

19

The fact that the strong races of Northern Europe did not repudiate the Christian God, certainly does not do any credit to their religious power, not to speak of their taste. They ought to have been able successfully to cope with such a morbid and decrepit offshoot of decadence. And a curse lies on their heads; because they were unable to cope with him, they made illness, decrepitude and contradiction a part of all their instincts – since then they have not *created* any other god! Two thousand years have passed and not a single new god! But still there exists, and as if by right – like an *ultimum* and *maximum* of god-creating power – the *creator spiritus* in man, this miserable God of Christian monotono-theism! This hybrid creature of decay, nonentity, concept and contradiction, in which all the instincts of decadence, all the cowardices and languors of the soul find their sanction!

20

With my condemnation of Christianity I should not like to have done an injustice to a religion which is related to it and the number of whose followers is even greater; I refer to Buddhism. As nihilistic religions, they are akin – they are religions of decadence – while each is separated from the other in the most extraordinary fashion. For being able to compare them at all, the critic of Christianity is profoundly grateful to Indian scholars. Buddhism is a hundred times more realistic than Christianity – it is part of its constitutional heritage to be able to face problems objectively and coolly, it is the outcome of centuries of lasting philosophical activity. The concept 'God' was already exploded when it appeared. Buddhism is the only really *positive* religion to be found in history, even in its epistemology (which is strict phenomenalism) – it no longer speaks of the 'struggle with *sin*', but fully recognising the true nature of reality it speaks of the 'struggle with *pain*'. It already has – and this distinguishes it fundamentally from Christianity – the self-deception of moral concepts beneath it – to use my own phraseology, it stands *Beyond Good and Evil.* The two physiological facts upon which it rests and upon which it bestows its attention are: in the first place excessive irritability of feeling, which manifests itself as a refined susceptibility to pain, *and also* as super-spiritualisation, an all-too-lengthy sojourn amid concepts and logical procedures, under the influence of which the personal instinct has suffered in favour of the 'impersonal'. (Both of these states will be known to a few of my readers, the objective ones, who, like myself, will know them from experience.) Thanks to these physiological conditions, a state of depression set in, which Buddha sought to combat by means of hygiene. Against it, he prescribes life in the open, a life of travel; moderation and careful choice in food; caution in regard to all intoxicating liquor, as also in regard to all the passions which tend to create bile and to heat the blood; and he deprecates care either on one's own or on other people's account. He recommends ideas that bring one either peace or good cheer – he invents means whereby the habit of contrary ideas may be lost. He understands goodness – being good – as promoting health. *Prayer* is out of the question, as is also *asceticism*; there is neither a Categorical Imperative nor any discipline whatsoever, even within the walls of a monastery (it is always possible to leave it if one wants to). All these things would have been only a means of accentuating the excessive irritability already referred to. Precisely on this account he does not exhort his followers to wage war upon those who do not share their views; nothing is more abhorred in his doctrine than the feeling of revenge, of aversion, and of resentment ('not through hostility doth hostility end': the touching refrain of the whole of Buddhism . . .). And in this he was right; for it is precisely these passions which are thoroughly unhealthy in view of the principal dietetic object. The mental fatigue which he finds already existent and which expresses itself in excessive 'objectivity' (*i.e.*, the enfeeblement of the individual's interest – loss of ballast and of 'egoism'), he combats by leading the spiritual interests as well imperatively back to the individual. In Buddha's doctrine egoism is a duty: the thing which is above all necessary, *i.e.* 'how canst thou be rid of suffering' regulates and defines the whole of the spiritual diet (let anyone but think of that Athenian who also declared war upon pure 'scientificality', Socrates, who made a morality out of personal egoism even in the realm of problems).

21

The pre-requisites for Buddhism are a very mild climate, great gentleness and liberality in the customs of a people and *no* militarism. The movement must also originate among the higher and even learned classes. Cheerfulness, peace and absence of desire, are the highest of inspirations, and they are *realised*. Buddhism is not a religion in which perfection is merely aspired to: perfection is the normal case. In Christianity all the instincts of the subjugated and oppressed come to the fore: it is the lowest classes who seek their salvation in this religion. Here the pastime, the manner of killing time is to practise the casuistry of sin, self-criticism, and conscience inquisition. Here the ecstasy in the presence of a *powerful being*, called 'god', is constantly maintained by means of prayer, while the highest thing is regarded as unattainable, as a gift, as an act of 'grace'. Here plain dealing is also entirely lacking: concealment and the darkened room are Christian. Here the body is despised, hygiene is repudiated as sensual; the church repudiates even cleanliness (the first Christian measure after the banishment of the Moors was the closing of the public baths, of which Cordova alone possessed 270). A certain spirit of cruelty towards one's self and others is also Christian: hatred of all those who do not share one's views; the will to persecute. Sombre and exciting ideas are in the foreground; the most coveted states and those which are endowed with the finest names, are really epileptic in their nature; diet is selected in such a way as to favour morbid symptoms and to over-excite the nerves. Christian, too, is the mortal hatred of the earth's rulers – the 'noble' – and at the same time a sort of concealed and secret competition with them (the subjugated leave the 'body' to their master – all they want is the 'soul'). Christian is the hatred of the intellect, of pride, of courage, freedom, intellectual *libertinage;* Christian is the hatred of the *senses*, of the joys of the senses, of joy in general.

22

When Christianity departed from its native soil, which consisted of the lowest classes, the *submerged masses* of the ancient world, and set forth in quest of power among barbaric nations, it no longer met with exhausted men but inwardly savage and self-lacerating men – the strong but bungled men. Here, dissatisfaction with one's self, suffering through one's self, is not, as in the case of Buddhism, excessive irritability and susceptibility to pain, but rather, conversely, it is an inordinate desire for inflicting pain, for a discharge of the inner tension in hostile deeds and ideas. Christianity was in need of *barbaric* ideas and values, in order to be able to master barbarians: such are for instance, the sacrifice of the first-born, the drinking of blood at communion, the contempt of the intellect and of culture; torture in all its forms, sensual and non-sensual; the great pomp of the cult. Buddhism is a religion for *senile* men, for races which have become kind, gentle, and over-spiritual, and which feel pain too easily (Europe is not nearly ripe for it yet); it calls them back to peace and cheerfulness, to a regimen for the intellect, to a certain hardening of the body. Christianity aims at mastering *beasts of prey*; its expedient is to make them *ill* – to render feeble is the Christian recipe for taming, for 'civilisation'. Buddhism is a religion for the close and exhaustion of civilisation; Christianity does not even find civilisation at hand when it appears, in certain circumstances it lays the foundation of civilisation.

Buddhism, I repeat, is a hundred times colder, more truthful, more objective. It no longer requires to justify pain and its susceptibility to suffering by the interpretation of sin – it simply says what it thinks, 'I suffer'. To the barbarian, on the other hand, suffering in itself is not a respectable thing: in order to acknowledge to himself that he suffers, what he requires, in the first place, is an explanation (his instinct directs him more readily to deny his suffering, or to endure it in silence). In his case, the word 'devil' was a blessing: man had an almighty and terrible enemy – he had no reason to be ashamed of suffering at the hands of such an enemy.

At bottom there are in Christianity one or two subtleties which belong to the Orient. In the first place it knows that it is a matter of indifference whether a thing be true or not; but that it is of the highest importance that it should be believed to be true. Truth and the belief that something is true: two totally separate worlds of interest, almost *opposite worlds,* the road to the one and the road to the other lie absolutely apart. To be initiated into this fact almost constitutes one a sage in the Orient: the Brahmins understood it thus, so did Plato, and so does every disciple of esoteric wisdom. If for example it give anyone pleasure to believe himself delivered from sin, it is *not* a necessary prerequisite thereto that he should be sinful, but only that he should *feel* sinful. If, however, *faith* is above all necessary, then reason, knowledge, and scientific research must be brought into evil repute: the road to truth becomes the *forbidden* road. Strong *hope* is a much greater stimulant of life than any single realised joy could be. Sufferers must be sustained by a hope which no actuality can contradict – and which cannot ever be realised: the hope of another world. (Precisely on account of this power that hope has of making the unhappy linger on, the Greeks regarded it as the evil of evils, as the most *mischievous* evil: it remained behind in Pandora's box.) In order that *love* may be possible, God must be a person. In order that the lowest instincts may also make their voices heard God must be young. For the ardour of the women a beautiful saint, and for the ardour of the men a Virgin Mary has to be pressed into the foreground. All this on condition that Christianity wishes to rule over a certain soil, on which Aphrodisiac or Adonis cults had already determined the *notion* of a cult. To insist upon *chastity* only intensifies the vehemence and profundity of the religious instinct – it makes the cult warmer, more enthusiastic, more soulful. Love is the state in which man sees things most widely different from what they are. The force of illusion reaches its zenith here, as likewise the sweetening and transfiguring power. When a man is in love he endures more than at other times; he submits to everything. The thing was to discover a religion in which it was possible to love: by this means the worst in life is overcome – it is no longer even seen. So much for three Christian virtues: Faith, Hope, and Charity. I call them the three Christian *precautionary measures*. Buddhism is too full of aged wisdom, too positivistic to be shrewd in this way.

24

Here I only touch upon the problem of the origin of Christianity. The first principle of its solution reads: Christianity can be understood only in relation to the soil out of which it grew – it is not a counter-movement against the Jewish instinct, it is the rational outcome of the latter, one step further in its appalling logic. In the formula of the Saviour: 'for Salvation is of the Jews'. The second principle is: the psychological type of the Galilean is still recognisable, but it was only in a state of utter degeneration (which is at once a distortion and an overloading with foreign features) that he was able to serve the purpose for which he has been used – namely, as the type of a Redeemer of mankind.

The Jews are the most remarkable people in the history of the world, because when they were confronted with the question of Being or non-Being, with simply uncanny deliberateness, they preferred Being *at any price:* this price was the fundamental *falsification* of all Nature, all the naturalness and all the reality, of the inner quite as much as of the outer world. They hedged themselves in behind all those conditions under which hitherto a people has been able to live, has been allowed to live; of themselves they created an idea which was the reverse of *natural* conditions – each in turn, they twisted first religion, then the cult, then morality, history and psychology, about in a manner so perfectly hopeless that they were made *to contradict their natural value*. We meet with the same phenomena again, and exaggerated to an incalculable degree, although only as a copy – the Christian Church as compared with the 'chosen people', lacks all claim to originality. Precisely on this account the Jews are the most *fatal* people in the history of the world: their ultimate influence has falsified mankind to such an extent, that even to this day the Christian can be anti-Semitic in spirit, without comprehending that he himself is the *final consequence of Judaism*.

It was in my *Genealogy of Morals* that I first gave a psychological exposition of the idea of the antithesis *noble-* and *resentment*-morality, the latter having arisen out of an attitude of negation to the former: but this is Judaeo-Christian morality heart and soul. In order to be able to say Nay to everything that represents the ascending movement of life, prosperity, power, beauty, and self-affirmation on earth, the instinct of resentment, become genius, had to invent *another* world, from the standpoint of which that *Yea-saying* to life appeared as *the* most evil and most abominable thing. From the psychological standpoint the Jewish people are possessed of the toughest vitality. Transplanted amid impossible conditions, with profound self-preservative intelligence, it voluntarily took the side of all the instincts of decadence – *not* as though dominated by them, but because it detected a power in them by means of which it could assert itself *against* 'the world'. The Jews are the opposite of all *decadents:* they have been forced to represent them to the point of illusion, and with a *non plus ultra* of histrionic genius, they have known how to set themselves at the head of all decadent movements (St Paul and Christianity for instance), in order to create something from them which is stronger than every party saying *Yea to life*. For the category of men which aspires to power in Judaism and Christianity – that is to say, for the sacerdotal class, decadence is but a *means:* this category of men has a vital interest in making men sick, and in turning the notions 'good' and 'bad', 'true' and 'false', upside down in a manner which is not only dangerous to life, but also slanders it.

25

The history of Israel is invaluable as the typical history of every *denaturalisation* of natural values: let me point to five facts which relate thereto. Originally, and above all in the period of the kings, even Israel's attitude to all things was the *right* one – that is to say, the natural one. Its Jehovah was the expression of its consciousness of power, of its joy over itself, of its hope for itself: victory and salvation were expected from him, through him it was confident that Nature would give what a people requires – above all rain. Jehovah is the God of Israel, and *consequently* the god of justice: this is the reasoning of every people which is in the position of power, and which has a good conscience in that position. In the solemn cult both sides of this self-affirmation of a people find expression: it is grateful for the great strokes of fate by means of which it became uppermost; it is grateful for the regularity in the succession of the seasons and for all good fortune in the rearing of cattle and in the tilling of the soil. – This state of affairs remained the ideal for some considerable time, even after it had been swept away in a deplorable manner by anarchy from within and the Assyrians from without. But the people still retained, as their highest desideratum, that vision of a king who was a good soldier and a severe judge; and he who retained it most of all was that typical prophet (that is to say, critic and satirist of the age), Isaiah. But all hopes remained unrealised. The old God was no longer able to do what he had done formerly. He ought to have been dropped. What happened? The idea of him was changed – the idea of him was denaturalised: this was the price they paid for retaining him. Jehovah, the god of 'Justice' – is no longer one with Israel, no longer the expression of a people's sense of dignity: he is only a god on certain conditions . . . The idea of him becomes a weapon in the hands of priestly agitators who henceforth interpret all happiness as a reward, all unhappiness as a punishment for disobedience to God, for 'sin': that most fraudulent method of interpretation which arrives at a so-called 'moral order of the Universe', by means of which the concept 'cause' and 'effect' is turned upside down. Once natural causation has been swept out of the world by reward and punishment, a causation *hostile to nature* becomes necessary; whereupon all the forms of unnaturalness follow. A god who *demands* – in the place of a god who helps, who advises, who is at bottom only a name for every happy inspiration of courage and of self-reliance . . . Morality is no longer the expression of the conditions of life and growth, no longer the most fundamental instinct of life, but it has become abstract, it has become the opposite of life – Morality as the fundamental perversion of the imagination, as the 'evil eye' for all things. What is Jewish morality, what is Christian morality? Chance robbed of its innocence; unhappiness polluted with the idea of 'sin'; well-being interpreted as a danger, as a 'temptation'; physiological indisposition poisoned by means of the canker-worm of conscience . . .

26

The concept of God falsified; the concept of morality falsified: but the Jewish priesthood did not stop at this. No use could be made of the whole *history* of Israel, therefore it must go! These priests accomplished that miracle of falsification, of which the greater part of the Bible is the document: with unparalleled contempt and in the teeth of all tradition and historical facts, they interpreted their own people's past in a religious manner – that is to say, they converted it into a ridiculous mechanical process of salvation, on the principle that all sin against Jehovah led to punishment, and that all pious worship of Jehovah led to reward. We would feel this shameful act of historical falsification far more poignantly if the ecclesiastical interpretation of history through millenniums had not blunted almost all our sense for the demands of uprightness *in historicis*. And the church is seconded by the philosophers: *the lie* of 'a moral order of the universe' permeates the whole development even of more modern philosophy. What does a 'moral order of the universe' mean? That once and for all there is such a thing as a will of God which determines what man has to do and what he has to leave undone; that the value of a people or of an individual is measured according to how much or how little the one or the other obeys the will of God; that in the destinies of a people or of an individual, the will of God shows itself dominant, that is to say it punishes or rewards according to the degree of obedience. In the place of this miserable falsehood, *reality* says: a parasitical type of man, who can flourish only at the cost of all the healthy elements of life, the priest abuses the name of God: he calls that state of affairs in which the priest determines the value of things 'the Kingdom of God'; he calls the means whereby such a state of affairs is attained or maintained, 'the Will of God'; with cold-blooded cynicism he measures peoples, ages and individuals according to whether they favour or oppose the ascendancy of the priesthood. Watch him at work: in the hands of the Jewish priesthood the Augustan Age in the history of Israel became an age of decline; the exile, the protracted misfortune transformed itself into eternal *punishment* for the Augustan Age – that age in which the priest did not yet exist. Out of the mighty and thoroughly freeborn figures of the history of Israel, they made, according to their requirements, either wretched bigots and hypocrites, or 'godless ones': they simplified the psychology of every great event to the idiotic formula 'obedient or disobedient to God'. A step further: the 'Will of God', that is to say the self-preservative measures of the priesthood, must be known – to this end a 'revelation' is necessary. In plain English: a stupendous literary fraud becomes necessary, 'holy scriptures' are discovered – and they are published abroad with all hieratic pomp, with days of penance and lamentations over the long state of 'sin'. The 'Will of God' has long stood firm: the whole of the trouble lies in the fact that the 'Holy Scriptures' have been discarded . . . Moses was already the 'Will of God' revealed . . . What had happened? With severity and pedantry, the priest had formulated once and for all – even to the largest and smallest contributions that were to be paid to him (not forgetting the daintiest portions of meat; for the priest is a consumer of beef-steaks) – *what he wanted*, 'what the Will of God was' . . . Henceforward everything became so arranged that the priests were *indispensable everywhere*. At all the natural events of life, at birth, at marriage, at the sick-bed, at death – not to speak of the sacrifice ('the meal') – the holy parasite appears in order to denaturalise, or in his language, to 'sanctify', everything . . . For this should be understood: every natural custom, every natural institution (the State, the administration of justice, marriage, the care of the sick and the poor), every demand inspired by the instinct of life, in short everything that has a value in itself, is rendered absolutely worthless and even dangerous through the parasitism of the priest (or of the 'moral order of the universe'): a sanction after the fact is required – a *power which imparts value* is necessary, which in so doing says Nay to nature, and which by this means alone *creates* a valuation . . . The priest depreciates and desecrates nature: it is only at this price that he exists at all. Disobedience to God, that is to say, to the priest, to the 'law', now receives the name of 'sin'; the means of 'reconciling one's self with God' are of course of a nature which render subordination to the priesthood all the more fundamental: the priest alone is able to 'save' . . . From the psychological standpoint, in every society organised upon a hieratic basis, 'sins' are indispensable: they are the actual weapons of power, the priest *lives* upon sins, it is necessary for him that people should 'sin' . . . Supreme axiom: 'God forgiveth him that repenteth' – in plain English: *him that submitteth himself to the priest.*

27

Christianity grew out of an utterly *false* soil, in which all nature, every natural value, every *reality* had the deepest instincts of the ruling class against it; it was a form of deadly hostility to reality which has never been surpassed. The 'holy people' which had retained only priestly values and priestly names for all things, and which, with a logical consistency that is terrifying, had divorced itself from everything still powerful on earth as if it were 'unholy', 'worldly', 'sinful' – this people created a final formula for its instinct which was consistent to the point of self-suppression; as *Christianity* it denied even the last form of reality, the 'holy people', the 'chosen people', *Jewish* reality itself. The case is of supreme interest: the small insurrectionary movement christened with the name of Jesus of Nazareth, is the Jewish instinct *over again* – in other words, it is the sacerdotal instinct which can no longer endure the priest as a fact; it is the discovery of a kind of life even more fantastic than the one previously conceived, a vision of life which is even more unreal than that which the organisation of a church stipulates. Christianity denies the church.

I fail to see against whom was directed the insurrection of which rightly or wrongly Jesus is understood to have been the promoter, if it were not directed against the Jewish church – the word 'church' being used here in precisely the same sense in which it is used today. It was an insurrection against the 'good and the just', against the 'prophets of Israel', against the hierarchy of society – not against the latter's corruption, but against caste, privilege, order, formality. It was the lack of faith in 'higher men', it was a 'Nay' uttered against everything that was tinctured with the blood of priests and theologians. But the hierarchy which was set in question if only temporarily by this movement, formed the construction of piles upon which, alone, the Jewish people was able to subsist in the midst of the 'waters'; it was that people's *last* chance of survival wrested from the world at enormous pains, the *residuum* of its political autonomy: to attack this construction was tantamount to attacking the most profound popular instinct, the most tenacious national will to live that has ever existed on earth. This saintly anarchist who called the lowest of the low, the outcasts and 'sinners', the Chandala of Judaism, to revolt against the established order of things (and in language which, if the gospels are to be trusted, would get one sent to Siberia even today) – this man was a political criminal in so far as political criminals were possible in a community so absurdly non-political. This brought him to the cross: the proof of this is the inscription found thereon. He died for *his* sins – and no matter how often the contrary has been asserted there is absolutely nothing to show that he died for the sins of others.

28

As to whether he was conscious of this contrast, or whether he was merely *regarded* as such, is quite another question. And here, alone, do I touch upon the problem of the psychology of the Saviour. I confess there are few books which I have as much difficulty in reading as the gospels. These difficulties are quite different from those which allowed the learned curiosity of the German mind to celebrate one of its most memorable triumphs. Many years have now elapsed since I, like every young scholar, with the sage conscientiousness of a refined philologist, relished the work of the incomparable Strauss. I was then twenty years of age; now I am too serious for that sort of thing. What do I care about the contradictions of 'tradition'? How can saintly legends be called 'tradition' at all! The stories of saints constitute the most ambiguous literature on earth: to apply the scientific method to them, *when there are no other documents to hand*, seems to me to be a fatal procedure from the start – simply learned fooling.

The point that concerns me is the psychological type of the Saviour. This type might be contained in the gospels, in spite of the gospels, and however much it may have been mutilated, or overladen with foreign features: just as that of Francis of Assisi is contained in his legends in spite of his legends. It is *not* a question of the truth concerning what he has done, what he has said, and how he actually died; but whether his type may still be conceived in any way, whether it has been handed down to us at all? The attempts which to my knowledge have been made to read the *history* of a 'soul' out of the gospels, seem to me to point only to disreputable levity in psychological matters. M. Renan, that buffoon *in psychologicis*, has contributed the two most monstrous ideas imaginable to the explanation of the type of Jesus: the idea of the *genius* and the idea of the *hero* ('*héros*'). But if there is anything thoroughly unevangelical surely it is the idea of the hero. It is precisely the reverse of all struggle, of all consciousness of taking part in the fight, that has become instinctive here: the inability to resist is here converted into a morality ('resist not evil', the profoundest sentence in the whole of the gospels, their key in a certain sense), the blessedness of peace, of gentleness, of not *being able* to be an enemy. What is the meaning of 'glad tidings'? True life, eternal life has been found – it is not promised, it is actually here, it is in *you;* it is life in love, in love free from all selection or exclusion, free from all distance. Everybody is the child of God – Jesus does not by any means claim anything for himself alone – as the child of God everybody is equal to everybody else . . . Fancy making

Jesus a *hero*! And what a tremendous misunderstanding the word 'genius' is! Our whole idea of 'spirit', which is a civilised idea, could have had no meaning whatever in the world in which Jesus lived. In the strict terms of the physiologist, a very different word ought to be used here . . . We know of a condition of morbid irritability of the sense of *touch*, which recoils shuddering from every kind of contact, and from every attempt at grasping a solid object. Any such physiological *habitus* reduced to its ultimate logical conclusion, becomes an instinctive hatred of all reality, a flight into the 'intangible', into the 'incomprehensible'; a repugnance to all formulae, to every notion of time and space, to everything that is established such as customs, institutions, the church; a feeling at one's ease in a world in which no sign of reality is any longer visible, a merely 'inner' world, a 'true' world, an 'eternal' world . . . 'The Kingdom of God is within you' . . .

30

The instinctive hatred of reality is the outcome of an extreme susceptibility to pain and to irritation, which can no longer endure to be 'touched' at all, because every sensation strikes too deep.

The instinctive exclusion of all aversion, of all hostility, of all boundaries and distances in feeling, is the outcome of an extreme susceptibility to pain and to irritation, which regards all resistance, all compulsory resistance as insufferable *anguish* (that is to say, as harmful, as *deprecated* by the self-preservative instinct), and which knows blessedness (happiness) only when it is no longer obliged to offer resistance to anybody, either evil or detrimental – love as the only ultimate possibility of life . . .

These are the two *physiological realities* upon which and out of which the doctrine of salvation has grown. I call them a sublime further development of hedonism, upon a thoroughly morbid soil. Epicureanism, the pagan theory of salvation, even though it possessed a large proportion of Greek vitality and nervous energy, remains the most closely related to the above. Epicurus was a *typical* decadent: and I was the first to recognise him as such. The terror of pain, even of infinitely slight pain – such a state cannot possibly help culminating in a *religion* of love . . .

31

I have given my reply to the problem in advance. The prerequisite thereto was the admission of the fact that the type of the Saviour has reached us only in a very distorted form. This distortion in itself is extremely feasible: for many reasons a type of that kind could not be pure, whole, and free from additions. The environment in which this strange figure moved, must have left its mark upon him, and the history, the *destiny* of the first Christian communities must have done so to a still greater degree. Thanks to that destiny, the type must have been enriched retrospectively with features which can be interpreted only as serving the purposes of war and of propaganda. That strange and morbid world into which the gospels lead us – a world which seems to have been drawn from a Russian novel, where the scum and dross of society, diseases of the nerves and 'childish' imbecility seem to have given each other rendezvous – must in any case have *coarsened* the type: the first disciples especially must have translated an existence conceived entirely in symbols and abstractions into their own crudities, in order at least to be able to understand something about it – for them the type existed only after it had been cast in a more familiar mould . . . The prophet, the Messiah, the future judge, the teacher of morals, the thaumaturgist, John the Baptist – all these were but so many opportunities of misunderstanding the type . . . Finally, let us not underrate the *proprium* of all great and especially sectarian veneration: very often it effaces from the venerated object, all the original and frequently painfully unfamiliar traits and idiosyncrasies – *it does not even see them*. It is greatly to be deplored that no Dostoevsky lived in the neighbourhood of this most interesting decadent – I mean someone who would have known how to feel the poignant charm of such a mixture of the sublime, the morbid, and the childlike. Finally, the type, as an example of decadence, may actually have been extraordinarily multifarious and contradictory: this, as a possible alternative, is not to be altogether ignored. Albeit, everything seems to point away from it; for, precisely in this case, tradition would necessarily have been particularly true and objective: whereas we have reasons for assuming the reverse. Meanwhile a yawning chasm of contradiction separates the mountain, lake, and pastoral preacher, who strikes us as a Buddha on a soil only very slightly Hindu, from that combative fanatic, the mortal enemy of theologians and priests, whom Renan's malice has glorified as '*le grand maître en ironie.*' For my part, I do not doubt but what the greater part of this venom (and even of *esprit*) was inoculated into the type of the Master only as the outcome of the agitated condition of Christian propaganda. For we have ample reasons for knowing the unscrupulousness of all sectarians when they wish to contrive their own *apology* out of the person of their master. When the first Christian community required a discerning, wrangling, quarrelsome, malicious and hair-splitting theologian, to oppose other theologians, it created its 'God' according to its needs; just as it did not hesitate to put upon his lips those utterly unevangelical ideas of his 'second coming', the 'last judgment' – ideas with which it could not then dispense – and every kind of expectation and promise which happened to be current.

32

I can only repeat that I am opposed to the importation of the fanatic into the type of the Saviour: the word '*impérieux*', which Renan uses, in itself annuls the type. The 'glad tidings' are simply that there is no longer any contradiction, that the Kingdom of Heaven is for the *children:* the faith which raises its voice here is not a faith that has been won by a struggle – it is to hand, it was there from the beginning, it is a sort of spiritual return to childishness. The case of delayed and undeveloped puberty in the organism, as the result of degeneration, is at least familiar to physiologists. A faith of this sort does not show anger, it does not blame, neither does it defend itself: it does not bring 'the sword' – it has no inkling of how it will one day establish feuds between man and man. It does not demonstrate itself, either by miracles, or by reward and promises, or yet 'through the scriptures': it is in itself at every moment its own miracle, its own reward, its own proof, its own 'Kingdom of God'. This faith cannot be formulated – it lives, it guards against formulae. The accident of environment, of speech, of preparatory culture, certainly determines a particular series of conceptions: early Christianity deals only in Judaeo-Semitic conceptions (the eating and drinking at the last super form part of these – this idea which like everything Jewish has been abused so maliciously by the church). But one should guard against seeing anything more than a language of signs, semiotics, an opportunity for parables in all this. The very fact that no word is to be taken literally, is the only condition on which this Antirealist is able to speak at all. Among Indians he would have made use of the ideas of Sankhyam, among Chinese, those of Lao-tze – and would not have been aware of any difference. With a little terminological laxity Jesus might be called a 'free spirit' – he cares not a jot for anything that is established: the word *killeth*, everything fixed *killeth*. The idea, *experience*, 'life' as he alone knows it, is, according to him, opposed to every kind of word, formula, law, faith and dogma. He speaks only of the innermost things: 'life' or 'truth', or 'light', is his expression for the innermost thing – everything else, the whole of reality, the whole of nature, language even, has only the value of a sign, of a simile for him. It is of paramount importance not to make any mistake at this point, however great may be the temptation thereto that lies in Christian – I mean to say, ecclesiastical – prejudice. Any such essential symbolism stands beyond the pale of all religion, all notions of cult, all history, all natural science, all experience of the world, all knowledge, all politics, all psychology, all books and all Art – for his 'wisdom' is precisely the complete ignorance of the existence of such things. He has not even heard speak of *culture*, he does not require to oppose it – he does not deny it . . . The same holds good of the state, of the whole of civil and social order, of work and of war – he never had any reason to deny the world, he had not the vaguest notion of the ecclesiastical concept 'the world' . . . Denying is precisely what was quite impossible to him. Dialectic is also quite absent, as likewise the idea that any faith, any 'truth' can be proved by argument (his proofs are inner 'lights', inward feelings of happiness and self-affirmation, a host of 'proofs of power'). Neither can such a doctrine contradict, it does not even realise the fact that there are or can be other doctrines, it is absolutely incapable of imagining a contrary judgment . . . Wherever it encounters such things, from a feeling of profound sympathy it bemoans such 'blindness' – for it sees the 'light' – but it raises no objections.

33

The whole psychology of the 'gospels' lacks the concept of guilt and punishment, as also that of reward. 'Sin', any sort of aloofness between God and man, is done away with – *this is precisely what constitutes the 'glad tidings'*. Eternal bliss is not promised, it is not bound up with certain conditions; it is the only reality – the rest consists only of signs wherewith to speak about it . . .

The results of such a state project themselves into a new practice of life, the actual evangelical practice. It is not a 'faith' which distinguishes the Christians: the Christian acts, he distinguishes himself by means of a *different* mode of action. He does not resist his enemy either by words or in his heart. He draws no distinction between foreigners and natives, between Jews and Gentiles ('the neighbour' really means the co-religionist, the Jew). He is angry with no one, he despises no one. He neither shows himself at the tribunals nor does he acknowledge any of their claims ('Swear not at all'). He never under any circumstances divorces his wife, even when her infidelity has been proved. All this is at bottom one principle, it is all the outcome of one instinct.

The life of the Saviour was naught else than this practice – neither was his death. He no longer required any formulae, any rites for his relations with God – not even prayer. He has done with all the Jewish teaching of repentance and of atonement; he alone knows the *mode* of life which makes one feel 'divine', 'saved', 'evangelical', and at all times a 'child of God'. *Not* 'repentance', *not* 'prayer and forgiveness' are the roads to God: the *evangelical mode of life alone* leads to God, it *is* 'God'. That which the gospels abolished was the Judaism of the concepts 'sin', 'forgiveness of sin', 'faith', 'salvation through faith' – the whole doctrine of the Jewish church was denied by the 'glad tidings'.

The profound instinct of how one must live in order to feel 'in Heaven', in order to feel 'eternal', while in every other respect one feels by *no* means 'in Heaven': this alone is the psychological reality of 'Salvation'. A new life and *not* a new faith . . .

34

If I understand anything at all about this great symbolist, it is this: that he regarded only *inner* facts as facts, as 'truths' – that he understood the rest, everything natural, temporal, material and historical, only as signs, as opportunities for parables. The concept 'the Son of Man', is not a concrete personality belonging to history, anything individual and isolated, but an 'eternal' fact, a psychological symbol divorced from the concept of time. The same is true, and in the highest degree, of the *God* of this typical symbolist, of the 'Kingdom of God', of the 'Kingdom of Heaven', and of the 'Sonship of God', Nothing is more un-Christlike than the *ecclesiastical crudity* of a personal God, of a Kingdom of God that is coming, of a 'Kingdom of Heaven' beyond, of a 'Son of God' as the second person of the Trinity. All this, if I may be forgiven the expression, is as fitting as a square peg in a round hole – and oh! what a hole! – the gospels: a *world-historic* cynicism in the scorn of symbols . . . But what is meant by the signs 'Father' and 'Son', is of course obvious – not to everybody, I admit: with the word 'Son', *entrance* into the feeling of the general transfiguration of all things (beatitude) is expressed; with the word 'Father', *this feeling itself*, the feeling of eternity and of perfection. I blush to have to remind you of what the Church has done with this symbolism: has it not set an Amphitryon story at the threshold of the Christian 'faith'? And a dogma of immaculate conception into the bargain? . . . *But by so doing it defiled conception.*

The 'Kingdom of Heaven' is a state of the heart – not something which exists 'beyond this earth' or comes to you 'after death'. The whole idea of natural death is lacking in the gospels. Death is not a bridge, not a means of access: it is absent because it belongs to quite a different and merely apparent world, the only use of which is to furnish signs, similes. The 'hour of death' is not a Christian idea – the 'hour', time in general, physical life and its crises do not exist for the messenger of 'glad tidings' . . . The 'Kingdom of God' is not something that is expected; it has no yesterday nor any day after tomorrow, it is not going to come in a 'thousand years' – it is an experience of a human heart; it is everywhere, it is nowhere . . .

35

This 'messenger of glad tidings' died as he lived and as he taught – *not* in order 'to save mankind', but in order to show how one ought to live. It was a mode of life that he bequeathed to mankind: his behaviour before his judges, his attitude towards his executioners, his accusers, and all kinds of calumny and scorn – his demeanour on the *cross*. He offers no resistance; he does not defend his rights; he takes no step to ward off the most extreme consequences, he does more – he provokes them. And he prays, suffers and loves with those, in those, who treat him ill . . . *Not* to defend one's self, *not* to show anger, *not* to hold anyone responsible . . . But to refrain from resisting even the evil one – to *love* him . . .

36

Only we spirits that have *become free*, possess the necessary condition for understanding something which nineteen centuries have misunderstood – that honesty which has become an instinct and a passion in us, and which wages war upon the 'holy lie' with even more vigour than upon every other lie . . . Mankind was unspeakably far from our beneficent and cautious neutrality, from that discipline of the mind, which, alone, renders the solution of such strange and subtle things possible: at all times, with shameless egoism, all that people sought was their *own* advantage in these matters, the Church was built up out of contradiction to the gospel . . .

Whoever might seek for signs pointing to the guiding fingers of an ironical deity behind the great Comedy of existence, would find no small argument in the *huge note of interrogation* that is called Christianity. The fact that mankind is on its knees before the reverse of that which formed the origin, the meaning and the *rights* of the gospel; the fact that, in the idea 'Church', precisely that is pronounced holy which the 'messenger of glad tidings' regarded as *beneath* him, as *behind* him – one might seek in vain for a more egregious example of *world-historic* irony.

37

Our age is proud of its historical sense: how could it allow itself to be convinced of the nonsensical idea that at the beginning Christianity consisted only of the *clumsy fable of the thaumaturgist and of the Saviour,* and that all its spiritual and symbolic side was only developed later? On the contrary: the history of Christianity – from the death on the cross onwards – is the history of a gradual and ever coarser misunderstanding of an original symbolism. With every extension of Christianity over ever larger and ruder masses, who were ever less able to grasp its first principles, the need of *vulgarising and barbarising* it increased proportionately – it absorbed the teachings and rites of all the *subterranean* cults of the *imperium Romanum*, as well as the nonsense of every kind of morbid reasoning. The fatal feature of Christianity lies in the necessary fact that its faith had to become as morbid, base and vulgar as the needs to which it had to minister were morbid, base and vulgar. *Morbid barbarism* at last braces itself together for power in the form of the Church – the Church, this deadly hostility to all honesty, to all loftiness of the soul, to all discipline of the mind, to all frank and kindly humanity. *Christian* and *noble* values: only we spirits *who have become free* have re-established this contrast in values which is the greatest that has ever existed on earth!

38

I cannot, at this point, stifle a sigh. There are days when I am visited by a feeling blacker than the blackest melancholy – the *contempt of man*. And in order that I may leave you in no doubt as to what I despise, *whom* I despise, I declare that it is the man of today, the man with whom I am fatally contemporaneous. The man of today, I am asphyxiated by his foul breath . . . Towards the past, like all knights of knowledge, I am profoundly tolerant – that is to say, I exercise a sort of *generous* self-control: with gloomy caution I pass through whole millennia of this madhouse world, and whether it be called 'Christianity', 'Christian Faith', or 'Christian Church', I take care not to hold mankind responsible for its mental disorders. But my feeling suddenly changes, and vents itself the moment I enter the modern age, *our* age. Our age *knows* . . . That which formerly was merely morbid, is now positively indecent. It is indecent nowadays to be a Christian. *And it is here that my loathing begins*. I look about me: not a word of what was formerly known as 'truth' has remained standing; we can no longer endure to hear a priest even pronounce the word 'truth'. Even he who makes but the most modest claims upon truth, *must* know at present, that a theologian, a priest, or a pope, not only errs but actually *lies*, with every word that he utters – and that he is no longer able to lie from 'innocence', from 'ignorance'. Even the priest knows quite as well as everybody else does that there is no longer any 'God', any 'sinner' or any 'Saviour', and that 'free will', and 'a moral order of the universe' are *lies*. Seriousness, the profound self-conquest of the spirit, no longer allows anyone to be *ignorant* about this . . . All the concepts of the Church have been revealed in their true colours – that is to say, as the most vicious frauds on earth, calculated to *depreciate* nature and all natural values. The priest himself has been recognised as what he is – that is to say, as the most dangerous kind of parasite, as the actual venomous spider of existence . . . At present we know, our *conscience* knows, the real value of the gruesome inventions which the priests and the Church have made, *and what end they served*. By means of them that state of self-profanation on the part of man has been attained, the sight of which makes one heave. The concepts 'Beyond', 'Last Judgment', 'Immortality of the Soul', the 'soul' itself, are merely so many instruments of torture, so many systems of cruelty, on the strength of which the priest became and remained master . . . Everybody knows this, *and nevertheless everything remains as it was*. Whither has the last shred of decency, of self-respect gone, if nowadays even our statesmen – a body of men who are otherwise so unembarrassed, and such thorough anti-Christians in deed – still declare themselves Christians and still flock to communion? . . . Fancy a prince at the head of his legions, magnificent as the expression of the egoism and self-exaltation of his people – but *shameless* enough to acknowledge himself a Christian! . . . What then does Christianity deny? What does it call 'world'? 'The world' to Christianity means that a man is a soldier, a judge, a patriot, that he defends himself, that he values his honour, that he desires his own advantage, that he is *proud* . . . The conduct of every moment, every instinct, every valuation that leads to a deed, is at present anti-Christian: what an *abortion of falsehood* modern man must be, in order to be able *without a blush* still to call himself a Christian!

39

I will retrace my steps, and will tell you the *genuine* history of Christianity. The very word 'Christianity' is a misunderstanding – truth to tell, there never was more than one Christian, and he *died* on the Cross. The 'gospel' *died* on the cross. That which thenceforward was called 'gospel' was the reverse of that 'gospel' that Christ had lived: it was 'evil tidings', a *dysangel*. It is false to the point of nonsense to see in 'faith', in the faith in salvation through Christ, the distinguishing trait of the Christian: the only thing that is Christian is the Christian mode of existence, a life such as he led who died on the Cross . . . To this day a life of this kind is still possible; for certain men, it is even necessary: genuine, primitive Christianity will be possible in all ages . . . *Not* a faith, but a course of action, above all a course of inaction, non-interference, and a different life . . . States of consciousness, any sort of faith, a holding of certain things for true, as every psychologist knows, are indeed of absolutely no consequence, and are only of fifth-rate importance compared with the value of the instincts: more exactly, the whole concept of intellectual causality is false. To reduce the fact of being a Christian, or of Christianity, to a holding of something for true, to a mere phenomenon of consciousness, is tantamount to denying

Christianity. *In fact there have never been any Christians*. The 'Christian', he who for two thousand years has been called a Christian, is merely a psychological misunderstanding of self. Looked at more closely, there ruled in him, *notwithstanding* all his faith, only instincts – and *what instincts*! – 'Faith' in all ages, as for instance in the case of Luther, has always been merely a cloak, a pretext, a *screen*, behind which the instincts played their game – a prudent form of *blindness* in regard to the dominion of *certain* instincts . . . 'Faith' I have already characterised as a piece of really Christian cleverness; for people have always spoken of 'faith' and acted according to their instincts . . . In the Christian's world of ideas there is nothing which even touches reality: but I have already recognised in the instinctive hatred of reality the actual motive force, the only driving power at the root of Christianity. What follows therefrom? That here, even *in psychologicis*, error is fundamental – that is to say capable of determining the spirit of things – that is to say, *substance*. Take one idea away from the whole, and put one realistic fact in its stead – and the whole of Christianity tumbles into nonentity! Surveyed from above, this strangest of all facts – a religion not only dependent upon error, but inventive and showing signs of genius only in those errors which are dangerous and which poison life and the human heart – remains a *spectacle for gods*, for those gods who are at the same time philosophers and whom I met for instance in those celebrated dialogues on the island of Naxos. At the moment when they get rid of their *loathing* (*and we do as well!*), they will be thankful for the spectacle the Christians have offered: the wretched little planet called Earth perhaps deserves on account of *this* curious case alone, a divine glance, and divine interest . . . Let us not therefore underestimate the Christians: the Christian, false *to the point of innocence in falsity*, is far above the apes – in regard to the Christians a certain well-known theory of Descent becomes a mere good-natured compliment.

40

The fate of the gospel was decided at the moment of the death – it hung on the 'cross' . . . It was only death, this unexpected and ignominious death; it was only the cross which as a rule was reserved simply for the *canaille* – only this appalling paradox which confronted the disciples with the actual riddle: *Who was that? What was that?* The state produced by the excited and profoundly wounded feelings of these men, the suspicion that such a death might imply the *refutation* of their cause, and the terrible note of interrogation: 'why precisely thus?' will be understood only too well. In this case everything *must* be necessary, everything must have meaning, a reason, the highest reason. The love of a disciple admits of no such thing as accident. Only then did the chasm yawn: 'Who has killed him?' 'Who was his natural enemy?' This question rent the firmament like a flash of lightning. Reply: *dominant* Judaism, its ruling class. Thenceforward the disciple felt himself in revolt *against* established order; he understood Jesus, after the fact, as one *in revolt against established order*. Heretofore this warlike, this nay-saying and nay-doing feature in Christ had been lacking; nay more, he was its contradiction. The small primitive community had obviously understood *nothing* of the principal factor of all, which was the example of freedom and of superiority to every form of *resentment* which lay in this way of dying. And this shows how little they understood him altogether! At bottom Jesus could not have desired anything else by his death than to give the strongest public *example* and *proof* of his doctrine . . . But his disciples were very far from *forgiving* this death – though if they had done so it would have been in the highest sense evangelical on their part – neither were they prepared, with a gentle and serene calmness of heart, to *offer* themselves for a similar death . . . Precisely the most unevangelical feeling, *revenge*, became once more ascendant. It was impossible for the cause to end with this death: 'compensation' and 'judgment' were required (and forsooth, what could be more unevangelical than 'compensation', 'punishment', 'judgment') The popular expectation of a Messiah once more became prominent; attention was fixed upon one historical moment: the 'Kingdom of God' descends to sit in judgment upon his enemies. But this proves that everything was misunderstood: the 'Kingdom of God' regarded as the last scene of the last act, as a promise! But the Gospel had clearly been the living, the fulfilment, the *reality* of this 'Kingdom of God'. It was precisely a death such as Christ's that was this 'Kingdom of God'. It was only now that all the contempt for the Pharisees and the theologians, and all bitter feelings towards them, were introduced into the character of the Master – and by this means he himself was converted into a Pharisee and a theologian! On the other hand, the savage veneration of these completely unhinged souls could no longer endure that evangelical right of every man to be the child of God, which Jesus had taught: their revenge consisted in *elevating* Jesus in a manner devoid of all reason, and in separating him from themselves: just as formerly, the Jews, with the view of revenging themselves on their enemies, separated themselves from their God, and placed him high above them. The Only God, and the Only Son of God: – both were products of resentment.

41

And from this time forward an absurd problem rose into prominence: 'how *could* God allow it to happen?' To this question the disordered minds of the small community found a reply which in its absurdity was literally terrifying: God gave his Son as a *sacrifice* for the forgiveness of sins. Alas! how prompt and sudden was the end of the gospel! Expiatory sacrifice for guilt, and indeed in its most repulsive and barbaric form – the sacrifice of the *innocent* for the sins of the guilty! What appalling Paganism! For Jesus himself had done away with the concept 'guilt' – he denied any gulf between God and man, he *lived* this unity between God and man, it was this that constituted *his* 'glad tidings' . . . And he did *not* teach it as a privilege! Thenceforward there was gradually imported into the type of the Saviour the doctrine of the Last Judgment, and of the 'second coming', the doctrine of sacrificial death, and the doctrine of *Resurrection*, by means of which the whole concept 'blessedness', the entire and only reality of the gospel, is conjured away – in favour of a state *after* death! . . . St Paul, with that rabbinic impudence which characterises all his doings, rationalised this conception, this prostitution of a conception, as follows: 'if Christ did not rise from the dead, our faith is vain.' And, in a trice, the most contemptible of all unrealisable promises, the *impudent* doctrine of personal immortality, was woven out of the gospel . . . St Paul even preached this immortality as a reward.

436

42

You now realise what it was that came to an end with the death on the cross: a new and thoroughly original effort towards a Buddhistic movement of peace, towards real and *not* merely promised *happiness on earth*. For, as I have already pointed out, this remains the fundamental difference between the two religions of *decadence:* Buddhism promises little but fulfils more, Christianity promises everything but fulfils nothing. The 'glad tidings' were followed closely by the absolutely *worst* tidings – those of St Paul. Paul is the incarnation of a type which is the reverse of that of the Saviour; he is the genius in hatred, in the standpoint of hatred, and in the relentless logic of hatred. And alas, what did this dysangelist not sacrifice to his hatred! Above all, the Saviour himself: he nailed him to *his* cross. Christ's life, his example, his doctrine and death, the sense and the right of the gospel – not a vestige of all this was left, once this forger, prompted by his hatred, had understood in it only that which could serve his purpose. *Not* reality: *not* historical truth! . . . And once more, the sacerdotal instinct of the Jew perpetrated the same great crime against history – he simply cancelled the yesterday, and the day before that, out of Christianity; he *contrived of his own accord a history of the birth of Christianity*. He did more: he once more falsified the history of Israel, so as to make it appear as a prologue to *his* mission: all the prophets had referred to *his* 'Saviour' . . . Later on the Church even distorted the history of mankind so as to convert it into a prelude to Christianity . . . The type of the Saviour, his teaching, his life, his death, the meaning of his death, even the sequel to his death – nothing remained untouched, nothing was left which even remotely resembled reality. St Paul simply transferred the centre of gravity of the whole of that great life, to a place *behind* this life – in the *lie* of the 'resuscitated' Christ. At bottom, he had no possible use for the life of the Saviour – he needed the death on the cross, *and* something more. To regard as honest a man like St Paul (a man whose home was the very headquarters of Stoical enlightenment) when he devises a proof of the continued existence of the Saviour out of a hallucination; or even to believe him when he declares that he had this hallucination, would amount to foolishness on the part of a psychologist: St Paul desired the end, consequently he also desired the means . . . Even what he himself did not believe, was believed in by the idiots among whom he spread *his* doctrine. What he wanted was power; with St Paul the priest again aspired to power – he could make use only of concepts, doctrines, symbols with which masses may be tyrannised over, and with which herds are formed. What was the only part of Christianity which was subsequently borrowed by Muhamed? St Paul's invention, his expedient for priestly tyranny and to the formation of herds: the belief in immortality – *that is to say, the doctrine of the 'Last Judgment'* . . .

43

When the centre of gravity of life is laid, *not* in life, but in a beyond – *in nonentity* – life is utterly robbed of its balance. The great lie of personal immortality destroys all reason, all nature in the instincts – everything in the instincts that is beneficent, that promotes life and that is a guarantee of the future, henceforward aroused suspicion. The very meaning of life is now construed as the effort to live in such a way that life no longer has any point . . . Why show any public spirit? Why be grateful for one's origin and one's forebears? Why collaborate with one's fellows, and be confident? Why be concerned about the general weal or strive after it? All these things are merely so many 'temptations', so many deviations from the 'straight path'. 'One thing only is necessary' . . . that everybody, as an 'immortal soul', should have equal rank, that in the totality of beings, the 'salvation' of each individual may lay claim to eternal importance, that insignificant bigots and three-quarter-lunatics may have the right to suppose that the laws of nature may be persistently *broken* on their account – any such magnification of every kind of selfishness to infinity, to *insolence*, cannot be branded with sufficient contempt. And yet it is to this miserable flattery of personal vanity that Christianity owes its *triumph* – by this means it lured all the bungled and the botched, all revolting and revolted people, all abortions, the whole of the refuse and offal of humanity, over to its side. The 'salvation of the soul' – in plain English: 'the world revolves around me' . . . the poison of the doctrine '*equal* rights for all' – has been dispensed with the greatest thoroughness by Christianity: Christianity, prompted by the most secret recesses of bad instincts, has waged a deadly war upon all feeling of reverence and distance between man and man – that is to say, the *prerequisite* of all elevation, of every growth in culture; out of the resentment of the masses it wrought its *principal weapons* against us, against everything noble, joyful, exalted on earth, against our happiness on earth . . . To grant 'immortality' to every St Peter and St Paul, was the greatest, the most vicious outrage upon *noble* humanity that has ever been perpetrated. And do not let us underestimate the fatal influence which, springing from Christianity, has insinuated itself even into politics! Nowadays no one has the courage of special rights, of rights of dominion, of a feeling of self-respect and of respect for his equals – of *pathos of distance*. Our politics are diseased with this lack of courage! The aristocratic attitude of mind has been most thoroughly undermined by the lie of the equality of souls; and if the belief in the 'privilege of the greatest number' creates and will continue to create *revolutions* – it is Christianity, let there be no doubt about it, and Christian values, which convert every revolution into blood and crime! Christianity is the revolt of all things that crawl on their bellies against everything that is lofty: the gospel of the 'lowly' *lowers* . . .

44

The Gospels are invaluable as a testimony of the corruption which was already persistent *within* the first Christian communities. That which St Paul, with the logician's cynicism of a Rabbi, carried to its logical conclusion, was nevertheless merely the process of decay which began with the death of the Saviour. These gospels cannot be read too cautiously; difficulties lurk behind every word they contain. I confess, and people will not take this amiss, that they are precisely on that account a joy of the first rank for a psychologist – as the reverse of all naïve perversity, as refinement *par excellence*, as a masterpiece of art in psychological corruption. The gospels stand alone. Altogether the Bible allows of no comparison. The *first* thing to be remembered if we do not wish to lose the scent here, is, that we are among Jews. The dissembling of holiness which, here, literally amounts to genius, and which has never been even approximately achieved elsewhere either by books or by men, this fraud in word and pose which in this book is elevated to an *art*, is not the accident of any individual gift, of any exceptional nature. These qualities are a matter of *race*. With Christianity, the art of telling holy lies, which constitutes the whole of Judaism, reaches its final mastership, thanks to many centuries of Jewish and most thoroughly serious training and practice. The Christian, this *ultima ratio* of falsehood, is the Jew over again – he is even three times a Jew . . . The fundamental will only to make use of concepts, symbols and poses, which are demonstrated by the practice of the priests, the instinctive repudiation of every other kind of practice, every other standpoint of valuation and of utility – all this is not only tradition, it is *hereditary*: only as an inheritance is it able to work like nature. The whole of mankind, the best brains, and even the best ages – (one man only excepted who is perhaps only a monster) – have allowed themselves to be deceived. The gospels were read as the *book of innocence* . . . this is no insignificant sign of the virtuosity with which deception has been practised here. Of course, if we could only succeed in seeing all these amazing bigots and pretended saints, even for a moment, all would be at an end – and it is precisely because *I* can read no single word of theirs, without seeing their pretentious poses, *that I have made an end of them* . . . I cannot endure a certain way they have of casting their eyes heavenwards. Fortunately for Christianity, books are for the greatest number, merely *literature*. We must not let ourselves be led away: 'judge not!' they say, but they dispatch all those to hell who stand in their way. Inasmuch as they let God do the judging, they themselves judge; inasmuch as they glorify God, they glorify themselves; inasmuch as they *exact* those virtues of which they themselves happen to be capable – nay more, of which they are in need in order to be able to remain on top at all – they assume the grand airs of struggling for virtue, of struggling for the dominion of virtue. 'We live, we die, we sacrifice ourselves for the good' ('the Truth', 'the Light', 'the Kingdom of God'): as a matter of fact they do only what they cannot help doing. Like sneaks they have to play a humble part: sit away in corners, and remain obscurely in the shade, and they make all this appear a *duty*; their humble life now appears as a duty, and their humility is one proof the more of their piety . . . Oh, what a humble, chaste and compassionate kind of falsity! 'Virtue itself shall bear us testimony.' . . . Only read the gospels as books calculated to seduce by means of morality: morality is appropriated by these petty people – they know what morality can do! The best way of leading mankind by the nose is with morality! The fact is that the most conscious *conceit* of people who believe themselves to be *chosen*, here simulates modesty: in this way they, the Christian community, the 'good and the just' place themselves once and for all on a certain side, the side 'of Truth' – and the rest of mankind, 'the world' on the other . . . This was the most fatal kind of megalomania that had ever yet existed on earth: insignificant little abortions of bigots and liars began to lay sole claim to the concepts 'God', 'Truth', 'Light', 'Spirit', 'Love', 'Wisdom', 'Life', as if these things were, so to speak, synonyms of themselves, in order to fence themselves off from 'the world'; little ultra-Jews, ripe for every kind of madhouse, twisted values round in order to suit themselves, just as if the Christian, alone, were the meaning, the salt, the standard and even the *'ultimate tribunal'* of all the rest of mankind . . . The whole fatality was rendered possible only because a kind of megalomania, akin to this one and allied to it in race – the Jewish kind – was already to hand in the world: the very moment the gulf between Jews and Judaeo-Christians was opened, the latter had no alternative left, but to adopt the same self-preservative measures as the Jewish instinct suggested, even *against* the Jews themselves, whereas the Jews, theretofore, had employed these same measures only against the Gentiles. The Christian is nothing more than an anarchical Jew.

45

Let me give you a few examples of what these paltry people have stuffed into their heads, what they have laid *on the lips of their Master.* Quite a host of confessions from 'beautiful souls' –

'And whosoever shall not receive you, nor hear you, when ye depart thence, shake off the dust under your feet for a testimony against them. Verily I say unto you, it shall be more tolerable for Sodom and Gomorrah in the day of judgment, than for that city.' (Mark 6:2) – How *evangelical*! . . .

'And whosoever shall offend one of these little ones that believe in me, it is better for him that a millstone were hanged about his neck, and he were cast into the sea.' (Mark 9:42) – How *evangelical*! . . .

'And if thine eye offend thee, pluck it out: it is better for thee to enter into the kingdom of God with one eye, than having two eyes to be cast into hell fire: where their worm dieth not, and the fire is not quenched.' (Mark 9:47, 48) – The eye is not precisely what is meant in this passage . . .

'Verily I say unto you, that there be some of them that stand here, which shall not taste of death, till they have seen the kingdom of God come with power.' (Mark 9:1) – Well *lied*, lion! . . .

'Whosoever will come after me, let him deny himself, and take up his cross, and follow me. *For* . . .' (*A psychologist's comment*: Christian morality is refuted by its 'For's': its 'reasons' refute – this is Christian.) (Mark 8:34)

'Judge not, that ye be not judged. For with what judgment ye judge, ye shall be judged.' (Matthew 7:1, 2) – What a strange notion of justice on the part of a 'just' judge! . . .

'For if ye love them which love you, what reward have ye? Do not even the publicans the same? And if ye salute your brethren only, what do ye more *than others?* Do not even the publicans so?' (Matthew 5:46, 47) The principle of 'Christian love': it insists upon being *well paid* . . .

'But if ye forgive not men their trespasses neither will your Father forgive your trespasses.' (Matthew 6:15) – Very compromising for the 'Father' in question.

'But seek ye first the kingdom of God, and his righteousness; and all these things shall be added unto you.' (Matthew 6:33) 'All these things' – that is to say, food, clothing, all the necessities of life. To use a moderate expression, this is an *error* . . . Shortly before this God appears as a tailor, at least in certain cases . . .

'Rejoice ye in that day, and leap for joy: for, behold, your reward *is* great in heaven: for in the like manner did their fathers unto the prophets.' (Luke 6:23) – *Impudent* rabble! They dare to compare themselves with the prophets . . .

'Know ye not that ye are the temple of God and that the Spirit of God dwelleth in you? If any man defile the temple of God, *him shall God destroy;* for the temple of God is holy, which *temple ye are.*' (St Paul, 1 Corinthians 3:16, 17) – One cannot have too much contempt for this sort of thing . . .

'Do ye not know that the saints shall judge the world? And if the world shall be judged by you, are ye unworthy to judge the smallest matters?' (St Paul, 1 Corinthians 4:2) – Unfortunately this is not merely the speech of a lunatic . . . This *appalling impostor* proceeds thus: 'Know ye not that we shall judge angels? How much more things that pertain to this life?'

'Hath not God made foolish the wisdom of this world? For after that in the wisdom of God, the world by wisdom knew not God, it pleased God by the foolishness of preaching to save them that believe . . . not many wise men after the flesh, not many mighty, not many noble *are called*: But God hath chosen the foolish things of the world to confound the wise; and God hath chosen the weak things of the world to confound the things which are mighty; And base things of the world, and things which are despised, hath God chosen; *yea*, and things which are not, to bring to nought things that are: That no flesh should glory in his presence.' (St Paul, 1 Corinthians 1:20 *et seq.*) – In order to *understand* this passage, which is of the highest importance as an example of the psychology of every Chandala morality, the reader should refer to my *Genealogy of Morals*: in this book, the contrast between a *noble* and a Chandala morality

445

born of *resentment* and impotent revengefulness, is
brought to light for the first time. St Paul was the
greatest of all the apostles of revenge . . .

46

What follows from this? That one does well to put on
one's gloves when reading the New Testament. The
proximity of so much pitch almost defiles one. We
should feel just as little inclined to hobnob with 'the
first Christians' as with Polish Jews: not that we need
explain our objections . . . They simply smell bad. –
In vain have I sought for a single sympathetic feature
in the New Testament; there is not a trace of freedom,
kindliness, open-heartedness and honesty to be found
in it. Humaneness has not even made a start in this
book, while *cleanly* instincts are entirely absent from
it . . . Only evil instincts are to be found in the New
Testament, it shows no sign of courage, these people
lack even the courage of their evil instincts. All is
cowardice, all is a closing of one's eyes and self-
deception. Every book becomes clean, after one has
just read the New Testament: for instance, immediately after laying down St Paul, I read with
particular delight that most charming and most wanton
of scoffers, Petronius, of whom someone might say
what Domenico Boccaccio wrote to the Duke of Parma
about Caesar Borgia: '*è tutto festo*' – immortally
healthy, immortally cheerful and well-constituted . . .
These petty bigots err in their calculations and in the
most important thing of all. They certainly attack;
but everything they assail is, by that very fact alone,
distinguished. He whom a 'primitive Christian' attacks,
is *not* thereby sullied . . . Conversely it is an honour to
be opposed by 'primitive Christians'. One cannot read

serpent, Heva' – every priest knows this: 'all evil came into this world through woman' – every priest knows this too. '*Consequently science* also comes from woman' . . . Only through woman did man learn to taste of the tree of knowledge. – What had happened? Panic had seized the old God. Man himself had been his *greatest* mistake, he had created a rival for himself, science makes you *equal to God* – it is all up with priests and gods when man becomes scientific! Moral: science is the most prohibited thing of all – it alone is forbidden. Science is the *first*, the germ of all sins, the original sin. *This alone is morality* – 'Thou shalt not know': the rest follows as a matter of course. God's panic did not deprive him of his intelligence. How can one *guard* against science? For ages this was his principal problem. Reply: man must be kicked out of paradise! Happiness, leisure leads to thinking – all thoughts are bad thoughts . . . Man must not think – And the 'priest-per-se' proceeds to invent distress, death, the vital danger of pregnancy, every kind of misery, decrepitude, and affliction, and above all *disease* – all these are but weapons employed in the struggle with science! Trouble prevents man from thinking . . . And notwithstanding all these precautions! Oh, horror! the work of science towers aloft, it storms heaven itself, it rings the death-knell of the gods – what's to be done? – The old God invents *war;* he separates the nations, and contrives to make men destroy each other mutually (the priests have always been in need of war . . .) War, among other things, is a great disturber of science! – Incredible! Knowledge, *the rejection of the sacerdotal yoke*, nevertheless increases. – So the old God arrives at this final decision: 'Man has become scientific – *there is no help for it, he must be drowned!*' . . .

the New Testament without feeling a preference for everything in it which is the subject of abuse – not to speak of the 'wisdom of this world', which an impudent windbag tries in vain to confound 'by the foolishness of preaching'. Even the Pharisees and the Scribes derive advantage from such opposition: they must certainly have been worth something in order to have been hated in such a disreputable way. Hypocrisy – as if this were a reproach which the 'first Christians' *were at liberty* to make! – After all the Scribes and Pharisees were the *privileged ones:* this was quite enough, the hatred of the Chandala requires no other reasons. I very much fear that the 'first Christian' – as also the '*last Christian' whom I may yet be able to meet* – is in his deepest instincts a rebel against everything privileged; he lives and struggles unremittingly for 'equal rights'! . . . Regarded more closely, he has no alternative . . . If one's desire be personally to represent 'one of the chosen of God' – or a 'temple of God', or a 'judge of angels' – then every *other* principle of selection, for instance that based upon a standard of honesty, intellect, manliness and pride, or upon beauty and freedom of heart, becomes the 'world' – *evil in itself.* Moral: every word on the lips of a 'first Christian' is a lie, every action he does is an instinctive falsehood – all his values, all his aims are pernicious; but the man he hates, *the thing* he hates, *has value* . . . The Christian, more particularly the Christian priest, is a *criterion of values* – Do I require to add that in the whole of the New Testament only *one* figure appears which we cannot help respecting? Pilate, the Roman Governor. To take a Jewish quarrel *seriously* was a thing he could not get himself to do. One Jew more or less – what did it matter? . . . The noble scorn of a Roman, in whose presence the word 'truth' had been shamelessly abused, has enriched the New Testament with the only saying which *is of value* – and this saying is not only the criticism, but actually the shattering of that Testament: 'What is truth' . . .

47

That which separates us from other people is not the fact that we can discover no God, either in history, or in nature, or behind nature – but that we regard what has been revered as 'God', not as 'divine', but as wretched, absurd, pernicious; not as an error, but as a *crime against life* . . . We deny God as God . . . If the existence of this Christian God were *proved* to us, we should feel even less able to believe in him. – In a formula: *deus qualem Paulus creavit, dei negatio.* – A religion such as Christianity which never once comes in touch with reality, and which collapses the very moment reality asserts its rights even on one single point, must naturally be a mortal enemy of the 'wisdom of this world' – that is to say, *science*. It will call all those means good with which mental discipline, lucidity and severity in intellectual matters, nobility and freedom of the intellect may be poisoned, calumniated and *decried*. 'Faith' as an imperative is a *veto* against science – *in praxi*, it means lies at any price. St Paul *understood* that falsehood – that 'faith' was necessary; subsequently the Church understood St Paul. – That 'God' which St Paul invented for himself, a God who 'confounds' the 'wisdom of this world' (in a narrower sense, the two great opponents of all superstition, philology and medicine), means, in very truth, simply St Paul's firm *resolve* to do so: to call his

own will 'God', *thora*, that is arch-Jewish. St Paul insists upon confounding the 'wisdom of this world': his enemies are the *good old* philologists and doctors of the Alexandrine schools; it is on them that he wages war. As a matter of fact no one is either a philologist or a doctor, who is not also an *Antichrist*. As a philologist, for instance, a man sees *behind* the 'holy books', as a doctor he sees *behind* the physiological rottenness of the typical Christian. The doctor says 'incurable', the philologist says 'forgery'.

48

Has anybody ever really understood the celebrated story which stands at the beginning of the Bible – concerning God's deadly panic over *science*? Nobody has understood it. This essentially sacerdotal book naturally begins with the great inner difficulty of the priest: *he* knows only one great danger, *consequently* 'God' has only one great danger.

The old God, entirely 'spirit', a high-priest through and through, and wholly perfect, is wandering in a leisurely fashion round his garden; but he is bored. Against boredom even the gods themselves struggle in vain. What does he do? He invents man – man is entertaining . . . But, behold, even man begins to be bored. God's compassion for the only form of misery which is peculiar to all paradises, exceeds all bounds: so forthwith he creates yet other animals. God's *first* mistake: man did not think animals entertaining – he dominated them, he did not even wish to be an 'animal'. Consequently God created woman. And boredom did indeed cease from that moment – but many other things ceased as well! Woman was God's *second* mistake. – 'Woman in her innermost nature is a

49

You have understood me. The beginning of the Bible contains the whole psychology of the priest. – The priest knows only one great danger, and that is science – the healthy concept of cause and effect. But, on the whole, science flourishes only under happy conditions – a man must have time, he must also have superfluous mental energy in order to 'pursue knowledge' . . . '*Consequently* man must be made unhappy' – this has been the argument of the priest of all ages. You have already divined what, in accordance with such a manner of arguing, must first have come into the world – 'sin' . . . The notion of guilt and punishment, the whole 'moral order of the universe', was invented against science – against the deliverance of man from the priest . . . Man must *not* cast his glance upon the outer world, he must turn it inwards into himself; he must not as a learner look cleverly and cautiously *into* things; he must not see at all: he must *suffer* . . . And he must suffer, so that he may be in need of the priest every minute. – Away with doctors! What is needed is a Saviour! – The notion of guilt and punishment, including the doctrine of 'grace', of 'salvation' and of 'forgiveness' – all *lies* through and through without a shred of psychological reality – were invented in order to destroy man's *sense of causality:* they are an attack on the concept of cause and effect! – And *not* an attack with the fist, with the knife, with honesty in hate and love! But one actuated by the most cowardly, most crafty, and most ignoble instincts! A *priest's* attack! A vampyrism of pale subterranean leeches! . . . When the natural consequences of an act are no longer 'natural', but are thought to be conjured up by phantom concepts of superstition, by 'God', by 'spirits', and by 'souls', as merely moral consequences, in the form of rewards, punishments, hints, and educational means – *then the greatest crime against man has been perpetrated.* – Sin, I repeat, this form of self-pollution *par excellence* on the part of man, was invented in order to make science, culture and every elevation and noble trait in man quite impossible; by means of the invention of sin the priest is able to *rule*.

50

I cannot here dispense with a psychology of 'faith' and of the 'faithful', which will naturally be to the advantage of the 'faithful'. If today there are still many who do not know how very *indecent* it is to be a 'believer' – *or* to what extent such a state is the sign of decadence, and of the broken will to Life – they will know it no later than tomorrow. My voice can make even those hear who are hard of hearing. If perchance my ears have not deceived me, it seems that among Christians there is such a thing as a kind of criterion of truth, which is called 'the proof of power'. 'Faith saveth; *therefore* it is true'. – It might be objected here that it is precisely salvation which is not proved but only *promised:* salvation is bound up with the condition 'faith' – one *shall* be saved, *because* one has faith . . . But how prove *that* that which the priest promises to the faithful really will take place, to wit: the 'Beyond' which defies all demonstration? – The assumed 'proof of power' is at bottom once again only a belief in the fact that the effect which faith promises will not fail to take place. In a formula: 'I believe that faith saveth – *consequently* it is true'. But with this we are at the end of our tether. This 'consequently' would be the *absurdum* itself as a criterion of truth. – Let us be indulgent enough to assume, however, that salvation is proved by faith (*not* only desired, and *not* merely promised by the somewhat suspicious lips of a priest): could salvation – or, in technical terminology, *happiness* – ever be a proof of truth? So little is it so that, when pleasurable sensations make their influence felt in replying to the question 'what is true', they furnish almost the contradiction of truth, or at any rate they make it in the highest degree suspicious. The proof through 'happiness', is a proof of happiness – and nothing else; why in the world should we take it for granted that *true* judgments cause more pleasure than false ones, and that in accordance with a pre-established harmony, they necessarily bring pleasant feelings in their wake? – The experience of all strict and profound minds teaches the *reverse*. Every inch of truth has been conquered only after a struggle, almost everything to which our heart, our love and our trust in life cleaves, has had to be sacrificed for it. Greatness of soul is necessary for this: the service of truth is the hardest of all services. – What then is meant by honesty in things intellectual? It means that a man is severe towards his own heart, that he scorns 'beautiful feelings', and that he makes a matter of conscience out of every Yea and Nay! – Faith saveth: *consequently* it lies . . .

51

The fact that faith may in certain circumstances save, the fact that salvation as the result of an *idée fixe* does not constitute a true idea, the fact that faith moves *no* mountains, but may very readily raise them where previously they did not exist – all these things are made sufficiently clear by a mere casual stroll through a *lunatic asylum*. Of course *no* priest would find this sufficient: for he instinctively denies that illness is illness or that lunatic asylums are lunatic asylums. Christianity is in *need* of illness, just as Ancient Greece was in need of a superabundance of health. The actual ulterior motive of the whole of the Church's system of salvation is to *make people ill*. And is not the Church itself the Catholic madhouse as an ultimate ideal? The earth as a whole converted into a madhouse? The kind of religious man which the Church aims at producing is a typical *decadent*. The moment of time at which a religious crisis attains the ascendancy over a people, is always characterised by nerve-epidemics; the 'inner world' of the religious man is ridiculously like the 'inner world' of over-irritable and exhausted people; the 'highest' states which Christianity holds up to mankind as the value of values, are epileptic in character – the Church has pronounced only madmen *or* great swindlers *in majorem dei honorem* holy. Once I ventured to characterise the whole of the Christian training of penance and salvation (which nowadays is best studied in England) as a *folie circulaire* methodically generated upon a soil which, of course, is already prepared for it – that is to say, which is thoroughly morbid. Not every one who likes can be a Christian: no man is 'converted' to Christianity – he must be sick enough for it . . . We others who possess enough courage both for health and for contempt, how rightly *we* may despise a religion which taught men to misunderstand the body! which would not rid itself of the superstitions of the soul! which made a virtue of taking inadequate nourishment! which in health combats a sort of enemy, devil, temptation! which persuaded itself that it was possible to bear a perfect soul about in a cadaverous body, and which, to this end, had to make up for itself a new concept of 'perfection', a pale, sickly, idiotically gushing ideal – so-called 'holiness' – holiness, which in itself is simply a symptom of an impoverished, enervated and incurably deteriorated body! . . . The movement of Christianity, as a European movement, was from first to last, a general accumulation of the ruck and scum of all sorts and kinds (and these, by means of Christianity, aspire to power). It does *not* express the downfall of a race, it is rather a conglomerate assembly of all the decadent elements from everywhere which seek each other and crowd together. It was not, as some believe, the corruption of antiquity, of *noble* antiquity, which made Christianity possible: the learned idiocy which now-adays tries to support such a notion cannot be too severely contradicted. At the time when the morbid and corrupted Chandala classes became Christianised in the whole of the *imperium*, the very *contrary type*, nobility, was extant in its finest and maturest forms. The greatest number became master; the democracy of Christian instincts triumphed . . . Christianity was not 'national', it was not determined by race – it appealed to all the disinherited forms of life, it had its allies everywhere. Christianity is built upon the rancour of the sick; its instinct is directed *against* the sound, against health. Everything well-constituted, proud, high-spirited, and beautiful is offensive to its ears and eyes. Again I remind you of St Paul's priceless words: 'And God hath chosen the *weak* things of the world, the *foolish* things of the world; and *base* things of the world, and things which are *despised*': this was the formula, *in hoc signo* decadence triumphed. *God on the Cross* – does no one yet understand the terrible ulterior motive of this symbol? – Everything that suffers, everything that hangs on the cross, is *divine* . . . All of us hang on the cross, consequently we are *divine* . . . We alone are divine . . . Christianity was a victory; a *nobler* type of character perished through it – Christianity has been humanity's greatest misfortune hitherto.

52

Christianity also stands opposed to everything happily constituted in the *mind* – it can make use only of morbid reason as Christian reason; it takes the side of everything idiotic, it utters a curse upon 'intellect', upon the *superbia* of the healthy intellect. Since illness belongs to the essence of Christianity, the typically Christian state, 'faith', *must* also be a form of illness, and all straight, honest and scientific roads to knowledge must be repudiated by the Church as forbidden . . . Doubt in itself is already a sin . . . The total lack of psychological cleanliness in the priest, which reveals itself in his look, is a *result* of decadence. Hysterical women, as also children with scrofulous constitutions, should be observed as a proof of how invariably instinctive falsity, the love of lying for the sake of lying, and the inability either to look or to walk straight, are the expression of decadence. 'Faith' simply means the refusal to know what is true. The pious person, the priest of both sexes, is false because he is ill: his instinct *demands* that truth should not assert its right anywhere. 'That which makes ill is good: that which proceeds from abundance, from superabundance and from power, is evil': that is the view of the faithful. The *constraint to lie* – that is the sign by which I recognise every predetermined theologian. – Another characteristic of the theologian is his lack of *capacity* for *philology*. What I mean here by the word philology is, in a general sense, to be understood as the art of reading well, of being able to take account of facts *without* falsifying them by interpretation, without losing either caution, patience or subtlety owing to one's desire to understand. Philology as *ephexis* in interpretation, whether one be dealing with books, newspaper reports, human destinies or meteorological records – not to speak of the 'salvation of the soul' . . . The manner in which a theologian, whether in Berlin or in Rome, interprets a verse from the 'Scriptures', or an experience, or the triumph of his nation's army for instance, under the superior guiding light of David's Psalms, is always so exceedingly *daring*, that it is enough to make a philologist's hair stand on end. And what is he to do, when pietists and other cows from Swabia explain their miserable everyday lives in their smoky hovels by means of the 'Finger of God', a miracle of 'grace', of 'Providence', of experiences of 'salvation'! The most modest effort of the intellect, not to speak of decent feeling, ought at least to lead these interpreters to convince themselves of the absolute childishness and unworthiness of any such abuse of the dexterity of God's fingers. However small an amount of loving piety we might possess, a god who cured us in time of a cold in the nose, or who arranged for us to enter a carriage just at the moment when a cloud burst over our heads, would be such an absurd god, that he would have to be abolished, even if he existed. God as a domestic servant, as a postman, as a general provider – in short, merely a word for the most foolish kind of accidents . . . 'Divine Providence', as it is believed in today by almost every third man in 'cultured Germany', would be an argument against God, in fact it would be the strongest argument against God that could be imagined. And in any case it is an argument against the Germans.

53

The notion that martyrs prove anything at all in favour of a thing, is so exceedingly doubtful, that I would fain deny that there has ever yet existed a martyr who had anything to do with truth. In the very manner in which a martyr flings his little parcel of truth at the head of the world, such a low degree of intellectual honesty and such obtuseness in regard to the question 'truth' makes itself felt, that one never requires to refute a martyr. Truth is not a thing which one might have and another be without: only peasants or peasant-apostles, after the style of Luther, can think like this about truth. You may be quite sure, that the greater a man's degree of conscientiousness may be in matters intellectual, the more modest he will show himself on this point. To *know* about five things, and with a subtle wave of the hand to refuse to know *others* . . . 'Truth' as it is understood by every prophet, every sectarian, every free thinker, every socialist and every churchman, is an absolute proof of the fact that these people haven't even begun that discipline of the mind and that process of self-mastery, which is necessary for the discovery of any small, even exceedingly small truth. – Incidentally, the deaths of martyrs have been a great misfortune in the history of the world: they led people astray . . . The conclusion which all idiots, women and common people come to, that there must be something in a cause for which someone lays down his life (or which, as in the case of primitive Christianity, provokes an epidemic of sacrifices) – this conclusion put a tremendous check upon all investigation, upon the spirit of investigation and of caution. Martyrs have *harmed* the cause of truth . . . Even to this day it only requires the crude fact of persecution, in order to create an honourable name for any obscure sect who does not matter in the least. What? Is a cause actually changed in any way by the fact that some one has laid down his life for it? An error which becomes honourable, is simply an error that possesses one seductive charm the more: do you suppose, dear theologians, that we shall give you the chance of acting the martyrs for your lies? – A thing is refuted by being laid respectfully on ice, and theologians are refuted in the same way. This was precisely the world-historic foolishness of all persecutors; they lent the thing they combated a semblance of honour by conferring the fascination of martyrdom upon it . . . Women still lie prostrate before an error today, because they have been told that some one died on the cross for it. *Is the cross then an argument?* – But concerning all these things, one person alone has said what mankind has been in need of for thousands of years – *Zarathustra*.

'Letters of blood did they write on the way they went, and their folly taught that truth is proved by blood.

'But blood is the very worst testimony of truth; blood poisoneth even the purest teaching, and turneth it into delusion and into blood feuds.

'And when a man goeth through fire for his teaching – what does that prove? Verily, it is more when out of one's own burning springeth one's own teaching.'

54

Do not allow yourselves to be deceived: great minds are sceptical. Zarathustra is a sceptic. Strength and the *freedom* which proceeds from the power and excessive power of the mind, *manifests* itself through scepticism. Men of conviction are of no account whatever in regard to any principles of value or of non-value. Convictions are prisons. They never see far enough, they do not look down from a sufficient height: but in order to have any say in questions of value and non-value, a man must see five hundred convictions *beneath* him – *behind* him . . . A spirit who desires great things, and who also desires the means thereto, is necessarily a sceptic. Freedom from every kind of conviction *belongs* to strength, to the *ability* to open one's eyes freely . . . The great passion of a sceptic, the basis and power of his being, which is more enlightened and more despotic than he is himself, enlists all his intellect into its service; it makes him unscrupulous; it even gives him the courage to employ unholy means; in certain circumstances it even allows him convictions. Conviction as a *means:* much is achieved merely by means of a conviction. Great passion makes use of and consumes convictions, it does not submit to them – it knows that it is a sovereign power. Conversely; the need of faith, of anything either absolutely affirmative or negative, Carlylism (if I may be allowed this expression), is the need of *weakness*. The man of beliefs, the 'believer' of every sort and condition, is necessarily a dependent man – he is one who cannot regard *himself* as an aim, who cannot postulate aims from the promptings of his own heart. The 'believer' does not belong to himself, he can be only a means, he must be *used up*, he is in need of someone who uses him up. His instinct accords the highest honour to a morality of self-abnegation: everything in him, his prudence, his experience, his vanity, persuade him to adopt this morality. Every sort of belief is in itself an expression of self-denial, of self-estrangement . . . If one considers how necessary a regulating code of conduct is to the majority of people, a code of conduct which constrains them and fixes them from outside; and how control, or in a higher sense, *slavery*, is the only and ultimate condition under which the weak-willed man, and especially woman, flourish; one also understands conviction, 'faith'. The man of conviction finds in the latter his *backbone*. To be *blind* to many things, to be impartial about nothing, to belong always to a particular side, to hold a strict and necessary point of view in all matters of values – these are the only conditions under which such a man can survive at all. But all this is the reverse of, the *antagonist* of, the truthful man – of truth . . . The believer is not at liberty to have a conscience for the question 'true' and 'untrue': to be upright on *this* point would mean his immediate downfall. The pathological limitations of his standpoint convert the convinced man into the fanatic – Savonarola, Luther Rousseau, Robespierre, Saint-Simon – these are the reverse type of the strong spirit that has become *free*. But the grandiose poses of these *morbid* spirits, of these epileptics of ideas, exercise an influence over the masses – fanatics are picturesque, mankind prefers to look at poses than to listen to reason.

55

One step further in the psychology of conviction of 'faith'. It is already some time since I first thought of considering whether convictions were not perhaps more dangerous enemies of truth than lies (*Human All-too-Human*, I, 54 and 483). Now I would fain put the decisive question: is there any difference at all between a lie and a conviction? All the world believes that there is, but what in Heaven's name does not all the world believe! Every conviction has its history, its preliminary stages, its period of groping and of mistakes: it becomes a conviction only after it has *not* been one for a long time, only after it has *scarcely* been one for a long time. What? Might not falsehood be the embryonic form of conviction? – At times all that is required is a change of personality: very often what was a lie in the father becomes a conviction in the son. – I call a lie, to refuse to see something that one sees, to refuse to see it exactly *as* one sees it: whether a lie is perpetrated before witnesses or not is beside the point. – The most common sort of lie is the one uttered to one's self; to lie to others is relatively exceptional. Now this refusal to see what one sees, this refusal to see a thing exactly as one sees it, is almost the first condition for all those who belong to a *party* in any sense whatsoever: the man who belongs to a party perforce becomes a liar. German historians, for instance, are convinced that Rome stood for despotism, whereas the Teutons introduced the spirit of freedom into the world: what difference is there between this conviction and a lie? After this is it to be wondered at, that all parties, including German historians, instinctively adopt the grandiloquent phraseology of morality – that morality almost owes its *survival* to the fact that the man who belongs to a party, no matter what it may be, is in need of morality every moment? – 'This is our conviction: we confess it to the whole world, we live and die for it – let us respect everything that has a conviction!' – I have actually heard antisemites speak in this way. On the contrary, my dear sirs! An antisemite does not become the least bit more respectable because he lies on principle . . . Priests, who in such matters are more subtle, and who perfectly understand the objection to which the idea of a conviction lies open – that is to say of a falsehood which is perpetrated on principle *because* it serves a purpose, borrowed from the Jews the prudent measure of setting the concept 'God', 'Will of God', 'Revelation of God', at this place. Kant, too, with his categorical imperative, was on the same road: this was his *practical* reason. – There are some questions in which it is *not* given to man to decide between true and false; all the principal questions, all the principal problems of value, stand beyond human reason . . . To comprehend the limits of reason – this alone is genuine philosophy. For what purpose did God give man revelation? Would God have done anything superfluous? Man cannot of his own accord know what is good and what is evil, that is why God taught man his will . . . Moral: the priest does *not* lie, such questions as 'truth' or 'falseness' have nothing to do with the things concerning which the priest speaks; such things do not allow of lying. For, in order to lie, it would be necessary to know *what* is true in this respect. But that is precisely what man cannot know: hence the priest is only the mouthpiece of God. – This

sort of sacerdotal syllogism is by no means exclusively
Judaic or Christian; the right to lie and the *prudent
measure* of 'revelation' belongs to the priestly type,
whether of decadent periods or of Pagan times (Pagans
are all those who say yea to life, and to whom 'God' is
the word for the great yea to all things). The 'law', the
'will of God', the 'holy book', and inspiration – all
these things are merely words for the conditions under
which the priest attains to power, and with which he
maintains his power – these concepts are to be found at
the base of all sacerdotal organisations, of all priestly
or philosophical and ecclesiastical governments. The
'holy lie', which is common to Confucius, to the law-
book of Manu, to Muhamed, and to the Christian
church, is not even absent in Plato. 'Truth is here'; this
phrase means, wherever it is uttered: *the priest lies* . . .

56

After all, the question is, to what *end* are falsehoods
perpetrated? The fact that, in Christianity, 'holy' ends
are entirely absent, constitutes *my* objection to the
means it employs. Its ends are only *bad* ends: the
poisoning, the calumniation and the denial of life, the
contempt of the body, the degradation and self-
pollution of man by virtue of the concept sin –
consequently its means are bad as well. My feelings are
quite the reverse when I read the law-book of *Manu*, an
incomparably superior and more intellectual work,
which it would be a sin against the *spirit* even to *mention*
in the same breath with the Bible. You will guess
immediately why: it has a genuine philosophy behind
it, *in* it, not merely an evil-smelling Jewish distillation
of Rabbinism and superstition – it gives something to
chew even to the most fastidious psychologist. And,

not to forget the most important point of all, it is fundamentally different from every kind of Bible: by means of it the *noble classes*, the philosophers and the warriors, guard and guide the masses; it is replete with noble values, it is filled with a feeling of perfection, with a saying of yea to life, and a triumphant sense of well-being in regard to itself and to life – the sun shines upon the whole book. All those things which Christianity smothers with its bottomless vulgarity: procreation, woman, marriage, are here treated with earnestness, with reverence, with love and confidence. How can one possibly place in the hands of children and women, a book that contains those vile words: 'to avoid fornication, let every man have his own wife, and let every woman have her own husband . . . it is better to marry than to burn.' And is it decent to be a Christian so long as the very origin of man is Christianised – that is to say, befouled, by the idea of the *immaculata conceptio*? . . . I know of no book in which so many delicate and kindly things are said to woman, as in the Law-Book of Manu; these old grey-beards and saints have a manner of being gallant to women which, perhaps, cannot be surpassed. 'The mouth of a woman', says Manu on one occasion, 'the breast of a maiden, the prayer of a child, and the smoke of the sacrifice, are always pure.' Elsewhere he says: 'there is nothing purer than the light of the sun, the shadow cast by a cow, air, water, fire and the breath of a maiden.' And finally – perhaps this is also a holy lie: 'all the openings of the body above the navel are pure, all those below the navel are impure. Only in a maiden is the whole body pure.'

The unholiness of Christian means is caught *in flagranti*, if only the end aspired to by Christianity be compared with that of the Law-Book of Manu; if only these two utterly opposed aims be put under a strong light. The critic of Christianity simply cannot avoid making Christianity *contemptible*. – A law-book like that of Manu comes into being like every good law-book: it epitomises the experience, the precautionary measures, and the experimental morality of long ages, it settles things definitely, it no longer creates. The prerequisite for a codification of this kind, is the recognition of the fact that the means which procure authority for *truth* to which it has cost both time and great pains to attain, are fundamentally different from those with which that same truth would be proved. A law-book never relates the utility, the reasons, the preliminary casuistry, of a law: for it would be precisely in this way that it would forfeit its imperative tone, the 'thou shalt', the first condition of its being obeyed. The problem lies exactly in this. – At a certain stage in the development of a people, the most far-seeing class within it (that is to say, the class that sees farthest backwards and forwards) declares the experience of how its fellow-creatures ought to live – *i.e. can* live – to be finally settled. Its object is, to reap as rich and as complete a harvest as possible, in return for the ages of experiment and *terrible* experience it has traversed. Consequently, that which has to be avoided, above all, is any further experimentation, the continuation of the state when values are still fluid, the testing, choosing, and criticising of values *in infinitum*. Against all this a double wall is built up: in the first place, *Revelation*,

466

which is the assumption that the rationale of every law is not human in its origin, that it was not sought and found after ages of error, but that it is divine in its origin, completely and utterly without a history, a gift, a miracle, a mere communication . . . And secondly, *tradition*, which is the assumption that the law has obtained since the most primeval times, that it is impious and a crime against one's ancestors to attempt to doubt it. The authority of law is established on the principles: God *gave* it, the ancestors *lived* it. – The superior reason of such a procedure lies in the intention to draw consciousness off step by step from that mode of life which has been recognised as correct (*i.e. proved* after enormous and carefully examined experience), so that perfect automatism of the instincts may be attained – this being the only possible basis of all mastery of every kind of perfection in the Art of Life. To draw up a law-book like Manu's, is tantamount to granting a people mastership for the future, perfection for the future – the right to aspire to the highest Art of Life. *To that end it must be made unconscious:* this is the object of every holy lie. – *The order of castes*, the highest, the dominating law, is only the sanction of a *natural order*, of a natural legislation of the first rank, over which no arbitrary innovation, no 'modern idea' has any power. Every healthy society falls into three distinct types, which reciprocally condition one another and which gravitate differently in the physio-logical sense; and each of these has its own hygiene, its own sphere of work, its own special feeling of perfection, and its own mastership. It is Nature, not Manu, that separates from the rest, those individuals preponderating in intellectual power, those excelling in muscular strength and temperament, and the third class which is distinguished neither in one way nor the other, the mediocre – the latter as the greatest number, the former as the *élite*. The superior caste – I call them the *fewest* – has, as the perfect caste, the privileges of the fewest: it devolves upon them to represent happiness, beauty and goodness on earth. Only the most intellectual men have the right to beauty, to the beautiful: only in them is goodness not weakness. *Pulchrum est paucorum hominum:* goodness is a privilege. On the other hand there is nothing which they should be more strictly forbidden than repulsive manners or a pessimistic look, a look that makes everything *seem ugly* – or even indignation at the general aspect of things. Indignation is the privilege of the Chandala, and so is pessimism. '*The world is perfect*' – that is what the instinct of the most intellectual says, the yea-saying instinct; 'imperfection, every kind of *inferiority* to us, distance, the pathos of distance, even the Chandala belongs to this perfection.' The most intellectual men, as the *strongest* find their happiness where others meet with their ruin: in the labyrinth, in hardness towards themselves and others, in endeavour; their delight is self-mastery: with them asceticism becomes a second nature, a need, an instinct. They regard a difficult task as their privilege; to play with burdens which crush their fellows is to them a *recreation* . . . Knowledge, a form of asceticism. – They are the most honourable kind of men: but that does not prevent them from being the most cheerful and most gracious. They rule, not because they will, but because they *are;* they are not at liberty to take a second place. – The second in rank are the guardians of the law, the custodians of order and of security, the noble warriors, the king, above all, as the highest formula of the warrior, the judge, and keeper of the law. The second in rank are the executive of the most intellectual, the nearest to them in duty, relieving them of all that is *coarse* in the work of ruling – their retinue, their right hand, their best disciples. In all this, I repeat, there is nothing arbitrary, nothing 'artificial', that which is *otherwise* is artificial – by that which is otherwise, nature is put to shame . . . The order of castes, and the order of rank, merely formulates the supreme law of life itself; the differentiation of the three types is necessary for the maintenance of society, and for enabling higher and highest types to be reared – the *inequality* of rights is the only condition of there being rights at all. – A right is a privilege. And in his way, each has his privilege. Let us not underestimate the privileges of the *mediocre*. Life always gets harder towards the summit – the cold increases, responsibility increases. A high civilisation is a pyramid: it can stand only upon a broad base, its first prerequisite is a strongly and soundly consolidated mediocrity. Handicraft, commerce, agriculture, science, the greater part of art – in a word, the whole range of professional and business callings, is compatible only with mediocre ability and ambition; such pursuits would be out of place among exceptions, the instinct pertaining thereto would oppose not only aristocracy but anarchy as well. The fact that one is publicly useful, a wheel, a function, presupposes a certain natural destiny: it is not *society*, but the only kind of *happiness* of which the great majority are capable, that makes them intelligent machines. For the mediocre it is a joy to be mediocre; in them mastery in one thing, a speciality, is a natural instinct. It would be absolutely unworthy of a profound thinker to see any objection in mediocrity *per se*. For in itself it is the first essential condition under which exceptions are possible; a high culture is determined by it. When the exceptional man treats the mediocre with more tender care than he does himself or his equals, this is not mere courtesy of heart on his part – but simply his *duty* . . . Whom do I hate most among the rabble of the present day? The socialistic rabble, the Chandala apostles, who undermine the working man's instinct, his happiness and his feeling of contentedness with his insignificant existence – who make him envious, and who teach him revenge . . . The wrong never lies in unequal rights; it lies in the claim to equal rights. What is *bad*? But I have already replied to this: everything that proceeds from weakness, envy and *revenge*. – The anarchist and the Christian are offspring of the same womb . . .

58

In point of fact, it matters greatly to what end one lies: whether one preserves or *destroys* by means of falsehood. It is quite justifiable to bracket the *Christian* and the *Anarchist* together: their object, their instinct, is concerned only with destruction. The proof of this proposition can be read quite plainly from history: history spells it with appalling distinctness. Whereas we have just seen a religious legislation, whose object was to render the highest possible means of making life *flourish*, and of making a grand organisation of society, eternal – Christianity found its mission in putting an end to such an organisation, *precisely because life flourishes through it*. In the one case, the net profit to the credit of reason, acquired through long ages of experiment and of insecurity, is applied usefully to the most remote ends, and the harvest, which is as large, as rich, as complete as possible, is reaped and garnered: in the other case, on the contrary, the harvest is *blighted* in a single night. That which stood there, *aere perennius*, the *imperium Romanum*, the most magnificent form of organisation, under difficult conditions, that has ever been achieved, and compared with which everything that preceded, and everything which followed it, is mere patchwork, gimcrackery, and dilettantism – those holy anarchists made it their 'piety', to destroy 'the world' – that is to say, the *imperium Romanum*, until no two stones were left standing one on the other – until even the Teutons and other clodhoppers were able to become masters of it. The Christian and the anarchist are both decadents; they are both incapable of acting in any other way than disintegratingly, poisonously and witheringly, like *blood-suckers;* they are both actuated by an instinct of *mortal hatred* of everything that stands erect, that is great, that is lasting, and that is a guarantee of the future . . . Christianity was the vampire of the *imperium Romanum* – in a night it shattered the stupendous achievement of the Romans, which was to acquire the territory for a vast civilisation which could *bide its time.* – Does no one understand this yet? The *imperium Romanum* that we know, and which the history of the Roman province teaches us to know ever more thoroughly, this most admirable work of art on a grand scale, was the beginning, its construction was calculated *to prove* its worth by millenniums – unto this day nothing has ever again been built in this fashion, nor have men even dreamt since of building on this scale *sub specie aeterni*! – This organisation was sufficiently firm to withstand bad emperors: the accident of personalities must have nothing to do with such matters – the *first* principle of all great architecture. But it was not sufficiently firm to resist the *corruptest* form of corruption, to resist the Christians . . . These stealthy canker-worms, which under the shadow of night, mist and duplicity, insinuated themselves into the company of every individual, and proceeded to drain him of all serious-ness for *real* things, of all his instinct for *realities*; this cowardly, effeminate and sugary gang have step by step alienated all 'souls' from this colossal edifice – those valuable, virile and noble natures who felt that the cause of Rome was their own personal cause, their own personal seriousness, their own personal *pride*. The stealth of the bigot, the secrecy of the conventicle, concepts as black as hell such as the sacrifice of the innocent, the *unio mystica* in the drinking of blood, above all the slowly kindled fire of revenge, of Chan-dala revenge – such things became master of Rome, the same kind of religion on the pre-existent form of which Epicurus had waged war. One has only to read Lucretius in order to understand what Epicurus combated, *not* Paganism, but 'Christianity', that is to say the corruption of souls through the concept of guilt, through the concept of punishment and immortality. He combated the *subterranean* cults, the whole of latent Christianity – to deny immortality was at that time a genuine *deliverance*. – And Epicurus had triumphed, every respectable thinker in the Roman Empire was an Epicurean: *then St Paul appeared* . . . St Paul, the Chandala hatred against Rome, against 'the world', the Jew, the eternal Jew *par excellence*, become flesh and genius . . . What he divined was how, by the help of the small sectarian Christian movement, independent of Judaism, a universal conflagration could be kindled; how, with the symbol of the 'God on the Cross', everything submerged, everything secretly insurrectionary, the whole offspring of anarchical intrigues could be gathered together to constitute an enormous power. 'For salvation is of the Jews'. – Christianity is the formula for the supersession, *and* epitomising of all kinds of subterranean cults, that of Osiris, of the Great Mother, of Mithras for example: St Paul's genius consisted in his discovery of this. In this matter his instinct was so certain, that, regardless of doing violence to truth, he laid the ideas by means of which those Chandala religions fascinated, upon the very lips of the 'Saviour' he had invented, and not only upon his lips – that he *made* out of him something which even a Mithras priest could understand . . . This was his moment of Damascus: he saw that he had *need* of the belief in immortality in order to depreciate 'the world', that the notion of 'hell' would become master of Rome, that with a 'Beyond' *this life* can be killed . . . Nihilist and Christian – they rhyme in German, and they do not only rhyme.

59

The whole labour of the ancient world *in vain:* I am at a loss for a word which could express my feelings at something so atrocious. – And in view of the fact that its labour was only preparatory, that with adamantine self-consciousness it laid the substructure, alone, to a work which was to last millenniums, the whole *significance* of the ancient world was certainly in vain! . . . What was the use of the Greeks? What was the use of the Romans? – All the prerequisites of a learned culture, all the scientific methods already existed, the great and peerless art of reading well had already been established – that indispensable condition to tradition, to culture and to scientific unity; natural science hand in hand with mathematics and mechanics was on the best possible road – the sense for facts, the last and most valuable of all senses, had its schools, and its tradition was already centuries old! Is this understood? Everything *essential* had been discovered to make it possible for work to be begun: methods, and this cannot be said too often, are the essential thing, also the most difficult thing, while they moreover have to wage the longest war against custom and indolence. That which today we have successfully reconquered for ourselves, by dint of unspeakable self-discipline – for in some way or other all of us still have the bad instincts, the Christian instincts, in our body – the impartial eye for reality, the cautious hand, patience and seriousness in the smallest details, complete *uprightness* in knowledge – all this was already there; it had been there over two thousand years before! And in addition to this there was also that excellent and subtle tact and taste! *Not* in the form of brain drilling! *Not* in the form of 'German' culture with the manners of a boor! But incarnate, manifesting itself in men's bearing and in their instinct – in short constituting reality . . . *All this in vain!* In one night it became merely a memory! – The Greeks! The Romans! Instinctive nobility, instinctive taste, methodic research, the genius of organisation and administration, faith, the *will* to the future of mankind, the great *yea* to all things materialised in the *imperium Romanum*, become visible to all the senses, grand style no longer manifested in mere art, but in reality, in truth, in *life*. – And buried in a night, not by a natural catastrophe! Not stamped to death by Teutons and other heavy-footed vandals!

But destroyed by crafty, stealthy, invisible anaemic vampires! Not conquered – but only drained of blood! . . . The concealed lust of revenge, miserable envy become *master*! Everything wretched, inwardly ailing, and full of ignoble feelings, the whole ghetto-world of souls, was in a trice *uppermost*! – One only needs to read any one of the Christian agitators – St Augustine, for instance – in order to realise, in order to *smell*, what filthy fellows came to the top in this movement. You would deceive yourselves utterly if you supposed that the leaders of the Christian agitation showed any lack of understanding – Ah! they were shrewd, shrewd to the point of holiness were these dear old Fathers of the Church! What they lack is something quite different. Nature neglected them – it forgot to give them a modest dowry of decent, of respectable and of *cleanly* instincts . . . Between ourselves, they are not even men. If Islam despises Christianity, it is justified a thousand times over; for Islam presupposes men.

60

Christianity destroyed the harvest we might have reaped from the culture of antiquity; later it also destroyed our harvest of the culture of Islam. The wonderful Moorish world of Spanish culture, which in its essence is more closely related to *us*, and which appeals more to our sense and taste than Rome and Greece, was *trampled to death* (– I do not say by what kind of feet), why? – because it owed its origin to noble, to manly instincts, because it said yea to life, even that life so full of the rare and refined luxuries of the Moors! . . . Later on the Crusaders waged war upon something before which it would have been more seemly in them to grovel in the dust – a culture, beside which even our Nineteenth Century would seem very poor and very 'senile'. – Of course they wanted booty: the Orient was rich . . . For goodness' sake let us forget our prejudices! Crusades – superior piracy, that is all! German nobility – that is to say, a Viking nobility at bottom, was in its element in such wars: the Church was only too well aware of how German nobility is to be won . . . German nobility was always the 'Swiss Guard' of the Church, always at the service of all the bad instincts of the Church; but it was *well paid for it all* . . . Fancy the Church having waged its deadly war upon everything noble on earth, precisely with the help of German swords, German blood and courage! A host of painful *questions* might be raised on this point. German nobility scarcely takes a place in the history of higher culture: the reason of this is obvious. Christianity, alcohol – the two *great* means of corruption. As a matter of fact, choice ought to be just as much out of the question between Islam and Christianity, as between an Arab and a Jew. The decision is already self-evident; nobody is at liberty to exercise a choice in this matter. A man is either of the Chandala or he is *not* . . . 'War with Rome to the knife! Peace and friendship with Islam': this is what that great free spirit, that genius among German emperors – Frederick II – not only felt but also *did*. What? Must a German in the first place be a genius, a free-spirit, in order to have *decent* feelings? I cannot understand how a German was ever able to have *Christian* feelings.

61

Here it is necessary to revive a memory which will be a hundred times more painful to Germans. The Germans have destroyed the last great harvest of culture which was to be garnered for Europe – it destroyed the *Renaissance*. Does anybody at last understand, *will* anybody understand what the Renaissance was? *The transvaluation of Christian values*, the attempt undertaken with all means, all instincts and all genius to make the *opposite* values, the *noble* values triumph . . . Hitherto there has been only *this* great war: there has never yet been a more decisive question than the Renaissance – *my* question is the question of the Renaissance: there has never been a more fundamental, a more direct and a more severe *attack*, delivered with a whole front upon the centre of the foe. To attack at the decisive quarter, at the very seat of Christianity, and there to place *noble* values on the throne – that is to say, to *introduce* them into the instincts, into the most fundamental needs and desires of those sitting there . . . I see before me a possibility perfectly magic in its charm and glorious colouring – it seems to me to scintillate with all the quivering grandeur of refined beauty, that there is an art at work within it which is so divine, so infernally divine, that one might seek through millenniums in vain for another such possibility; I see a spectacle so rich in meaning and so wonderfully paradoxical to boot, that it would be enough to make all the gods of Olympus rock with immortal laughter – *Caesar Borgia as Pope* . . . Do you understand me? . . . Very well then, this would have been the triumph which *I* alone am longing for today – this would have *swept* Christianity *away*! – What happened? A German monk, Luther, came to Rome.

This monk, with all the vindictive instincts of an abortive priest in his body, foamed with rage over the Renaissance in Rome . . . Instead of, with the profoundest gratitude, understanding the vast miracle that had taken place, the overcoming of Christianity at its *headquarters* – the fire of his hate knew only how to draw fresh fuel from this spectacle. A religious man thinks only of himself. – Luther saw the corruption of the Papacy when the very reverse stared him in the face: the old corruption, the *peccatum originale*, Christianity *no longer* sat upon the Papal chair! But Life! The triumph of Life! The great yea to all lofty, beautiful and daring things! . . . And Luther reinstated the Church; he attacked it. The Renaissance thus became an event without meaning, a great *in vain*! – Ah these Germans, what have they not cost us already! In vain – this has always been the achievement of the Germans. – The Reformation, Leibniz, Kant and so-called German philosophy, the Wars of Liberation, the Empire – in each case are in vain for something which had already existed, for something which *cannot be recovered* . . . I confess it, these Germans are my enemies: I despise every sort of uncleanliness in concepts and valuations in them, every kind of cowardice in the face of every honest yea or nay. For almost one thousand years, now, they have tangled and confused everything they have laid their hands on; they have on their conscience all the half-measures, all the three-eighth measures of which Europe is sick; they also have the most unclean, the most incurable, and the most irrefutable kind of Christianity – Protestantism – on their conscience . . . If we shall never be able to get rid of Christianity, the *Germans* will be to blame.

478

62

With this I will now conclude and pronounce my judgment. I *condemn* Christianity and confront it with the most terrible accusation that an accuser has ever had in his mouth. To my mind it is the greatest of all conceivable corruptions, it has had the will to the last imaginable corruption. The Christian Church allowed nothing to escape from its corruption; it converted every value into its opposite, every truth into a lie, and every honest impulse into an ignominy of the soul. Let anyone dare to speak to me of its humanitarian blessings! To *abolish* any sort of distress was opposed to its profoundest interests; its very existence depended on states of distress; it created states of distress in order to make itself immortal . . . The cancer germ of sin, for instance: the Church was the first to enrich mankind with this misery! – The 'equality of souls before God', this falsehood, this *pretext* for the *rancunes* of all the base-minded, this anarchist bomb of a concept, which has ultimately become the revolution, the modern idea, the principle of decay of the whole of social order – this is *Christian* dynamite . . . The 'humanitarian' blessings of Christianity! To breed a self-contradiction, an art of self-profanation, a will to lie at any price, an aversion, a contempt of all good and honest instincts out of *humanitas*! Is this what you call the blessings of Christianity? – Parasitism as the only method of the Church; sucking all the blood, all the love, all the hope of life out of mankind with anaemic and sacred ideals. A 'Beyond' as the will to deny all reality; the cross as the trademark of the most subterranean form of conspiracy that has ever existed – against health, beauty, well-constitutedness, bravery, intellect, kindliness of soul, *against Life itself* . . .

This eternal accusation against Christianity I would fain write on all walls, wherever there are walls – I have letters with which I can make even the blind see . . . I call Christianity the one great curse, the one enormous and innermost perversion, the one great instinct of revenge, for which no means are too venomous, too underhand, too underground and too *petty* – I call it the one immortal blemish of mankind . . .

And *time* is reckoned from the *dies nefastus* upon which this fatality came into being – from the first day of Christianity! – *Why not rather from its last day?* – *From today?* – Transvaluation of all Values! . . .